The Art of *Musical* Conducting

BOOKS BY DAVID WHITWELL

Philosophic Foundations of Education
Foundations of Music Education
Music Education of the Future
The Sousa Oral History Project
The Art of Musical Conducting

The History and Literature of the Wind Band and Wind Ensemble Series
A Concise History of the Wind Band
Volume 1 *The Wind Band and Wind Ensemble Before 1500*
Volume 2 *The Renaissance Wind Band and Wind Ensemble*
Volume 3 *The Baroque Wind Band and Wind Ensemble*
Volume 4 *The Wind Band and Wind Ensemble of the Classic Period (1750–1800)*
Volume 5 *The Nineteenth-Century Wind Band and Wind Ensemble*

For a complete list of the currently available works of David Whitwell visit:
whitwellbooks.com

David Whitwell

The Art of *Musical* Conducting

SECOND EDITION

EDITED BY CRAIG DABELSTEIN

WHITWELL BOOKS • AUSTIN, TEXAS, USA

The Art of Musical Conducting
Second Edition
David Whitwell
Edited by Craig Dabelstein
www.whitwellbooks.com

Whitwell Books
P.O. Box 342673
Austin, Texas, USA

Copyright © David Whitwell 2011
All rights reserved

All images used in this book are in the public domain except where otherwise noted.

Composed in Bembo Book
Published in the United States of America

The Art of Musical Conducting (paperback) isbn 978-1-936512-12-6

The public was pouring into the Hall … then began the extraordinary. For two hours the hearts of the friends of music were lifted higher and higher. Conductor, David Whitwell, conducted the entire concert from memory. Already from his very first motion, it was apparent that he conducts with an inimitable elegance and clarity. He shapes on a foundation of very precise pulse and attacks, sometimes with broad inviting gestures, sometimes with minute indications. The 52 young players follow, at the slightest wink, with discipline full of temperament.

One hears every note, even every little note! Everything is perfect: Intonation, Articulation, Dynamics, Rhythm and Tempo …

The Schönberg Theme and Variations was a masterpiece masterfully interpreted. The Schmitt Dionysiaques was as fresh as if the notes had just come from the printer …

Everyone said, 'It was an unforgettable evening.'

Schwäbische Zeitung, Germany, 20 July 1981

Foreword

IN THE BEGINNING it is composers who instigate the writing and publishing of books on conducting, as—indeed they are responsible for all in the creation of the whole of the music art. Coming to grips with rhythm of the body, together with that challenging science of mathematics, and the forever open-endedness of the human urge to create, the rash of books about conducting amidst the rise of music in the closing decades of the twentieth century was to be expected.

If you're on the hunt for endless graphic time signature aids, program and repertory suggestions or advice for proper length of baton be you long-armed at 6'2" you will find no such prescriptions in this book. But it *is* a unique narrative book about innumerable aspects of the art and about music education that are sure to find you hastening to copious footnote sources with ample reward.

Dr. David Whitwell has set out to assure, re-assure, entice, convince, convert, set-to-thinking and acting on the acceptance of his text as a positive plea for the truth of his belief that music is *feeling*. No innocent word, it is—to him and his legion of great thinkers and clear-headed listeners from Confucius (551–479 BC) to Georg Solti (1912–1997) the true essence of nature's incredible gift we call music.

In his life of work as a scholar, composer, conductor and teacher this book is his expression of belief in a subject that has been brewing in his mind these many years. It is this long, deep plunge into that most inhabited sea, of books on conducting, coupled to long-time observation, beginning as a player, of the conductor's art as it is taught and practiced which have made this a book he simply had to write.

Frederick Fennell
Miami
18 May 1998

Contents

Foreword   v

PART I: SOME PRELIMINARY CONSIDERATIONS
1   *In the beginning*   3
2   *The paramount purpose of music*   17
3   *Thoughts on the failure of American music education*   33

PART II: ON THE ORIGINS OF CONDUCTING
4   *On the heritage of movement and gesture as expression of emotion*   55
5   *On the early history of conducting*   77

PART III: ON THE NATURE AND PURPOSE OF SCORE STUDY
6   *The four paramount enigmas of the score*   105
7   *How not to study a score*   127
8   *How to study a score, I*   139
    The Paramount Object of Score Study
9   *How to study a score, II*   151
    The Five Steps of Musical Score Study
10 *How to study a score, III*   177
    On Thinking of Conceptual Detail as Music

PART IV: ON CONDUCTING TECHNIQUE
11 *On the purpose of rehearsal*   195
12 *The technique of **musical** conducting*   209
13 *On 'standard conducting technique'*   223

PART V: ON PERFORMANCE AND THE PUBLIC
14 *Regarding performance*   237
15 *On programming*   259

Afterword   279
About the Author   283

Part I

Some Preliminary Considerations

1   *In The Beginning*

THE NATURE OF CONDUCTING has its basis in the physiological relationship of music to our species. We might therefore begin by asking, 'How old is Music?' Charles Darwin not only believed it very old, but believed the emotions we feel in hearing music today are a bridge to very remote ancestors.

> Music has a wonderful power ... of recalling in a vague and indefinite manner, those strong emotions which were felt during long-past ages, when, as is probable, our early progenitors courted each other by the aid of vocal tones.[1]

Our oldest extant records of music are in the prehistoric cave paintings of France and Spain, where we not only see musicians pictured but the visible prints of dancing feet, suggesting that music was involved in the rituals associated with these paintings. Contemporary with these caves are the Cro-Magnon humans, who played on percussion instruments made from mammoth bones, in addition to the flute-types pictured in the caves, so it seems clear these people were musical. They must have been perceptive listeners as well, for it has been observed that the most resonant caves have the most paintings.

Much more recent are the oldest surviving specimens of actual instruments. They are of a nature which one might associate with very early man, as they are all made from natural objects—flutes of clay, tree branches and bones; percussion instruments from shells; and trumpet-types from large sea shells. Curiously, there are surviving clay flutes with holes cut for *diatonic* pitches which are thousands of years older than Pythagoras, to whom we give credit for 'discovering' the overtone series. How is this possible? The answer is that Pythagoras only worked out the mathematics of describing the overtone series, while the overtone series itself, as a genuine physical law of nature, was of course always present. Early man needed to be able to hear only the fourth overtone to be able to be in touch with the principle of the major key tonal system.

Charles Darwin, artist unknown

[1] Charles Darwin, *The Expression of Emotions in Man and Animals* [1872] (New York: St Martin's Press, 1979), 219; also *The Descent of Man*, II, 336.

Simple vocal sounds reflecting emotions would logically seem to be the first recognizable oral sounds, as is suggested by Richard Cytowic, MD:

> Consciousness, language, and higher mental functions are the *consequences of our ability to express emotion*.[2]

[2] Richard Cytowic, MD, *The Man who Tasted Shapes* (New York: Putnam, 1993), 196.

Richard Wagner, among others, suggested that these simple vocal sounds[3] uttered in succession became melodic in character.

[3] All modern languages use the same five vowel sounds.

> The primal organ of utterance of the inner man, however, is music, as the most spontaneous expression of the inner feeling stimulated from without. A mode of expression similar to that still proper to the beasts was alike first employed by man [and this we can demonstrate at any moment] by removing from our language its dumb articulations [consonants] and leaving nothing but the open sounds [of the vowels]. In these vowels, if we think of them as stripped of their consonants, and picture to ourselves the manifold and vivid play of inner feelings, with all their range of joy and sorrow, we shall obtain an image of man's first emotional language; a language in which the stirred and high-strung Feeling could certainly express itself through nothing but a combination of ringing tones, which altogether of itself must take the form of Melody. This melody, which was accompanied by appropriate bodily gestures in such a way as the gestures would also appear a simultaneous inner expression, and from these gestures we get rhythm.[4]

[4] Ashton Ellis, *The Prose Works of Richard Wagner* (New York: Broude), II, 224ff.

Richard Wagner, by Franz Hanfstaegl, ca. 1870–1883

The great language scholar, Otto Jespersen, points out that in passionate speech the voice still tends toward pitch fluctuation, that civilization attempts to reduce this effect by reducing passionate utterance and that savages still use a sing-song manner of speaking.

> These facts and considerations all point to the conclusion that there was once a time when all speech was song, or rather when these two actions were not yet differentiated.[5]

Perhaps the strongest evidence for this theory that music preceded language is found in the fact that we still form melodic contours with each sentence we 'speak' today. In this regard, Roger Bacon (b. ca. 1214), made the interesting comment that 'accent is a kind of singing.'[6]

This topic continued to hold great interest for later philosophers. The fifteenth-century Scholastic philosopher, Nicholas of Cusa, found it interesting that lower animals still communicate emotions by vowel-like sounds.[7] The impressive French writer, Jean-Baptiste Du Bos (1670–1742), placed great importance in the relationship of vocal sounds with Nature herself. It is a particularly important point he makes when he reminds his readers that spoken words are mere symbols of emotion, but carry no actual emotional content in themselves. Sung words, on the other hand, carry the direct emotional meaning of the music.

> Just as the painter imitates the forms and colors of nature so the musician imitates the tones of the voice—its accents, sighs and inflections. He imitates in short all the sounds that nature herself uses to express the feelings and passions. All these sounds, as we have already shown, have a wonderful power to move us because they are the signs of the passions that are the work of nature herself, from whence they have derived their energy. Spoken words, on the other hand are only arbitrary symbols of the passions.[8]

Voltaire, who was very interested in this topic, suggested that language began with simple emotional utterances which were later clarified by the addition of gesture.

---

[5] Otto Jespersen, *Language: Its Nature, Development and Origin* (New York: Henry Holt, 1922), 420. Deryck Cooke, *The Language of Music* (Oxford: Oxford University Press, 1990), 26, observes that in some cases little differentiation yet exists:
> A groan of 'Ah!' uttered by a character in an opera on a two-note phrase of definite pitch is hardly different from a groan of 'Ah!' uttered by a character in a play at indefinite pitch; the effect is equally emotive in both cases.

[6] *The Opus Majus of Roger Bacon*, trans., Robert Burke (New York: Russell & Russell, 1962), I, 259ff.

[7] Nicholas of Cusa, 'Compendium,' XIV, trans., William Wertz, Jr., in *Toward a New Council of Florence* (Washington, D.C.: Schiller Institute, 1993), 539ff.

Jean-Baptiste Du Bos

[8] Jean-Baptiste Du Bos, *Réflexions critiques sur la poësie et sur la peinture* [Paris, 1719], quoted in Peter le Huray and James Day, *Music and Aesthetics in the Eighteenth and Early-Nineteenth Centuries* (Cambridge: Cambridge University Press, 1981), 18.

> May we not, without offending anyone, suppose that the alphabet originated in cries and exclamations? Infants of themselves articulate one sound when an object catches their attention, another when they laugh, and a third when they are whipped, which they ought not to be ...
>
> From exclamations formed by vowels as natural to children as croaking is to frogs, the transition to a complete alphabet is not so great as may be thought. A mother must always have said to her child the equivalent of come, go, take, leave, hush!, etc. These words represent nothing; they describe nothing; but a gesture makes them intelligible.

He adds that he is astonished when he reflects on the ages it must have taken to go from this to sentences. He concludes his discussion by observing that as words were invented they soon became charged with subjective inferences, from their association with religion, from magic, from necromancy, etc., thus losing their value as invariable symbols. Thus, he says, 'the alphabet was the origin of all man's knowledge, and of all his errors.'[9]

William Shenstone (1714–1763) seemed to suggest that instead of saying speech developed after music, perhaps we should regard speech as a form of music.

> Harmony of period and melody of style have greater weight than is generally imagined in the judgment we pass upon writing and writers. As proof of this, let us reflect, what texts of scripture, what lines in poetry, or what periods we most remember and quote, either in verse or prose, and we shall find them to be only musical ones.[10]

How old, then, is Music? Perhaps it is so ancient that we should perhaps think of its origin in biological terms. A very interesting proposal in this regard has been made by the French doctor, Alfred A. Tomatis. He once lived near the Solesmes monastery known to all musicians for their work in the notation of chant early in the last century. This Order, which today engages in agriculture work, had for centuries maintained the practice of chanting six hours a day. A new head man, an efficiency expert, proposed to the brothers that if they reduced their chanting to two hours a day they would have four additional hours for agriculture work and could thereby increase their income for needs of the monastery. So they began doing this and after a period of time they all began to get sick. A local doctor was called in, but could find nothing

[9] The discussion is found under 'The Alphabet,' in his *Philosophical Dictionary*.

William Shenstone from the frontispiece of *The Works in Verse and Prose of William Shenstone, Esq.*, Vol. I, Second Edition (London, J Dodsley, 1765)

[10] William Shenstone, *Men and Manners* (Boston: Houghton Mifflin, 1927), 49.

wrong. An engineer was called to check ventilation, etc., but could find nothing. Finally Tomatis volunteered to come by, looked everything over, and suggested they return to six hours of chanting. They did and they all got well, and of course accomplished more work in less time as a result of being well.

Tomatis then began to reflect on the fact that so many societies engage in some sort of chanting, began to wonder why this should be and began to study chanting throughout the world. He finally offered the proposition that perhaps music is a kind of 'food' for the brain, that it 'warms up' the brain for enhanced activity. A similar conclusion had been made by Disraeli, during the nineteenth century, when he observed that 'Music is a stimulant to mental exertion.' There is some clinical evidence for this kind of physical impact on the brain by music, for we know listening to music can cause the pleasant release of endorphins. Perhaps such dimly felt physical associations with music, together with the ancient observation that music is the only Art you cannot see, help explain why music from the earliest times was thought to have some association with the divine.[11]

One physicist believes that music is so ancient as to be related to the very essence of nature itself.

> Analyzing music from many different cultures and historical periods, Richard Voss of IBM's Thomas J. Watson Research Center found that a simple mathematical relationship describes how the notes of any musical piece rise and fall in relation to the composition as a whole. This same mathematical relationship is also found in a wide variety of other natural patterns, such as the changes in the electrical patterns of brain cells, the fluctuations in sunspots and the growing of tree rings …
>
> Voss's research suggests that the essence of music may be its subtle reflection of nature.[12]

Music, he says, is as old as nature. Perhaps so, for modern physics has discovered that every organ of the body, even every molecule, atom and subatomic particle actually vibrates to specific pitches which can be heard under great amplification. One of these physicists, Dr. Hans Jenny of Switzerland, believed that it is the combination of these pitches, our harmony if you will, which, together with gravity, accounts for our body being shaped as it is.[13] It has been further suggested that, since we are made up of these vibrating systems, many

[11] The civilization of Sumeria, ca. 3,000 BC, believed music was of divine origin. They created temples for a number of gods, all of whom they believed had to be entertained, to keep them in good spirits, by singing and playing of instruments. Among these gods was one called *Enlil*, the father of humanity, who governed with a musical instrument called *al*. [See Alfred Sendrey, *Music in the Social and Religious Life of Antiquity* (Rutherford: Fairleigh Dickson University Press, 1974), 31]

[12] 'The Musical Brain,' op. cit.

[13] This reminds us that some ancient Greeks thought of the lyre as a symbol of the human form, with strings representing the nerves and the player the spirit. See Manly P. Hall, *The Secret Teachings of All Ages* (Los Angeles: The Philosophical Research Society, 1972), 81-83.

health problems may have some relationship to our literally being 'out-of-tune.' Is this also why we use expressions such as muscle *tone*? Or we say, 'She is *in tune* with everyone,' or '*I am disconcerted*,' or '*I am in concert with that decision*' and why Aristotle once said, 'Beauty is visible harmony.' We should also mention that the late fifteenth-century scholar, Franchino Gaffurio, in his *Theorica musice*, quotes a remarkable passage from Cicero, who had apparently reached this same idea by deduction.

> A certain tuning pitch exists in one's body like that of the voice and instruments called harmony; just as sounds are made in singing, so out of the nature and form of the whole body issue various vibrations.[14]

So, if our very molecules and atoms produce pitches, then music must be older than them. Perhaps it was the pitch created by the vibration of the rotation of the earth which stirred that primordial 'soup' that began the chain of evolution. A vibrating pitch may have been the mid-wife of us all!

In view of this physiological connection between man and his music, it should perhaps be no surprise that many early philosophers believed that music was both genetic and universal in character. 'Why,' Aristotle asks, 'do all men love music?'

> Is it because we naturally rejoice in natural movements? This is shown by the fact that children rejoice in [rhythm and melody] as soon as they are born. Now we delight in the various types of melody for their moral character, but we delight in rhythm because it contains a familiar and ordered number and moves in a regular manner; for ordered movement is naturally more akin to us than disordered, and is therefore more in accordance with nature.[15]

The first century AD philosopher, Philodemus of Gadara, not only recognized the universality of music, but suspected that this universality was genetic in origin as well.

> We have an innate affinity with the Muses, one which does not have to be learned. This is clearly shown by the way infants are lulled to sleep with wordless singing.[16]

[14] 'Tusculan Disputations,' 1.9.19–20, quoted in Paolo Cortese, 'De cardinalatu libri tres,' quoted in Nino Pirrotta, in *Music and Culture in Italy from the Middle Ages to the Baroque* (Cambridge: Harvard University Press, 1984), 177ff.

[15] *Problemata*, 920b.28.

[16] Quoted in Warren D. Anderson, *Ethos and Education in Greek Music* (Cambridge: Harvard University Press, 1966), 173.

Erasmus (1469–1536) also found the effect of music on children to be evidence of innate understanding.

> [This is its nature] just as children too are affected by the modes of music through some natural affinity, even when they have no idea what music is.[17]

[17] 'Adages,' in *The Collected Works of Erasmus* (Toronto: University of Toronto Press, 1992), XXXI, 167.

Believing that everything was made by God, it is no surprise to find the early Church fathers also mentioning the innate understanding of music found in man. St. John Chrysostom argued that the pleasure man finds in music is divinely implanted.[18] St. Augustine makes a similar argument, discussing it from the perspective of both players and the listening public.

[18] St. John Chrysostom, 'Exposition of Psalm XLI,' quoted in Oliver Strunk, *Source Readings in Music History* (New York: Norton, 1950), 68.

[19] *On Music*, trans., Robert Taliaferro in *Writings of Saint Augustine* (New York: Fathers of the Church), I, v.

> AUGUSTINE. How do you explain the fact that an ignorant crowd hisses off a flute player letting out futile sounds, and on the other hand applauds one who sings well, and finally that the more agreeably one sings the more fully and intensely it is moved? For it isn't possible to believe the crowd does all this by the art of music, is it?
> STUDENT. No.
> AUGUSTINE. How then?
> STUDENT. I think it is done by nature giving everyone a sense of hearing by which such things are judged.
> AUGUSTINE. You are right.[19]

St. Augustine in his studio, by Sandro Botticelli, 1480

The great Italian Renaissance theorist, Zarlino, thought it might be some genetic memory of the music of the angels which impels man to sing as a means of easing labor.

> Many were of the opinion that in this life every soul is won by music, and, although the soul is imprisoned by the body, it still remembers and is conscious of the music of the heavens, forgetting every hard and annoying labor.[20]

[20] 'Le Istitutioni harmoniche.'

This idea of the genetic understanding of music being a kind of memory in us, was also mentioned by the great German philosopher, Gottfried Wilhelm Leibniz (1646–1716). He believed genetic knowledge explained why 'we need only the beginning of a song to remember it,'[21] and why hearing a musical performance seems to create 'a sympathetic echo in us.'[22]

[21] Leibniz, *New Essays Concerning Human Understanding*, in Leroy Loemker, *Philosophical Papers and Letters* (Dordrecht: Reidel, 1956), preface.

[22] Leibniz, 'On Wisdom' (ca. 1690–1698), in ibid., 425ff.

The Baroque writers tended to concentrate on the genetic understanding of specific elements of music. The brilliant thinker, Jean-Philippe Rameau (1683–1764), was absorbed for years with the idea that man is born with a genetic pitch template, something which modern research seems also to suggest.[23] In 1734, Rameau was clearly pondering observations which he had made along these lines.

> In music the ear obeys only nature. It takes account of neither measure nor range. Instinct alone leads it.
>   Whether a novice or the most experienced person in music, the moment one sings an improvisation, one ordinarily places the first tone in the middle register of the voice and then continues up, even though the voice range above or below this first tone is about equal; this is completely consistent with the resonance of any sounding body from which all emanating overtones are above its fundamental tone which one thinks one is hearing alone.
>   On the other hand, inexperienced as one may be, one hardly ever fails, when improvising on an instrument, immediately to play, ever ascending, the perfect chord made up of the overtones of the sounding body, the major form of which is always preferred to the minor, unless the latter is suggested by some reminiscence.[24]

Twenty-five years later he was still struggling with this idea. He begins by discounting the ancient explanations based on faith and wonders why these early philosophers did not pursue natural rules, that is, understanding based on Nature.

> [The ancient writers] found the relationships between sounds in divinely inspired order; they discoursed a great deal on that subject, and every reason they were able to advance evaporated like a wisp of smoke. Finally the geometricians and the philosophers became disheartened. Can it be true that up to the present time man has always been so enthralled by this single inspiration that it never occurred to anyone to seek the reason why, despite ourselves, we should be compelled to prefer certain intervals to others after certain sounds, especially after the first sound? Allow your natural feelings to operate in yourself with no preconceived expectation and then try to see if you can ever ascend a semitone after a given semitone, and whether you can do the same thing after two successive tones. Why was this suggested to me in this way? Whence this sensation? What could have given rise to this sensation in me, if it was not in the moment itself? It was necessary to test the effect of the sound, and from it three sounds would have been distinguished which form that enchanting harmony, and from there one would have proceeded with certainty, as I believe I have done.

[23] St. Augustine, in his treatise, *On Music*, also suspected a genetic template:
> I believe, while we were discussing these things, a fifth kind appeared from somewhere, a kind in the natural judgment of perceiving when we are delighted by the equality of numbers or offended at a flaw in them. [See *On Music*, trans., Robert Taliaferro in *Writings of Saint Augustine* (New York: Fathers of the Church), VI, iv]

[24] Jean Philippe Rameau, *Observations sur notre instinct pour la musique et sur son principe* (1734), quoted in Sam Morgenstern, *Composers on Music* (New York: Pantheon, 1956), 44.

Jean-Philippe Rameau, by Jean-Baptiste van Loo

The principle is inexhaustible and holds true for theology as well as geometry and physics. Anyone more enlightened than myself should be able to draw the most far-reaching conclusions from this and already I can envision the origin of that final knowledge which cannot be denied without denying the phenomenon from which it is derived.[25]

Another French composer of the Baroque, Michel de Saint-Lambert, in his *Les Principes du Clavecin* of 1702, adds rhythm to pitch as genetic information. After briefly mentioning some of the abilities needed in performance, he says,

> Though this at first sight may appear a large order, it is nevertheless sure that this extreme accuracy in intonation and rhythm is a gift given to almost all men, like sight and speech. There are very few who do not sing and dance naturally; if it is not with the delicacy and correctness that Art has sought, it is at least with the correctness which Art dictates and which Art itself has derived from Nature. It is already a great asset for those who want to learn music or to play some instrument that they know they have discernment of the ear by nature, that is, the first and most important of these aptitudes.[26]

The French philosopher, Charles Batteaux (1713–1780), in reference to the innate character of music, quotes, without source, a Latin expression, 'We are led to melody by natural instinct.'[27]

Modern medical research has identified in more specific terms the nature of the musical information we carry genetically into birth. For one thing, there is pitch awareness itself, which must have been critical to early man. The actual affinity for a musical language can also be tested at a very early age. Dennis Molfese of the University of Pennsylvania has conducted studies on infants less than forty-eight hours after birth.[28] University of California researchers believe that infants are born with a genetic ability to recognize and respond to music, even before language.[29] Psychologists have found that even before age *one*, infants can detect errors in music![30] Among the most interesting findings are those which have to do with the acquisition of 'perfect pitch.'

> There is evidence that almost all musicians who began their training before the age of 6 possess absolute pitch, compared with none of those who began after the age of 11.[31]

[25] Letter to A. M. Beguillet, October 6, 1762, quoted in Gertrude Norman and Miriam Shrifte, *Letters of Composers* (New York, Knopf, 1946), 20.

[26] Michel de Saint-Lambert, *Les Principes du Clavecin* (1702), quoted in Carol MacClintock, *Readings in the History of Music in Performance* (Bloomington: Indiana University Press, 1979), 212.

[27] Charles Batteaux (1713–1780), *Les beaux-arts réduits à un même principe* [Paris,1746], quoted in Peter le Huray and James Day, *Music and Aesthetics in the Eighteenth and Early-Nineteenth Centuries* (Cambridge: Cambridge University Press, 1981), 50ff.

[28] Craig Buck, 'Knowing the LEFT from the RIGHT,' *Human Behavior*, June, 1976.

[29] *Associated Press*, January 23, 1992.

[30] 'The Musical Brain,' *U. S. News & World Report*, June 11, 1990.

[31] D. Sergeant, 'Experimental Investigation of Absolute Pitch,' in *Journal of Research in Musical Education*, 1969, 17, 135–143.

Research by Dr. Jamshed Bharucha, of Dartmouth College has found that we have a biological affinity for *melodic patterns*. It is interesting that this idea of genetic preference for certain kinds of melody was mentioned by the great English philosopher, Thomas Hobbes (1588–1679).

> That which pleases is called a tune [*air*]; but for what reason one succession in tone and measure is a more pleasing tune than another, I confess I know not; but I conjecture the reason to be, for that some of them imitate and revive some passion which otherwise we take no notice of, and the other not.[32]

32 'Human Nature,' VIII, 2.

This biological affinity for musical patterns is present in the brains of other species as well. A study by Stewart Hulse of Johns Hopkins University found that starlings have the ability to recognize a simple melody in different keys, and other studies suggest that dolphins recognize octaves. In another experiment, pigeons were trained to distinguished random excerpts of music by J. S. Bach from excerpts by Igor Stravinsky, and they were even able to correctly categorize music by other composers as being either 'Bach-like' or 'Stravinsky-like'.[33]

33 'The Musical Brain,' *U. S. News & World Report*, June 11, 1990.

Jay Dowling, of the University of Texas at Dallas, has discovered clinical evidence to suggest that ordinary people perceive these melodic patterns on the basis of the relationship between the notes themselves, and not on the basis of precise pitches. Thus, almost everybody can sing 'Happy Birthday' starting from any note on the piano.[34] But, with bad news for the twelve-tone composers, research by John Pierce at Stanford has demonstrated that the brain has little ability to recognize melodic patterns played backwards. For example, most people don't realize that the sound of the word *we* is the reverse of the sound of *you*.[35]

34 ibid.

35 ibid.

It would seem, then, that there is a great deal about the nature of music which cannot be explained as a learned art. And if none of this research existed, the point would still be obvious in the fact that people all over the world listen to music, even though they 'know' nothing at all about music.

Finally, there is the fundamental issue of the two hemispheres of our brain, a bicameral nature found already in the very earliest of ancient fossils. Every reader must be familiar with the medical research of the past forty years, research which won the Nobel Prize in medicine, on the left and right hemispheres of the brain. While more recent research suggests there is some cross-over possible, nevertheless it does appear that the left hemisphere is best adapted for rational activity and the right hemisphere for non-rational activity. Written music, like any symbolic language, is found in the left; music performed, being experiential, is understood in the right.[36] While the most recent clinical findings suggest this is more complex in the brain, nothing yet departs from the basic division I have suggested.

These findings answer many questions, such as why it is difficult to *talk* about music or to write an adequate love letter, why Erasmus observed that one cannot listen to music if someone is talking[37] and why he also observed 'My tongue is not adequate to my feelings'[38] and why Martin Luther found he could not write while his son, Hans, was singing.[39] Much is also explained by the fact that the left hemisphere (the talking and writing half) does not recognize the existence of the right hemisphere and therefore does not understand the world of the right hemisphere. Blaise Pascal (1623–1662) was thus prompted to comment,

> The heart has its reason, which reason does not know. We feel it in a thousand things.[40]

If we remember the fact that our left hemisphere controls the right hand and the right hemisphere the left, then we understand why the Indians of the American Southwest distinguished between the functions of the hands, the right for writing and the left for music, and why the French word for Law, one of the most conceptual, logical and left hemisphere oriented of professions, is *droit* ('Right,' as in right hand). For the same reason we have the traditional phrases 'He received a *left*-handed compliment,' or the more positive, 'The Favorite sat on the *right*-hand of the King.' Since sight and hearing cross to opposite brains, similar to the operation of the hands, we find most remarkable indeed a poem by Thomas Sheridan (1687–1738), a priest and schoolmaster friend of Swift. He was absolutely, and astonishingly, correct in his assigning of right or left eye and ear functions vis-a-vis their actual relationship with the brain hemispheres.

[36] See Craig Buck, 'Knowing the LEFT from the RIGHT,' in *Human Behavior*, June, 1976. Some research suggests that trained musicians who listen for conceptual detail hear music with the left hemisphere. Thus, among other things, music schools ruin musicians as listeners.

[37] 'The Tongue,' [1525] in *The Collected Works of Erasmus* (Toronto: University of Toronto Press, 1992), XXIX, 279.

[38] 'A Congratulatory Poem [for] Prince Philip, Upon his Happy Return,' in ibid., LXXXV, 139.

[39] In a conversation of 1532 reported by Veit Dietrich, in *Luther's Works* (St. Louis: Concordia, 1961), LIV, 21.

[40] Blaise Pascal, *Pensées* (New York: Modern Library, 1941), III, 277.

Thomas Sheridan, ca. 1700s

With my left eye, I see you sit snug in your stall,
With my right I'm attending the lawyers that scrawl.
With my left I behold your bellower a cur chase;
With my right I'm reading my deeds for a purchase.
My left ear's attending the hymns of the choir,
My right ear is stunned with the noise of the crier.[41]

Since some remain concerned over the sometimes confusing and conflicting data of this research, perhaps for the moment we might simply all agree that man has his rational and experiential sides of his personality, however they are organized physiologically. Certainly this aspect of man has been observed and commented on by a wide range of writers. Roger Bacon (b. ca. 1214) wrote of the two sides of man being the 'cogitative faculty' and that of 'experience.'[42] There were several fifteenth-century works of English literature which explored 'Reson and Sensuallyte.' Francis Bacon (1561–1626) believed the brain to be divided into understanding and reason on one hand, and appetite and affection on the other.[43] And Wagner wrote at some length on 'understanding' versus 'feeling.'[44] In another place, Wagner observed,

> The Understanding tells us: '*So it is*,'—only when the Feeling has told us: '*So it must be*.'[45]

Each of these two sides of our personality has its own form of communication. The 'understanding side' has language. The 'feeling side' has music. We chose between language and music depending on what we wish to communicate. A play communicates rational thought through language. An opera communicates feeling through music. This is why when we attend a great opera we don't pay much attention to the actual words of the libretto. The words can even be in a language we do not speak, yet it detracts little from our enjoyment of the music. It was this fact upon which Rossini once observed:

> If the magic of music has really seized the listener, the word undoubtedly will always come off second best. But if the music doesn't seize the listener, what good is it? It is useless then, if not superfluous or even detrimental.[46]

---

[41] Quoted in *The Poetical Works of Jonathan Swift* (London: Bell and Daldy, n.d.), III, 245.

[42] 'Experimental Science,' in *The Opus Majus of Roger Bacon*, trans., Robert Burke (New York: Russell & Russell, 1962), I.

[43] *The Works of Francis Bacon* (Cambridge: Cambridge University Press, 1869), VI, 258ff.

[44] 'A Communication to my Friends,' in William Ellis, *Wagner's Prose Works* (New York: Broude), I, 271ff.

[45] 'The Play and Dramatic Poetry,' in ibid., II, 209.

[46] Reported by Wagner, in ibid., VIII, 377.

2   The Paramount Purpose of Music

THE EXTANT WRITINGS OF THE ANCIENT GREEKS document that civilization had concluded by some earlier time that the paramount purpose of music is to communicate emotions, as we see already in the oldest literature of Western Europe, where Homer describes Ulysses crying as a minstrel sings. Plato, in *Ion*,[1] presents a valuable discussion between Socrates and a Rhapsodist, the ancient singer of epic poetry, during which the singer describes the emotions of the audience while he performs.

[1] 534c–535e.

> ION. I look down upon them from the stage, and behold the various emotions of pity, wonder, sternness, stamped upon their faces when I am performing.

Plato, in fact, defined music as, 'a science of the phenomena of love in its application to harmony and rhythm.'[2]

[2] Plato, *Symposium*, 187b.

The ancient writers also clearly recognized the fact that the ability to appreciate and understand music is not dependent on any technical knowledge whatsoever. Petrarch, for example, quotes Cicero as saying the music 'tickles their ears, without their knowing why.'[3] It is remarkable that an almost identical statement was made by Mozart in a letter to his father:

[3] Letter to Boccaccio, in James Robinson, *Petrarch, The First Modern Scholar and Man of Letters* (New York: Putnam, 1914), 184.

[4] 28 December 1782.

> These passages are written in such a way that the less learned cannot fail to be pleased, though without knowing why.[4]

With the beginning of the Christian Era, the construction of concert halls, private and public concerts of secular art music, together with popular music and sung poetry, all continued, although one would never discover this in reading music history texts which describe the Middle Ages. There was however a new development which had far reaching consequences in music practice. The new Christian Church, consumed with the desire to rid Western Europe of all things 'pagan' (meaning the values of ancient Greece and Rome), took a very strong stand against all expressions of emotion. Emotions, the Church fathers proclaimed, were the path to sin. St. Basil even proposed that the proper Christian should not even laugh, because laughing is a form of emotion and because nowhere in the New Testament is Jesus described as laughing. After the fall of Rome, the new Church attacked art in general, reasoning that the Christian cannot love art—for to love art is to love the present life, which is inconsistent with believing in the future life.[5]

The Church rather grudgingly accepted vocal music, as indeed it had to not only because of the legend of the choir of angels singing at the time of the birth of Jesus but also because Jesus himself is described as singing in the New Testament,[6] so it stressed that in church singing it is the words that matter, not the music. Augustine wrote that whenever he found himself listening to the music, instead of thinking about the words, he felt he had 'sinned penally.'[7] Regarding the music itself there was the additional problem that it 'disappeared' when the performance ended, as mentioned by the third-century Church philosopher, Lactantius.

> For all those things which are unconnected with words, that is, pleasant sounds of the air and of strings, may be easily disregarded, because they do not adhere to us, and cannot be written.[8]

For its schools, the early Church could therefore only admit the study of music when it was presented in conceptual terms, and, in particular, as mathematics. The influential Boethius (475–524 AD), although he acknowledges in passing the power of the emotional aspect in music by noting 'that we cannot be free from it even if we so desired,'[9] nevertheless clearly sought to establish the principle that it is not enough for a musician to know *music*, he must know *about* music. From this judgment, his conclusion followed:

> How much nobler, then, is the study of music as a rational discipline than as composition and performance![10]

From this nonsense, Church philosophers established the definition of 'musician' to be not one who makes music, but one who *knows about* music. The mere performer was given a much lower social status, thus Aurelian of Réome, in his

---

[5] St. John Chrysostom, 'Commentary on Saint John,' trans., Sister Thomas Aquinas Goggin (New York: Fathers of the Church, 1960), 227.

[6] Together with his disciples in Matthew 26:30.

[7] *The Confessions*, X.

[8] Lactantius, 'The Divine Institutes,' trans., William Fletcher in *The Works of Lactantius* (Edinburgh: T. & T. Clark, 1886), I, Book VI, xxi.

[9] Boethius, *Fundamentals of Music*, trans., Calvin Bower (New Haven: Yale University Press), I, i.

[10] ibid., I, xxxiv. Fifteen centuries later our music schools still labor under these misconceptions.

Musica Disciplina (ca. 843 AD), could observe, 'The singer seems to stand before the musician like a prisoner before the judge.'[11] John Cotton, in his music treatise of 1100 AD, says the musician who doesn't know about music is a beast by definition.[12]

There must have been many who regarded this official thinking as nonsense. One was the tenth-century nun, Hrotswitha, who has left a play, *Paphnutius*, which contains an extensive dialog on the subject of music.[13] The passage begins with a group of students asking the teacher, 'What *is* music?' The teacher responds with various mathematical complexities based on Boethius, each one of which causes the students to object to this conceptual language and respond, 'What has this got to do with *music*?,' implying, we presume, that they understood that music has to do with feelings and emotions, not mathematics. The teacher answers in frustration, 'But that is how you *talk* about music!'

When the first Church universities began to be established, music was placed in the faculty of mathematics and all music courses were taught by, and music treatises written by, mathematicians. But these professors were very much aware that the actual performance of music which they *heard* included elements, such as feeling, which were not easily represented or explained by numbers, or any other conceptual symbols. Hence they simply separated the discipline of music at this time into two branches: *musica speculativa* and *musica practica*. They said, in effect, 'We will teach the first, and leave to you players the second.'

Thus we have inherited two forms of music: a *speculativa* form, which includes notation and all of 'theory' which we can talk and write about, and which we learn by eye, and a *practica* form which is mostly learned by ear (the private studio teacher says, 'No, it goes like this'). But in truth, the *speculativa* form does not exist. It is only a conceptual symbolic language which *represents* the *practica* form, which is *real* music! Thus, when music schools teach the conceptual form, while they *call* it music, they are not really teaching music. Harmony, for example, is not music and might better be identified as another symbolic language.

[11] Aurelian of Réome, *The Discipline of Music*, trans., Joseph Ponte (Colorado Springs: Colorado College Music Press, 1968), VII.

[12] John gives the source as the *Micrologus*, but it actually comes from the beginning of Guido's *Regulae rhythmicae*.

[13] *The Plays of Hrotswitha of Gandersheim,* trans., Larissa Bonfante (New York: New York University Press, 1979), 108ff.

These views of music are still found as late as the famous Johannes Tinctoris (1435–1511), who identified himself as one who professes 'the mathematical sciences.'[14] It is particularly interesting that after the publication of his mathematics-based book on proportions, *Proportionale Musices*, he was criticized by a singer, a 'practical' musician. Indeed, Tinctoris confides this man 'has not been afraid to menace me with a violent meal of this little book if ever I should return to my native land.'

It was only the rediscovery and publication of the ancient Greek treatises which finally led to the rejection of the old Church nonsense about music and restored an understanding of the true nature of music. It was this Renaissance movement which we call Humanism. We can clearly see a change is in the air in the first decade of the fourteenth century, in the writings of Marchetto of Padua. In considering the etymology of the word 'voice' [*vox*] he notes that it comes from 'vows' [*vota*], 'because it expresses vows of the heart.' He then quotes Aristotle as saying of the spoken voice, 'Things spoken are symbols of the passions of the soul.'[15] He concludes it is appropriate, therefore, that we speak of 'notes' of music, which derives from *nota* ('symbol').

In Petrarch we find a passage in which 'Joy' and 'Reason' are clearly representatives of Humanism and the Church.

> JOY: Song moves me.
> REASON: But to what purpose? Without doubt music has great power over the noble hearts of men. But its effects are various beyond belief. And, to omit what is of no concern, it moves some to shallow mirth, others to pure and devout joy and, sometimes, even to pious tears.[16]

An especially interesting reference to the importance of *feeling* in music is found in Chaucer's 'Nun's Priest's Tale.' A fox, who has come to hear a rooster sing, declares that the rooster sings with more feeling in his music than Boethius or any other singer.

> Therwith ye han in musyk moore feelynge
> Than hadde Boece, or any that kan synge.[17]

[14] *Concerning the Nature and Propriety of Tones*, trans., Albert Seay (Colorado Springs, 1976), 1.

[15] Marchetto of Padua, *Lucidarium*, Jan W. Herlinger, trans., (Chicago: University of Chicago Press, 1985), I, 10, iiiff.

[16] 'Remedies for Fortune Fair and Foul,' trans., Conrad Rawski (Bloomington: Indiana University Press, 1991), I, xxiii, 71.

[17] 'Nun's Priest's Tale,' 4483

By the fifteenth century Humanism had made the emotions a topic of general discussion. The Florentine philosopher, Leon Battista Alberti (b. 1404), gives an interesting testimonial to the power of love and, more significantly, points out that it is only by *experience* that one can understand such an emotion.

> Who would believe, except by the experience of his own feelings, how great and intense is the love of a father toward his children? Every kind of love seems to me no small matter. Many have been known to risk all their possessions, to give time and fortune, to undergo terrible hardships, dangers, and troubles only to display their loyalty and the quality of their love for a friend. And it is said that there have been men who, for desire of things loved which they thought they had lost, refused to continue living.[18]

Leonardo da Vinci observed,

> The tears come from the heart and not from the brain.[19]

By the sixteenth century the paramount purpose of music had been restored to what it had been understood to be by the ancient Greeks. Galilei wrote in 1581, 'True music has a primary purpose to express the passions' and, secondarily, 'to communicate these with equal force to the minds of mortals for their benefit and advantage.'[20] Certainly in no medieval music treatise does one find a statement such as this one by Martin Luther: 'Only music deserves being extolled as the mistress and governess of the feelings of the human heart.'[21] Galilei's book on lute intabulation, by the way, gives an almost startling description of the emotions capable on the lute. No organist, he observes, can produce,

> the cries, laments, shrieks, tears, and finally quietude and rage—with so much grace and skill as excellent players do on the lute.[22]

The university treatises of the Renaissance still speak of music as being mathematics, but finally one is quite different. The *Compendium Musices* by Adrian Coclico (ca. 1550–1562) documents the beginning of a shift away from the old Scholastic complexities of speculative music to the more modern emphasis on expressive, practical musicianship.[23] In this work, written for the training of boys, he constantly warns against

---

[18] Leon Battista Alberti, *I Libri dela Famiglia*, trans., Renée Watkins (Columbia: University of South Carolina Press, 1969), I, 45.

[19] Quoted in Jean Paul Richter, ed., *The Literary Works of Leonardo da Vinci* (London: Phaidon, 1970), II, 93. Found together with notes on anatomy!

[20] Oliver Strunk, *Source Readings in Music History* (New York: Norton, 1950), 306ff.

[21] Luther, Preface to a collection of part-songs (1538) based on the suffering and death of Jesus.

[22] Vincenzo Galilei, *Fronimo* (1584), trans., Carol MacClintock (Neuhasen-Stuttgart: Hänssler-Verlag, 1985), 87.

[23] Adrian Coclico, *Musical Compendium*, trans., Albert Seay (Colorado Springs: Colorado College Music Press, 1973), 30.

rules-based learning. No sooner has he begun writing of scales, for example, than he stops and observes that this can only be understood in performance.

> I have wished to train these boys in music through but few words and precepts on that account, so that no youth running to the books of musician-mathematicians will waste his life in reading them and never arrive at the goal of singing well.[24]

[24] ibid., 10.

Of all the periods of music history, none has been more inaccurately portrayed by musicologists than the Renaissance. Music history texts give the impression that Church music *was* renaissance music, whereas in fact there was a great deal more than that. A composer such as Machaut would have been utterly astonished if he could have known that he would be remembered today for his Church music, an insignificant portion of his music upon which he placed little value in comparison to his love songs. It is also because scholars concentrate only on Church music, that we never read that the people who actually knew Leonardo da Vinci considered him the greatest *musician* they knew. And why have these same books kept from us descriptions of such powerful performances of art music as that by Francesco da Milano in 1555?

Francesco da Milano, ca. 1535

[25] Pontus de Tyard, *Solitaire second* (1555).

> He made the very strings to swoon beneath his fingers and transported all who listened into such gentle melancholy that one present buried his head in his hands, another let his entire body slump into an ungainly posture with members all awry, while another, his mouth sagged open and his eyes more than half shut, seemed, one would judge, as if transfixed upon the strings, and yet another, with chin sunk upon his chest, hiding the most sadly taciturn visage ever seen, remained abstracted in all his senses save his hearing, as if his soul had fled from all the seats of sensibility to take refuge in his ears where more easefully it could rejoice in such enchanting symphony.[25]

Who has ever read a description of listeners of Renaissance church music which compares with that? The truth of the matter is that the Church polyphony, upon which our modern music history texts are based, was music heard by the actual people living during the Renaissance as being already old-fashioned and scholastic. This was because this music was composed upon principles of mathematics, and not of feeling. For example, Pontus de Tyard, a member of the group of French poets known as the Pléiade, observed,

> Contrapuntal music most often brings to the ears only a lot of noise, from which you feel no vivid effect.[26]

26 Pontus de Tyard, *Les Discours philosophiques* (Paris, 1587).

Similarly, Zarlino wrote,

> At times nothing is heard but a jumbled din of voices and diverse instrumental sounds, singing without taste or discretion, and an unseemly pronunciation of words, so that he hears only a tumult and uproar. Music practiced in this way cannot have any effect on us worth remembering.[27]

27 *Le Istitutioni harmoniche*, II, ix, 75.

It was in the Renaissance, then, that Europe began to rediscover the fundamental role of the emotions in music. The story of the Baroque is one of an obsession for emotions in music by both composers and philosophers alike. Again, the view of the Baroque given us by musicologists over the past hundred years is so incomplete, and therefore misleading, that many musicians today do not even think of Baroque music as being emotional at heart. Many musicians have been misled by their teachers into thinking of Baroque music as math, now called counterpoint and functional-bass chord progressions.

28 Quoted in Nino Pirrotta and Elena Povoledo, *Music and Theatre from Poliziano to Monteverdi* (Cambridge: Cambridge University Press, 1982), 241.

But the better Baroque composers never talked like that! Cavalieri, in the preface to his *La rappresentatione di Anima* (1600) says his goal is to 'move listeners to different emotions, such as pity and joy, tears and laughter.'[28] And Caccini, in his *Le Nuove Musiche*, writes that the goal of his solo songs was 'to move the affect of the soul.'[29] Charles Butler wrote, in 1636,

29 *Le Nuove Musiche*, 45.

> [Good composing is impossible] unless the Author, at the time of Composing, be transported as it were with some Musical fury; so that himself scarce knoweth what he doth, nor can presently give a reason for his doing.[30]

Le Nuove Musiche, Caccini

30 Charles Butler, *The Principles of Musik in Singing and Setting* [1636] (New York: Da Capo Press, 1970), 92.

Angelo Berardi wrote in 1681 that 'Music is the ruler of the passions of the soul.'[31] Speaking of his *Il Gran Tamerlano* (1706), Scarlatti relates that he tried to achieve, 'naturalness and beauty, together with the expression of the passion.'[32] And Karl Philipp Emanuel Bach wrote,

> It appears to me that it is the special province of music to move the heart.[33]

We might also add that in his biographical work, *Ehrenpforte* (Hamburg, 1740), in reference to a person who had claimed both a goal of making 'music a scientific or scholarly pursuit' and an association with J. S. Bach, Johann Mattheson objects that Bach certainly did not teach this man 'the supposed mathematical basis of composition.' 'This,' Mattheson testifies, 'I can guarantee.'[34]

It is at this time also that we find philosophers focusing on the emotions when writing of the purpose of music. Even that left-brained, mechanically obsessed Descartes, in his definition of music, had to admit,

> The basis of music is sound; its aim is to please and to arouse various emotions in us.[35]

But the real evidence for the consuming interest in the emotions among Baroque musicians is found in the contemporary descriptions of their performance. To begin with singers, Severo Bonini has left this description of the singing of one of the first opera composers.

> A much learned singer and composer was Signor Jacopo Peri, who would have moved and brought to tears the hardest heart by singing his works.[36]

And consider the range of emotions mentioned by Christoph Bernhard, in his singing treatise of 1649.

> In the recitative style, one should take care that the voice is raised in moments of anger, and to the contrary dropped in moments of grief. Pain makes it pause; impatience hastens it. Happiness enlivens it. Desire emboldens it. Love renders it alert. Bashfulness holds it back. Hope

[31] Angelo Berardi, *Ragionamenti Musicali* (Bologna, 1681), 87.

[32] Quoted in Claude Palisca, *Baroque Music* (Englewood Cliffs: Prentice Hall, 1981), 236ff.

[33] Quoted in Nat Shapiro, *An Encyclopedia of Quotations About Music* (New York: Da Capo, 1978), 192.

[34] Quoted in Hans T. David and Arthur Mendel, *The Bach Reader* (New York: Norton, 1966), 440.

Rene Descartes, portrait after Frans Hals, ca. 1649–1700

[35] 'Compendium of Music,' Walter Robert, trans. (American Institute of Musicology, 1961), 11.

[36] Quoted in Nino Pirrotta and Elena Povoledo, op. cit., 246.

strengthens it. Despair diminishes it. Fear keeps it down. Danger is fled with screams. If, however, a person faces up to danger, then his voice must reflect his daring and bravery.[37]

A manuscript by Diderot describes the nephew of Rameau as an amateur singing in a cafe.

> While singing fragments of Jomelli's *Lamentations*, he reproduced with incredible precision, fidelity, and warmth the most beautiful passages of each scene. In that magnificent recitative in which Jeremiah describes the desolation of Jerusalem he was drenched in tears, which drew their like from every onlooker. His art was complete—delicacy of voice, expressive strength, true sorrow …
>
> Worn out, exhausted, like a man emerging from a deep sleep or a prolonged reverie, he stood motionless, dumb, petrified. He kept looking around him like a man who has lost his way and wants to know where he is. He waited for returning strength and wits, wiping his face with an absent-minded gesture.[38]

The most dramatic descriptions of Baroque performers are those of violinists, such as this one heard by a French critic in 1702, as,

> an ecstatic who was so carried away with the piece that he was playing that he not only martyred his instrument but also himself. No longer master of his own being, he became so transported that he gyrated and hopped around like someone overcome by a demon.[39]

The critic, François Raguenet, describes another.

> The artist himself, whilst he is performing it, is seized with an unavoidable agony; he tortures his violin; he racks his body; he is no longer master of himself, but is agitated like one possessed with an irresistible motion.[40]

If there is still a reader anywhere who is under the impression that Baroque music was mechanical and boring, perhaps this eyewitness description of the famous Corelli will make him wonder if he has been misinformed.

> I never met with any man that suffered his passions to hurry him away so much whilst he was playing on the violin as the famous Arcangelo Corelli, whose eyes will sometimes turn as red as fire; his countenance will be distorted, his eyeballs roll as in an agony, and he gives in so much to what he is doing that he doth not look like the same man.[41]

[37] Quoted in Ellen Harris, 'Voices,' in *Performance Practice: Music after 1600* (New York: Norton, 1989), 110.

[38] Quoted in *Rameau's Nephew and Other Works*, trans., Jacques Barzun (Garden City: Doubleday, 1956), 69.

[39] Quoted in Hans-Peter Schmitz, *Die Kunst der Verzierung im 18. Jahrhundert* (Kassel: Bärenreiter, 1955), 12.

[40] François Raguenet, 'Parallèle des Italiens et des Français,' (1702), quoted in Strunk, op. cit., 478ff.

[41] O. Strunk, 'François Raguenet, *Comparison between the French and Italian Music* (1702),' in The Musical Quarterly XXXII (1946), 419fn.

Arcangelo Corelli, by Jan Frans van Douven

In some cases, accounts by contemporary listeners suggest an emotional impact much greater than we might experience in hearing the same music today. The English actor, Betterton, found,

> Purcell penetrates the heart, makes the blood dance through your veins, and thrill with the agreeable violence offered by his Heavenly Harmony.[42]

[42] Charles Gildon, *The Life of Mr. Thomas Betterton, the Late Eminent Tragedian* [1710] (London: Frank Cass Reprint, 1970), 155ff.

And consider the impact of mere incidental music in a play, as recalled by Pepys in a 27 February 1668 entry in his famous *Diary*.

> What did please me beyond anything in the whole world was the wind-musique when the Angel comes down, which is so sweet that it ravished me; and indeed, in a word, did wrap up my soul so that it make me really sick, just as I have formerly been when in love with my wife; that neither then, nor all the evening going home and at home, I was able to think of anything, but remained all night transported, so as I could not believe that ever any music has that real command over the soul of a man as this did upon me; and makes me resolve to practice wind-music and to make my wife do the same.

One vivid portrait of an attentive audience is found in a description of a performance of Handel.

> The audience was so enchanted with this performance, that a stranger who should have seen the manner in which they were affected, would have imagined they had all been distracted.[43]

[43] J. Mainwaring, *Memoirs of Handel* (1760), quoted in Robert Donnington, *The Interpretation of Early Music* (New York, 1964), 96.

Finally, there is this rather remarkable advice to the listener by Rameau, himself famous during his lifetime as a theoretician.

> Often we think we hear in music only what exists in the words, or in the interpretation we wish to give them. We try to subject music to forced inflections, but that is not the way to be able to judge it. On the contrary, we must not think but let ourselves be carried away by the feeling which the music inspires; without our thinking at all, this feeling will become the basis of our judgment.[44]

[44] Jean Philippe Rameau, *Observations sur notre instinct pour la musique et sur son principe.*

The strong focus on the emotions demonstrated in Italian opera helped prepare the melodically expressive music of the Classic Period. Equally significant was the influence of the Enlightenment which encouraged even the Catholic composers to write music which expressed their own feelings, instead of thinking of themselves as surrogates for God. Now, in expressing emotions, the composers no longer sought the exaggeration of the Baroque, and Italian opera in particular, but instead sought to express more natural and true emotions. Thus, Mozart, describing his *Die Entführung aus dem Serail* for his father, wrote,

> Now, as for Belmonte's aria in A major, do you know how it is expressed—even the throbbing of his loving heart is indicated—the two violins in octaves … One sees the trembling—the wavering—one sees how his swelling breast heaves—this is expressed by a crescendo—one hears the whispering and the sighing—which is expressed by the first violins, muted, and a flute in unison. Nothing could be more definite than that.[45]

[45] Letter to his father, September 26, 1781.

And it is no surprise to find Mozart complimenting Mlle. Weber's singing, by remarking that her singing 'goes to the heart.'[46]

[46] Letter to his father, February 19, 1778.

From this time until the twentieth century, no one questioned the fact that the paramount role of music was to express the emotions. When Beethoven finished his *Missa Solemnis*, he wrote on the score, 'From the heart, may it go to the heart.' Subsequent composers clearly made the expression of emotions through music their credo. Consider the following:

Schumann:
> Music is to me the perfect expression of the soul.[47]

[47] Letter to his mother, Leipzig, May 8, 1832.

Berlioz:
> The prevailing characteristics of my music are passionate expression, intense ardor, rhythmical animation, and unexpected turns.[48]

[48] *Memoirs*.

Chopin:
> A long time ago I decided that my universe will be the soul and heart of man.[49]

Verdi:
> I should compose with utter confidence a subject that set my blood going, even though it were condemned by all other artists as anti-musical.[50]

[49] Letter to Delphine Potocka. Chopin's last words were reported to be, 'Play Mozart in memory of me.'

[50] Letter of 1854.

Mahler:
What is best in music is not to be found in the notes.[51]

Gustav Mahler, photograph by Leonhard Berlin-Bieber, 1892

Paul Dukas:
Be it laughter or tears, feverish passion or religious ecstasy, nothing, in the category of human feelings, is a stranger to music.[52]

Max Reger:
Music, in and by itself, should generate a flow of pure emotion without the least tinge of extraneous rationalization.[53]

Ravel:
Music, I feel, must be emotional first and intellectual second.[54]

Frederick Delius:
Music is an outburst of the soul.[55]

Because it was so evident that the purpose of music was to express emotion, over a long period of time some philosophers had been speaking of music as an actual language of the emotions. Already in the sixteenth century, Martin Luther had observed, 'Music is a language of feelings without words.'[56] Subsequent philosophers in France, Descartes, Chénier, Nodier, Chabanon, De Vismes and J.-J. Rousseau in particular, began to speculate on the possibility of an international language based on music which might replace traditional languages. The extraordinary attempts of Jean-François Sudre

[51] A frequent observation by Mahler, according to Bruno Walter, *Gustav Mahler* (New York: Greystone Press, 1941), 83.

[52] Quoted in Nat Shapiro, op. cit., 194.

[53] Letter to Adalbert Lindner (June 6, 1891)

[54] Quoted in Nat Shapiro, op. cit., 197.

[55] ibid., 11.

[56] Luther, Preface to Rhau's *Symphoniae iucundae* (1538).

to realize this dream with his 'Langue Musicale Universelle' had no successor, with the exception of Wagner, who almost certainly found his leitmotif concept here.

Some other familiar persons commented on the idea of music as a language, among them:

Mendelssohn:
People usually complain that music is so ambiguous; that it is so doubtful what they ought to think when they hear it; whereas everyone understands words. With me it is entirely the reverse. And not only with regard to an entire speech, but also with individual words; these, too, seem to me to be so ambiguous, so vague, and so easily misunderstood in comparison with genuine music, which fills the soul with a thousand things better than words. The thoughts which are expressed to me by a piece of music which I love are not too indefinite to be put into words, but on the contrary too definite.[57]

[57] Letter to Marc André Souchay (October 5, 1842).

Mussorgsky:
Music is a means of communicating with people, not an aim in itself.

Edward MacDowell:
Music ... is a language, but a language of the intangible, a kind of soul-language.[58]

[58] *Critical and Historical Essays* (1912).

Wagner:
Music is the speech of Passion.[59]

...

It is a truth forever, that where the speech of man stops short, there Music's reign begins.[60]

[59] Wagner, 'Judaism in Music.'

[60] Wagner, 'A Happy Evening.'

Hans Christian Anderson:
Where words fail, music speaks.

Leo Tolstoy:
Music is the shorthand of emotion. Emotions which let themselves be described in words with such difficulty, are directly conveyed to man in music, and in that is its power and significance.[61]

[61] Quoted in Nat Shapiro, op. cit., 199.

Listeners during the nineteenth century had become fully conditioned to hear music as a synonymous expression of feeling. From an endless supply of possible quotations, consider only these two remarkable testimonies to the experience of hearing the music of Mozart.

Tchaikovsky:
> Here are things which can bring tears to our eyes. I will only mention the adagio of the D minor string quintet. No one else has ever known as well how to interpret so exquisitely in music the sense of resigned and inconsolable sorrow. Every time Laub played the adagio I had to hide in the farthest corner of the concert-room, so that others might not see how deeply this music affected me.[62]

[62] Letter to von Meck, March 16, 1878.

Pyotr Ilyich Tchaikovsky, by Nikolai Dimitriyevich Kuznetsov, 1893

Sören Kierkegaard:
> I am in love with Mozart like a young girl. Immortal Mozart! I owe you everything; it is thanks to you that I lost my reason, that my soul was awestruck in the very depths of my being … I have you to thank that I did not die without having loved.[63]

[63] *Either/Or* (1843).

Three thousand years of experience were not enough to discourage radical new departures during the twentieth century. One new school of composers championed 'objective' music, which had never ever existed before. Their credo was that music can be understood only as C♯s and B♭s. For the most part, however, the composers of 'objective' music found their greatest admirers and followers among the academic community and not among the general public, who never responded as it did for traditional music. For the general public there is not a single work from this school which communicates as directly as the weakest Beethoven symphony.

The twelve-tone school was, of course, a return to math, in so far as the process was concerned. This school is now completely dead and nearly forgotten. It lasted exactly as long as the Classic Period, which produced numerous masterpieces which will be performed forever. How many compositions from the fifty years of twelve-tone music will be performed forever?

Another significant new influence of the twentieth century has been the recording industry, which has made technical accuracy a higher goal than feeling. The impact of this influence can be clearly seen in the criticism of the later recordings by Karajan. Peter Davis, in New York Magazine, called Karajan,

> master of the recorded cult which has purged the spirit from the music.

A senior British critic considered the absence of feeling in a Karajan performance of the Beethoven *Eroica* as amounting to fraud.

> Beauty without form, sound without meaning, power without reason, reason without soul—it is the deadly logic of hi-fi. Machines, we are told, will one day compose symphonies. At present they merely perform them.

Herbert von Karajan, Bundesarchiv, Bild 183-R92264

And do we not, even today, still hear some concerts and recordings which are characterized by great demonstrations of technical skill and precision but lacking in genuine feeling?

3 *Thoughts on the Failure of American Music Education*

CONSIDER A FEW BENCHMARKS on the progress of American Music Education since the 1950s:

Item: During the 1970s the participation of high school students in music courses declined from 25.1 to 21.6 percent, and fell even more during the 1980s.[1]

[1] *The American School Board Journal*, December, 1988, 15.

Item: A 1985 survey by the National Endowment for the Arts found:
- 61% of adults do not attend one cultural event per year
- 68% say their parents never listened to classical music
- 80% say they never had music appreciation courses.

But!
- 57 million (1 out of 4) were playing an instrument
- Sales of music recordings were at an all time high.

Item: The Report of the National Commission on Music Education (Reston: MENC, 1991) provided some very disturbing information about our country's progress in art education.

- Of the 29 states requiring some instruction in music and the other arts for graduation, 13 accept courses in domestic science, industrial arts, humanities, foreign languages, or computer science as alternative ways to meet the requirement. Only 9 states require arts courses per se for all high school students.

- The six broad education goals advanced by President Bush and the nation's governors in 1990 do not mention the arts.

- The US government is willing to spend on support for the arts only .095% of what it spends on support for science.

- In student–teacher ratio in music, South Dakota ranked best at 151:1; California last at 1,535:1.

- Only 15 percent of California music classes were taught by a qualified music teacher.

Item: American university music education students are given the impression by their teachers that America is a model for successful music education. An objective examination of the results of our educational system tells a different story.

- Music has never become a core subject, even though all adults will consume music their entire lives, while hardly any will use 'core subjects' like calculus.

- All children love music. Why are relative few of the entire student body found in our music classes?

From these kinds of reports, taken together with what one learns on the current state of music education in discussion with almost any public school music teacher who has been in the business twenty years or more, one can only conclude that American Music Education has failed dramatically during the past fifty years. How is this to be explained?

Beginning with the late Renaissance the influence of humanism caused the professional art music field to return to the values of the ancient Greeks in which music was understood to be performance, and its paramount purpose to be the communication of feeling. At the very same time, however, the universities of Europe continued on the wrong track they had inherited from their Catholic Church sponsors, making music a branch of mathematics in order to qualify it as a rational and conceptual subject like other university subjects.

The universities generally remained locked in the old medieval Scholastic notion that music belonged to mathematics. Thus, in 1505, the University of Leipzig appointed Sebastianus Müchelon as '*lector musicae et aritmetice*,'[2] a document of the University of Köln in 1515 specifies the teaching of 'the books on mathematics, that is geometry, arithmetic, music and astronomy' and in 1558 the University of Heidelberg employed a lecturer in mathematics who was expected to include music in his teaching.

The most influential of the radical English religious books which attack music is Stephen Gosson's *The Schoole of Abuse* of 1579, which declares that the student must forget performance and return to the study of 'speculative music,' meaning what we call music theory today. First, he quotes Pythagoras, in

[2] Nan Cooke Carpenter, *Music in the Medieval and Renaissance Universities* (Norman: University of Oklahoma Press, 1958), 251. Carpenter documents the association with mathematics extensively.

something the philosopher surely never said, as 'condemning as fools, anyone who judges Music by sound and by ear.' Then, he concludes,

> If you wish to be good Scholars, and to profit from the Art of Music, shut your fiddle cases.[3]

A French philosopher, Nicholas Malebranche (1638–1715), writes that music can only be judged by conceptual knowledge, not by the ear. Hence he concludes, 'Musicians know nothing.'[4]

We are happy to report that some humanists satirized these old-fashioned and incorrect views. Ben Jonson, in his *Cynthia's Revels* (act 2, scene 3) in a humorous discussion of the facial expressions needed by a courtier, satirizes the pedagogy of the academic world by referring to a courier who only knows 'the court by speculation rather than through practice.' This uninformed courtier, we are told, doesn't know the '*ut-re-me-fa-sol-la* of courtship.'

In 'The Blind as Judges of Color,' Voltaire presents a brief story of the blind in a hospital who pretend to be authorities on color. This is a satire on self-proclaimed academic experts, who know nothing of a practical nature. In particular he was thinking of the Scholastic views of the University of Paris, which held that one can only 'know' music in its conceptual form ('speculative music') rather than by the ear. This story concludes with the observation by a deaf man that the 'deaf were the only proper judges of music.'[5] Petrarch, in his 'Remedies for Fortune Fair and Foul' (II, xcvii), comments in satire of the old Church position:

> A deaf person can know the tones and numbers characterizing the intervals of fifth and octave, as well as the other proportions of the musical scale with which musicians work. Although one does not hear the sounds of the human voice, of strings or the organ, he nevertheless may understand in his mind their fundamental canon and, doubtless, will prefer the intellectual pleasure to a mere titillation of the ear.

[3] Stephen Gosson, *The Schoole of Abuse* (1579), ed., Edward Arber (London, 1868), 26

[4] Nicolas Malebranche, *Elucidations of the Search after Truth*, quoted in *Malebranche, Philosophical Selections*, trans., Thomas Lennon and Paul Olscamp (Indianapolis: Hacket Publishing Company, 1992), 89.

Ben Jonson, by George Vertue after Gerard van Honthorst, 1730

[5] 'The Blind as Judges of Color,' in *The Works of Voltaire* (New York: St. Hubert Guild, 1901), IV, 13ff.

Voltaire, by Catherine Lusurier after Nicolas de Largillière, 1778

One is amazed at the number of otherwise brilliant minds who continued to think of music as a branch of mathematics. The list includes Shakespeare,[6] Mersenne,[7] Isaac Newton,[8] Defoe[9] and Samuel Pepys.[10] Even in the nineteenth century one finds Hegel writing of music that,

> besides the deepest feeling, there reigns also a rigorous mathematical intelligence.[11]

Music education in young, protestant America began without obligation to the long heritage of European universities and consequently enjoyed a good start. The early church schools were practical, and not academic, in purpose. When the broader forms of public music education began to grow during the nineteenth century, America had the lucky chronological coincidence to be under strong European influence at a time when European music and music education values were completely experiential in nature. It is one reason why important nineteenth-century American music educators, such as Lowell Mason, understood and stressed the moral values of music.

During the first decades of the twentieth century, which saw the great expansion of public school music, the driving force were leaders who were performers and conductors. Some of the greatest leaders were even without formal education in music, but were dedicated to performance. The music conferences were organized around concerts by the finest models and the model was performance. This was a period of great growth in music education and strong civic support.

After World War II the entire philosophy of music education in America began to change. Music education began to be dominated not by performers of music, but by professional educators, persons with an EdD. These professional educators returned to the late medieval university model, centering the discussion on concepts and math (now called statistics) rather than performance. They began to make music like the other conceptual core subjects, rather than distinguishing its originality.

But there are fundamental problems with concept based music teaching, the first of which is that the student is led to understand music from the perspective of the teacher, rather

---

[6] *The Taming of the Shrew*, act 2, scene 2, line 57.

[7] *Harmonie universelle* (1636).

[8] In his ideal university curriculum music is taught by the mathematics lecturer. See *Unpublished Scientific Papers of Isaac Newton*, ed., Rupert Hall (Cambridge: University Press, 1962), 369ff.

[9] Daniel Defoe, 'Augusta Triumphans: or, the Way to make London the Most Flourishing City in the Universe.'

[10] *Private Correspondence of Samuel Pepys*, ed., J. Tanner (London: Bell and Sons, 1926), II, 109.

[11] Quoted in Nat Shapiro, *An Encyclopedia of Quotations about Music* (New York: Da Capo, 1977), 276.

than from his own perspective—where *his* understanding of music must, in the end, lie. This is exactly the point Schumann makes in a note in his Diary in thinking about theory teachers. They are, he says,

> not satisfied when a young student works out the old classic form, as a master, and according to his own understanding of it; he must do so according to theirs.[12]

The result will always be that the gifted student finds frustration, not enlightenment, in being forced to write music by someone else's rules. Schumann himself was particularly sensitive to criticism of parallel fifths.

> For all I care, the fifths may ascend or descend chromatically, the melody may be doubled in every interval in octaves, but …! Yes, recently I heard in a dream angelic music filled with heavenly fifths, and this happened because, the angels assured me, they had never found it necessary to study thorough bass.[13]

Berlioz, in an article on the music of Gluck, tells of a similar anecdote about Beethoven.

> Though Gluck was not, strictly speaking, the equal of some of those who came after him, he was certainly enough of a musician to have the right of answering his critics as Beethoven once did:
> 'Who forbids this harmony?'
> 'Why, Fux, Albrechtsberger, and a dozen other theorists.'
> 'Well, I allow it.'[14]

Liszt also commented on this incident.

> Beethoven was quite right to assert *his right* to allow that which was forbidden by Kirnberger, Marpurg, Albrechtsberger, etc.![15]

And Liszt was quite right! It should be the student's right to write anything he *feels*. 'Rules' should come afterward, as a vehicle for the student to discover, by the comparison of his work with examples from earlier masters, the necessary musical insights. Under conceptual teaching theory we usually do this the other way around, presenting lists of rules to students who do not have the experiential background to understand

Robert Schumann, daguerreotype, 1850

[12] Schumann's Diary, 1833 or before.

[13] Robert Schumann, 'Trios,' in *Neue Zeitschrift für Musik* (1836).

[14] 'The *Alcestis* of Euripides' (1862).

[15] Letter to Franz Brendel, December 1, 1859.

them. The result, as Schumann says, is that later, 'The young mind must often unlearn theory, before it can be put in practice.' George Bernard Shaw was more adamant on this point:

> People would compose music skillfully enough if only there were no professors in the world.[16]

[16] *Music in London, 1890–1894.*

An even more fundamental problem is that by approaching the subject of music as a series of concepts we pretend to be teaching music, when we are not.

We say we are teaching music when we teach rhythm, but we are teaching mathematics.

We call music history a music course, but it is a history course. And the playing of records in a history class is not music—which by definition must be live. Recordings are to real music as photographs are to real people.

We say we are teaching music when we teach harmony, but we are teaching a foreign, symbolic language. And when have you heard a theory professor use words like 'pain' and 'sorrow'?

We say we are teaching music when we teach instrumental technique, but we are teaching a mechanical discipline.

In taking what is an experiential art and translating it into rational concepts, the result is often concepts which the student is unsuccessful in applying in actual practice. Consequently, since we teach rhythm as mathematics, the young musicians cannot *feel* rhythm. When we teach harmony as a symbolic language, the young musicians do not learn to *hear* harmony. The teaching of form is perhaps the most vivid example. We teach the sonata form, for example, as data, spreading it out on a blackboard looking like a family tree as it branches down into smaller units. And while this information is perfectly true as data, it is completely useless information. By this we mean it is information which can never be used, with the sole exception being if the student becomes a teacher of a university form class. It is useless information because neither the composer, the performer nor the listener ever experience a sonata form as it appears on the blackboard. The sonata form is experienced as something moving through time, in the present tense,[17] from the beginning of the movement through to the end of the

[17] Stravinsky emphasizes this point: 'Music is the sole domain in which man realizes the present.' See *Chronicle of My Life* (1935).

movement. But we do not teach the perception of form sequentially. It was exactly this kind of problem which caused Mahler to remark,

> It is a peculiarity of the interpretation of works of art that the rational element in them is almost never their true reality.[18]

Thus in turning music into rational concepts we take the precious voice of our experiential self and turn it from *feeling* into *concepts*; from *us* into *it*; from the wordless into words; and from the right hemisphere to the left hemisphere. In fact, we are teaching everything except *music*. Here is an illustration:

Gustav Mahler, photograph by studio A. Dupont, New York, Library of Congress

[18] Alma Mahler, *Gustav Mahler* (New York: Viking Press, 1969), 320.

> When we talk about concept learning, however, we move into the cognitive domain, where our interest is in helping students develop their thinking processes ...
>
> People perform essentially three different kinds of thinking or knowing operations. The first of these, and undoubtedly the most critical, is discrimination, which is the ability to tell that one thing isn't another ...
>
> The second thought operation is sequence learning—placing things in a particular order so that one event or object or situation naturally follows the preceding one ...
>
> Concept formation—the third type of thought operation—is the ability to identify those characteristics that classify otherwise dissimilar objects or events.[19]

[19] James C. Carlsen, 'Concept Learning—It Starts with a Concept of Music,' *Music Educators Journal*, November, 1973.

Aesthetics, which belong to the realm of the listener–student, in conceptual theory now becomes an aspect of teaching. In our view, nothing could be more wrong-headed than the following:

> [The] teacher–director will find his aesthetic attitude constantly challenged in the selection of didactic materials, in problems of musical description, and in related matters of value both as voiced by the experiencing subject and as embodied within the musical object. He is in a singular position to introduce into contexts of performance practical applications of aesthetic theories: of play, empathy, imagery, psychical distance. The actual shaping of sounds, the dramatic unfolding of musical form, the consideration of immediate and refined judgments, values, and responses—all could take on pedagogical import via the performance–analysis process.[20]

[20] Abraham A. Schwadron, 'Music Education and Teacher Preparation,' *Journal of Musicological Research*, 1982.

Such philosophizing in music education is in reality the philosophy of education or of learning, but not the philosophy of *music* education. Such conceptual efforts have often resulted in a considerable waste of human effort. Consider the fact that American music education went through a brief period of flirting with the ideas of the dehumanizing behaviorists—ten years after the field of psychology itself had finished considering and had dismissed the whole idea. This was followed with much fanfare by the era of 'Comprehensive Musicianship.' Never has a movement in music education been so short lived, leaving closets all over the country filled with unused publications paid for by government grants.

The result of nearly a half-century of conceptual music teaching is declining numbers of music students, relative to the population, with little discernible civic support. The reason for this, a reason intuitively grasped by students and parents alike, is that music is not a conceptual subject, it is experiential. A conceptual philosophy of music education can only mean teaching *about* music, not teaching *music*.

This is the first problem when we conceptualize music. These things are the rational, left hemisphere associations with music. They are necessary to write the notes on paper and we use them as means of conceptualizing about music. But they are not *music*. This is the point once made by the German poet, Heine:

> Nothing is more futile than theorizing about music. No doubt there are laws, mathematically strict laws, but these laws are not music; they are only its conditions—just as the art of drawing and the theory of colors, even the brush and palette, are not painting, but only its necessary means. The essence of music is revelation; it does not admit of exact reckoning.[21]

[21] Heinrich Heine, 'Letters on the French Stage' (1837).

Mahler adds the warning that conceptualizing, placing the focus on what you can talk about, only serves to mislead us and distract one from what is important in music.

> It is a peculiarity of the interpretation of works of art that the rational element in them is almost never their true reality.[22]

[22] Alma Mahler, *Gustav Mahler* (New York: Viking Press, 1969), 320.

Saint-Saëns reminds us of the very obvious fact that the reverse is also true: music cannot communicate rational ideas. The question follows, if music cannot convey concepts, why do we think we can explain music by concepts?

> Nothing is more difficult than to speak about music. The attempt is very arduous for musicians themselves and nearly impossible for others …
>
> I have invariably found this art by nature unable to convey purely abstract ideas … whereas, on the contrary, music is all-powerful when it comes to expressing the several degrees of passion, the infinite nuances of feeling. Insight into the soul, the exploration of its inmost recesses, is precisely its most congenial task, the scene of its triumphant success. Music takes up where speech leaves off, it utters the ineffable, makes us discover in ourselves depths we had not suspected, conveys impressions and states of being that no words can render.[23]

[23] *Portraits et Souvenirs* (1903).

The teaching of *music* can *only* occur through the performance of music, including in the classroom and in rehearsals, because music does not exist except in performance. But this is a form of music education for which university teacher training does not prepare its students. Consider the average school band rehearsal. The band plays for a few moments, then stops while the conductor makes comments. Then they play for a while and stop again, play and stop, etc. Ironically, all of current music educational theory is focused on *the intervals where there is no music*.

We should like to propose that the focus of music education needs to be returned to direct experience in the *playing* of music. Conceptual teaching is important only in its supporting role, but it must never be confused with the core values of music teaching. Otherwise, Wagner concluded,

> If one needs a science for it, then Art is useless.[24]

[24] William Ashton Ellis, *Wagner's Prose Works* (New York: Broude, VIII, 392.

Real music education must be learned through personal experience, not through the contemplation of concepts and math. History is very rich in teachers of this basic truth. Leonardo da Vinci (1452–1519), for example, observed,

> To me it seems that all sciences are vain and full or errors that are not born of experience, mother of all certainty, and that are not tested by experience.[25]

[25] Jean Paul Richter, ed., *The Literary Works of Leonardo da Vinci* (London: Phaidon, 1970), I, 33ff.

The greatest French writer of the sixteenth century, Michel de Montaigne (1533–1592), ridicules those who think they can teach experiential arts, such as music and dance, through conceptual teaching alone.[26] Extending this thought in humor, he quotes Plato[27] as saying we should never submit ourselves to a doctor unless he himself had had the same illness and cured himself. Thus, says Montaigne,

> If doctors want to know how to cure syphilis it is right that they should first catch it themselves!

Erasmus (1469–1536) calls practice, 'the best teacher of any subject,' with the specific example, that one learns music by playing.[28] In this regard, Franchino Gaffurio (1451–1518), in his *Practica musicae*, notes that performing musicians had been ignoring the academic *musica speculativa* anyway. But having come from this latter tradition himself, he is somewhat astonished that musicians could learn such things as harmony without the conceptual instruction.

> It is incredible that musicians could have attained the practical skill in harmony which they did attain without any study of theory.[29]

Gaffurio's explanation for this 'incredible' fact is the correct one: musicians learn the fundamentals of music experientially.[30]

The Flemish theorist Adrian Coclico, a music teacher at the university in Wittenberg in 1545, documents in his *Compendium Musices* (1552) actual examples of the sixteenth-century shift away from the old Scholastic complexities of speculative music to practical musicianship.[31] He mentions that in Belgian cities no music is written down or prescribed by precept. Especially interesting is his reference to his own training:

> My teacher, Josquin des Près, never rehearsed or wrote out any musical procedures, yet in a short time made perfect musicians, since he did not hold his students back in long and frivolous precepts, but taught precepts in a few words at the same time as singing through exercise and practice.[32]

Michel de Montaigne

[26] Michel de Montaigne, *Essays*, trans., M. A. Screech (London: Penguin, 1993), I, xxvi, 171.

[27] *Republic*, III, 408 D-E.

[28] 'Adages,' in *The Collected Works of Erasmus* (Toronto: University of Toronto Press, 1992), XXXII, 25.

[29] Irwin Young, trans., *The Practica musicae of Franchinus Gafurius* (Madison: University of Wisconsin Press, 1969), 11.

[30] It is this same explanation, we might add, that accounts for the fact that the world is filled with musicians who have never taken music classes!

[31] In Adrian Coclico, *Musical Compendium*, trans., Albert Seay (Colorado Springs: Colorado College Music Press, 1973), 30.

[32] ibid., 16.

The Baroque writers were even more outspoken against the old academic *musica speculativa*. Johann Mattheson (1681–1764) begins his first important book, *Das Neu-Eröffnete Orchestre*, with a startling chapter entitled, 'The Fall of Music and its Cause.' His basic view was that music is something very close to Nature, but the student is led to believe that he knows nothing of music unless he knows the academic conceptual form of it. Mattheson writes of these professors:

Johann Mattheson, engraving by Johann Jacob Haid after a painting by J.S. Wahl, 1746

> For they are persuaded that this beautiful and perfect creation, which a beneficent God has given us men for our pleasure, and likewise as a model of the eternal, harmonious Splendor, depends solely upon deep learning and laborious knowledge. To prove this, they dispense their philosophical rules and scholarly vagaries, not only with great authority, but likewise with such obscurity that one has a rightful aversion for the stuff, and would rather remain in permanent ignorance than to go through such *horrenda*.[33]

33 *Das Neu-Eröffnete Orchestre*, in Beekman Cannon, *Johann Mattheson, Spectator in Music* (Archon Books, 1968), 2ff.

In another place he argues that those concepts which are necessary should be centered in performance.

> That type of contemplation or theory is however to be preferred to all others which does not delve so deeply into shallow, mental considerations that action is forgotten; but turns its main aim toward actual practice and usage … Whoever wants to make good use of both aspects must never separate them, but keep them fast together, like body and soul.[34]

34 Johann Mattheson, *Der vollkommene Capellmeister* (1739), trans., Ernest Harris (Ann Arbor: UMI Research Press, 1981), I, i, 5.

He observes that while it is an intelligent thing to ponder, contemplate and reflect on a piece of music before performing it, it sometimes works the other way around. That is, the study seems to be a 'corroboration of that which one finds to be true in practice.' The same conclusion is given by King James I, in his book of advice to his son 'that Art is better learned by practice than speculation.'[35]

Two Baroque writers emphasize that musical understanding does not come from books. François Fénelon (1651–1715), thinking of the listener, observes that one does not learn music from books, but from observing musicians.[36] And in a letter to Père Porée, Voltaire (1694–1778) also contends that the artist learns by experience, and not from books.

35 James I, *Basilicon Doron* (1599) (Menston: Scolar Press, 1969), 67.

36 François de Salignac de La Mothe-Fénelon, *The Adventures of Telemachus, Son of Ulysses*, Book XII, (London: Garland Publishing, 1979, facsimile of the 1720 edition), XXIV, ii, 270.

No matter how many books are written on the technique of painting by those who know their subject, not one of them will afford as much instruction to the pupil as will the sight of a single head by Raphael.

The principles of all the arts, which depend upon imagination, are simple and easy; they are based upon nature and reason ... The composer of *Armide* and *Issé* [Lully], and the worst of composers, worked according to the same musical rules.[37]

By the end of the Baroque, we see Charles Avison (1709–1770), in a complete break with Scholastic dogma, state that musical communication is *not* of the realm of Reason.

After all that has been, or can be said, the energy and grace of musical expression is of too delicate a nature to be fixed by words: it is a matter of taste, rather than of reasoning, and is, therefore, much better understood by example than by precept.[38]

The great value of music is that its revelation is on a *personal* level. Joseph Campbell wrote about how the importance of personal revelation is lost in academic conceptualization.

People talk about trying to learn the meaning of life. Life has no meaning. What's the meaning of a flower? What we are looking for is an experience of life, getting the experience. But we're shoving ourselves off the experience by naming, translating and classifying every experience that comes to us.[39]

And this is what Debussy had in mind, when he wrote, 'Music must never be shut in and become an academic art.'[40] Aaron Copland presented a great lesson on this importance of personal revelation in music.

Listen ... to the forty-eight fugue themes of Bach's Well-Tempered Clavichord. Listen to each theme, one after another. You will soon realize that each theme mirrors a different world of feeling. You will also soon realize that the more beautiful a theme seems to you the harder it is to find any word that will describe it to your complete satisfaction. Yes, you will certainly know whether it is a gay theme or a sad one ... Now study the sad one a little closer. Try to pin down the exact quality of its sadness. Is it pessimistically or resignedly sad; is it fatefully sad or smilingly sad? Let us suppose that you are fortunate and can describe to your own satisfaction in so many words the exact meaning of your chosen theme. There is still no guarantee that anyone else will be satisfied. Nor need they be. The important thing is that each one feel for himself

[37] Letter to Père Porée (1730), quoted in Barrett Clark, *European Theories of the Drama* (New York: Crown, 1959), 279.

Charles Avison

[38] Charles Avison, *An Essay on Musical Expression* [London, 1753] (New York: Broude Reprint, 1967), 81.

[39] Joseph Campbell, *Transformations of Myth Through Time* (New York: Harper & Row, 1990), 204ff. With regard to how the academic world often fails to connect its precepts with real life, Robert Ornstein, responding to a friend's question about taping a box, suggested using 'the Pythagorean theorem and compute the length of the diagonal compared with the sum of the two sides.' His friend responded, 'Is that what geometry was all about?' [Robert Ornstein, *The Right Mind* (New York: Harcourt Brace, 1997), 171]

[40] Quoted in Nat Shapiro, *An Encyclopedia of Quotations About Music* (New York, Da Capo, 1977), 268.

the specific expressive quality of a theme, or, similarly, of an entire piece of music. And if it is a great work of art, don't expect it to mean exactly the same thing to you each time you return to it.[41]

[41] Aaron Copland, *What to Listen For in Music*, Chapter 2.

Aaron Copland and David Whitwell, 1975

We believe this is essentially what Wagner meant when he concluded, 'We cannot accept a thing conceptually if we have not already grasped it intuitively.'[42] It was for this reason that in his proposal for the design of a music school for Munich, he found that only in the context of live performance did all the conceptual teaching make sense.

[42] Letter to August Röckel (August 23, 1856).

> The invisible bond, uniting the various branches of study, will always have to be performance.[43]

[43] 'A Music School for Munich,' William Ellis, *Wagner's Prose Works* (New York: Broude), IV, 197.

The second change which urgently needs to be made is the reintroduction of something believed for thousands of years but which has totally fallen from discussion in American music education. The subject is the moral values which derive from music. Again, history is rich with great minds who argued that this was a basic characteristic of music itself. Confucius (551–479 BC) once observed,

> If you would know if a people be well governed, if its laws be good or bad, examine the music it practices.[44]

[44] Quoted in Shapiro, op. cit., 233.

In the West, one finds the power of music to impact character mentioned in the oldest literature of Western Civilization, in the *Odyssey* of Homer. According to Strabo, the government of ancient Egypt placed musicians in charge of the development of character in the young.[45] And in one place, Plato seems to have made this purpose part of the very definition of music.

> And the sound of the voice which reaches and educates the soul, we have ventured to term music.[46]

The early Christians emphasized the power of music to affect manners, as we see already in the second century in the writings of Clement of Alexandria.

> Music is then to be handled for the sake of the embellishment and composure of manners.[47]

By late Middle Ages fantastic stories of the power of music to change manners appear, such as Guido's claim[48] that music saved a young lady in stopping a rapist by changing his intent and Cotton's belief that music can disarm bandits.[49] By the end of the Middle Ages we find in Johannes de Grocheo's *De Musica* (ca. 1300) the same belief.

> Music is also good in a practical sense, for it corrects and improves the customs of men if used in the proper way.[50]

During the Renaissance, we find the sixteenth-century Italian philosopher, Giulio del Bene, recommending 'Through music learn to be well ordered and constituted in our minds.'[51] In fact, Vincenzo Galilei (1533–1591) believed it was impossible to find a man who is truly a musician who is also of a vicious character.[52]

Among the French humanists known as the Pléiade was an important philosopher, Pontus de Tyard. In his *Solitaire premier, ou, Prose des Muses & de la fureur Poetique* (1552), he contended that the purpose of music, in particular, was to raise the soul from the lowest point from which it has fallen.[53] Similar references to the power of music to affect the soul can be found in Calvin and Luther, the latter observing,

---

[45] Quoted in Lise Manniche, *Music and Musicians in Ancient Egypt* (London: British Museum Press, 1991), 41.

[46] *Laws*, 672e.

[47] Clement of Alexandria, 'The Miscellanies,' Book VI, xi.

[48] See *Hucbald, Guido, and John on Music*, trans., Warren Babb (New Haven: Yale University Press, 1978), 160.

[49] ibid., 114ff.

[50] Johannes de Grocheo, *De Musica*, trans., Albert Seay (Colorado Springs: Colorado College Music Press, 1967), 1.

[51] Quoted in Claude V. Palisca, *Humanism in Italian Renaissance Musical Thought* (New Haven: Yale University Press, 1985), 337.

[52] Galilei, 'Dialogo della musica antica e della moderna.'

[53] Quoted in Frances Yates, *The French Academies of the Sixteenth Century* (London: University of London, 1947; Nendeln: Kraus Reprint, 1968), 80ff.

> There is no doubt that there are many seeds of good qualities in the minds of those who are moved by music. Those, however, who are not moved by music I believe are definitely like stumps and blocks of stone.[54]

[54] Letter to Ludwig Senfl [1530].

Similarly, Nicholaus Listenius (ca. 1500–1550), who studied at Wittenberg in 1529, when both Luther and Melancthon were teaching there, wrote in his treatise, *Musica* (1537),

> Music influences souls to humanity, suavity, even-temper; it restrains all immoderate affections, grief, wrath; it represses violence and obscene desires … This art invites the soul to virtue.[55]

[55] Nicolaus Listenius, *Musica*, trans., Albert Seay (Colorado Springs: Colorado College Music Press, 1975), 1.

At the beginning of the Baroque we find the philosopher Francis Bacon (1561–1626) attempting to explain why music has the power to affect the manners of men.

> It has been anciently held and observed, that the sense of hearing and the kinds of music most in operation upon manners … The cause is, for that the sense of hearing strikes the spirits more immediately than the other senses.[56]

[56] *Natural History*, Section 114.

John Milton (1608–1674), recognizing this power of music, recommends in his treatise, *On Education*, the employment of music to improve the character of students during their times of rest.

> The interim of unsweating themselves regularly, and convenient rest before meat may both with profit and delight be taken up in recreating and composing their travailed spirits with the solemn and divine harmonies of Musick heard or learned … which if wise men and Prophets be not extremely out, have a great power over the dispositions and manners, to smooth and make them gentle from rustic harshness and distempered passions.

And then there is that memorable comment by Handel, made in a letter to Lord Kinnoull, after the first London performance of the Messiah, on 23 March 1743:

> I should be sorry, my lord, if I have only succeeded in entertaining them; I wished to make them better.

This influence of music on man is also mentioned by the great composers of the nineteenth century. Let us only mention Wagner, who wrote,

> Music is able to work on taste, but also on *manners*: the first point will be disputed by no one, even in our day; but a direct relation to morality has not as yet been generally ascribed to Music, in fact it has even been judged as morally quite harmless. That is not so.[57]

[57] 'A National Theater,' in *Prose Works of Wagner*, op. cit., VII, 355.

We find the moral influence of music also mentioned in the statutes of the new civic musical organizations of the nineteenth century. The civic band in Nuremburg, Germany, in 1878, gives the purpose of the organization 'to awaken the sense of that which is lovely and noble in the people through the performance of selected musical compositions.' The famous Viennese critic, Eduard Hanslick, in an article discussing the French civic musical societies known as 'Orphéon,' comments on their value to society:

> Only the best of the French Band Societies achieve that which is musically perfect, but even the least of them can take pride in drawing some souls away from drink and card playing. For the working man, even a crude encounter with art has something which frees and ennobles.[58]

[58] Quoted in Eugen Brixel, 'Musikpapst und Blasmusik,' in *Österreichische Blasmusik* (October, 1975), 5.

And as all musicians today must realize, the moral values of music are still strongly believed in the Far East. Shinichi Suzuki, for example, observed, 'Teaching music is not my main purpose. I want to make good citizens.'[59]

[59] *Reader's Digest*, November, 1973.

It is important to observe carefully what the above persons were describing. These were first-hand testimonies reflecting observed change in the character and behavior in actual people, including listeners, as a result of hearing and experiencing music. They were not describing ethical concepts taught through rational instruction in association with music education. These particular values in music are not rendered convincing through words alone. Indeed, Solti recalls that after World War II, Hindemith was touring several cities in Europe lecturing on this subject. His lecture, on 'ethos of music,' apparently found little success.

It was quite dry and academic in content, to say the least. I was told that after he had delivered the lecture in Zurich he asked if there were any questions, and Otto Klemperer, the conductor, who was in the audience, stood up—a tall, imposing figure—and said, '*Herr Hindemith, wo sind hier die Toiletten?*,' which sadly reflected his opinion of Hindemith's lecture.[60]

This subject has fallen from discussion in American music education primarily because music educators have failed to confront two other basic issues.

The first we have discussed, the need to understand and admit that music is performance and exists in no other form. The second issue which music educators have failed to honestly confront, is the educational consequences of the *quality* of the music performed. Music education has failed to confront this even though the importance of this issue has been recognized for more than two thousand years. In *The Clouds*, by Aristophanes (450–366 BC), we get a glimpse of the education of boys destined to be professional lyre players. The quality of the music used for instruction was already an important issue, for we read,

> Their lyres were strung
> Not to ignoble melodies, for they were taught
> A loftier key.[61]

The question of quality also seems evident in Polybius (200–118 BC), in his history of Arcadia, when he writes 'For the practice of music, I mean real music, is beneficial to all men.'[62]

The real educational significance of this issue lies, of course, in the opportunity for the student to be exposed to the greatest possible minds through the music. The importance of this issue was described by Montaigne (1533–1592), in his essay on Beauty.

> Just as our mind is strengthened by contact with vigorous and well-ordered minds, so too it is impossible to overstate how much it loses and deteriorates by the continuous commerce and contact we have with mean and ailing ones. No infection is as contagious as that is.[63]

In more recent times we find Wagner making this same point in reference to school literature.

[60] Sir Georg Solti, *Memoirs* (New York: Knopf, 1997), 71.

[61] *Clouds*, 961ff.

[62] Polybius, *The Histories*, IV.20.5ff, trans., W. R. Paton (Cambridge: Harvard University Press, 1954).

[63] Michel de Montaigne, *Essays*, trans., M. A. Screech (London: Penguin, 1993), III, viii, 1045.

The acceptance of the empty for the sound is stunting everything we possess in the way of schools, tuition, academies and so on, by ruining the most natural feelings and misguiding the faculties of the rising generation.[64]

[64] 'On Poetry and Composition,' *Wagner's Prose Works*, op. cit., VI, 147.

In terms of music education, his answer was clear.

The true aesthetics and the sole intelligible history of music we must teach in no other way but by beautiful and correct performances of works of classical music.[65]

[65] 'A Music School for Munich,' ibid., IV, 200.

An appropriate analogy by Schumann makes the same point.

No children can be brought to healthy manhood on candy and pastry. Spiritual like bodily nourishment must be solid. The masters have provided it; cleave to them.

George Bernard Shaw could not understand why we should want to expose our children to anything but beautiful music.

The notion that you can educate a child musically by any other means whatsoever except that of having beautiful music finely performed within its hearing, is a notion which I feel constrained to denounce.[66]

George Bernard Shaw, LIFE Photo Archive, 1914

[66] *Music in London, 1890–1894*.

We agree and contend that the quality of music education cannot be separated from the quality of the music itself.

In summary, the moral values which exist in music are obtainable only through the experience of live music, either in listening or playing. These values, being experiential in nature, are not obtainable by rational, conceptual discussion. Educationally speaking, therefore, the process must begin with the conductor. We must make the necessary changes in the training of conductors for music education in order to produce conductors who think of themselves first and foremost as artists. Of course, a professional conductor such as Ricardo Muti works with a different kind of ensemble, with different music and with different purpose. But after decades of contemplating the question, we can think of no reason why the high school or university conductor, when he is on the podium, should think of himself as any less an artist than Muti. When the baton rises, their purpose must be the same.

Until this problem in self-identity is changed, the higher goals of music education will be unobtainable.

Part II

On The Origins Of Conducting

4 Heritage of Movement and Gesture as Expression of Emotion

BECAUSE INSTRUCTION IN MUSIC in the modern universities is founded on the late Medieval perspective of music as rational concepts, including mathematics, rather than on its true origin as an expression of the feeling–experiential nature of man, we have come to think of the primary role of the conductor as being also mathematics-related—he gives the metrical 'beats.' But it is far more accurate to say the conductor expresses the *duration* of the beat. That is, the conductor is a personification of the *movement* of music through time. One might go further and say the conductor is a modern symbol of the ancient relationship between movement and music.[1] Movement itself is a form of communication, which, of course, is what the conductor above all engages in. Therefore, to understand both the evolution of conducting and the artistic function of the modern conductor, one must begin with the consideration of movement itself.

One might suppose that the close relationship between movement and music begins in the fetus, where both hearing and movement develop in the inner ear. Therefore it should be no surprise to find the earliest of early men using movement as a form of communication long before the earliest speech. Lower animals, of course, also use movement as a means of communication, in particular with regard to mating ritual. Since musical communication also dates before speech, we must imagine the association of music and movement as not only a natural one but one understood quite early. Curt Sachs, in his discussion of dance in primitive societies, notes,

> Whether we speak of individuals or of entire tribes, peoples, and races, their melodies and dances must always be closely related. For both are determined by the same impulse to motion.[2]

The association of music and dance is so close, and so ancient, for centuries some writers remained unable to think of music without this association. Jean Paul Richter, the writer who so influenced nineteenth-century Romantic composers,

---

[1] Shortly after writing this, the author attended a solo dance recital by the great Mikhail Baryshnikov. It was interesting to observe not only numerous hand and arm movements which are identical to those of conductors, but also various relationships between movement and music. In particular, these included the correspondence of movement with melody, the obvious correspondence of tempi with emotion, and, of course, form.

[2] Curt Sachs, *World History of the Dance* (New York: Norton, 1937), 183.

considered that 'music is invisible dance, as dancing is silent music.'[3] Some early philosophers, focusing on the communicative nature of music, go even further. Agnolo Segni, in 1573, advanced the idea that music, language and dance are all imitations of each other.[4] Johannes Cochlaeus, in 1511, defined four categories of musician: orators, poets, mimes and (what *we* call) musicians.[5]

The association between movement and music is documented in the oldest extant literature. For example, a stone relief from the Assyrian Empire (750–606 BC) pictures two male harpists who are dancing while playing. The lyric poets of ancient Greece, who flourished during the sixth and seventh centuries BC, were poets who sang their works in public performance. Athenaeus reports that while they performed with few facial expressions, they were active with their feet, 'both in marching and in dance steps.'[6]

The most interesting ancient medium which combined music and movement were the Greek choirs, because what we know of their movements suggests they were used to specifically to express, or amplify, the emotions of the music they sang.[7] We first find reference to the Greek choral movements in a poem by the lyric poet, Alkman, in which he complains that he is too old and weak to *dance* with the chorus.

The historian, Xenophon (434–355 BC) suggests that a social value was placed on coordinated motions by the choir.

> There is nothing so convenient nor so good for human beings as order. Thus, a chorus is a combination of human beings; but when the members of it do as they choose, it becomes mere confusion, and there is no pleasure in watching it; but when they act and sing in an orderly fashion, then those same men at once seem worth seeing and worth hearing.[8]

Plato, in a lengthy discussion of music competitions (*Laws*, 659d) was concerned that the choirs not use the gestures of freemen and that the rhythms of the dance correspond with those of the melody.

After the rediscovery and republication of the ancient Greek treatises, Western European philosophers took note of the Greek's use of movement and music. Roger Bacon (b. ca. 1214) wrote of a category of music which he calls 'visual music,'

[3] *Levana* (1807).

[4] 'Lezioni intorno alla poesia,' quoted in Claude V. Palisca, *Humanism in Italian Renaissance Musical Thought* (New Haven: Yale University Press, 1985), 401.

[5] *Tetrachordum Musices.*

[6] Athenaeus, *Deipnosophistae*, I, 22.

[7] Curt Sachs believed the development of choirs from the solo singers was begun by the Dorians, as a reflection on the higher emphasis on social order than on individual freedom, and that the Greek choral dance was used to vent youthful exuberance (*choreia*, which he believed came from *chara*, 'joy'). [op. cit., 239, 237]

Xenophon, marble bust in the Altes Museum, Berlin

[8] 'Oeconomicus,' VIII, trans., E. C. Marchant, *Memorabilia and Oeconomicus* (Cambridge: Harvard University Press, 1953).

which is of great significance. The ancient Greek philosophers never discussed this topic at length, but there are sufficient hints in their descriptions of choral performance to suggest that the inevitable movements by the singers were thought of not as a kind of dance, but as the part of music you could see. One must remember that the Greeks placed considerable significance in the fact that one cannot *see* music and it was for this reason that music was so closely associated with religion (whose principal mysteries also cannot be seen). Bacon's discussion supplies important insights into this ancient association of music and movement.

> Music, moreover, consisting in what is visible, is necessary; and that it is such is evident from the book on the Origin of the Sciences. For whatever can be conformed to sound in similar movements and in corresponding formations, so that our delight may be made complete not only by hearing, but by seeing, belongs to music. Therefore dances and all bendings of bodies are reduced to gesture, which is a branch of music, since these are conformed to sound in similar movements and corresponding formations, as the author of the aforesaid book maintains. Therefore Aristotle says in the seventh book of the Metaphysics that the art of dancing is not complete without another art, that is, without another kind of music to which the art of dancing is conformed.[9]

9 'Mathematics,' XVI, in *The Opus Majus of Roger Bacon*, trans., Robert Burke (New York: Russell & Russell), I, 259.

Girolamo Cardano (1501–1576) wrote that, 'In antiquity dancing was called a sixth part of music.'[10] He also adds an interesting observation on the relationship of ancient dance and music which we have not found in extant ancient literature, that the movements of Greek choral performances were patterned on even earlier statues.

10 Quoted in Clement Miller, *Hieronymus Cardanus, Writings on Music* (American Institute of Musicology, 1973), 117.

> Dancing and gesticulation express the ample movements that were left from antique statues, and the movements were then transferred from the figures to choral dances, and from choral dances to wrestling schools.[11]

11 ibid., 119.

The ancient relationship between movement and music, particularly with respect to the communication of emotions, served as the foundation for later reflection on the more specific gestures used by actors and orators. In these writings we find ideas which have a very close correspondence to the gestures of conducting. It was in Elizabethan England that modern theater had its revival and in *Hamlet* (act 3, scene 2) Shakespeare provides a brief discussion of the gestures of the actor, which of course came from his own experience on the stage. He seems primarily concerned that the gestures of the actor not communicate emotions at a higher level than the ordinary viewers can identify with. He pleas for natural gestures for which he advises the actor to 'hold, as it were, the mirror up to nature.'

From the early eighteenth century, Johann Mattheson (1681–1764) provides, under the title, 'On the Art of Gesticulation,'[12] an extraordinary discussion of the emotions as expressed by gesture. His frequent reference to music is typical of most early discussion of oratory.

The proper term for the art of gesticulation, according to Mattheson, is *Hypocritica*, which he says Cassiodorus defined as 'silent music.' Quintillian defined it as 'the science of hand gesticulation,' but used the term *chironomy*—a term which, as we shall see below, we specifically associate with the beginning of conducting.

But the word *Hypocritica*, for Mattheson, means more than chironomy, for *Hypo* (under) and *Crisis* (criticism) suggests the submission of one's thoughts for judgment. This should be thought of in a positive sense, as a form of stimulation, and not in the ill-meant 'hypocrisy.' The origin, and source of power, for gesture is found in its universality. First, Mattheson points out that language itself only developed as a shadow of action.[13] Second, he touches on a very important point:

> Words do not move a person who does not understand the language; discriminating words are good only for discriminating minds; but everyone understands the well-used facial expression, even young children with whom neither words nor beatings have as much effect as a glance.[14]

This observation is more important than Mattheson realized, with respect to universality, for modern research has shown that both facial expressions and the basic emotions are universal and the latter are formed before birth and are thus not learned, but genetic.

[12] Johann Mattheson, *Der Volkommene Capellmeister* (1739), trans., Ernest Harris (Ann Arbor: UMI Research Press, 1981), I, vi.

[13] ibid., I, vi, 5.

[14] ibid., I, vi, 6.

Mattheson classifies this subject under *oratorical*, which directs the movement of the body; the *histrionic*, which belongs to plays and requires much stronger gesturing than the first; and the *saltatorial*, which deals with all kinds of steps and leaps.

The oratorical he considered to be closely related to music, for music is 'an oratory in tones' and the ancient orators 'gleaned their best rules from music.' As he pauses at this point to discuss music, he seems to include under the concept of gesture the actions of the entire body. Regarding the singers in church he observes,

> It would be desirable that if no proper gestures take place out of bad habit, at least nothing of a quite inappropriate, indecent, or cold and indifferent mien would occur: of which unfortunately! we are so little lacking that often the most serious and sacred pieces are sung and played in such a shameless manner, chattering, smirking, trifling, so that devout listeners are very annoyed.
>
> I have attended many, many a Passion and Requiem which to my great chagrin evoked audible joking and laughter.[15]

[15] ibid., I, vi, 11ff.

Secular concert music is criticized for similar reasons.

> If we go from the church to the concert room, one likewise encounters quite marvelous and diverse unseemly poses at Concerts which sometimes do not have anything in common with what is going on ... [Most players] seem to me like people who care only about filling their stomach and not about elegant taste.
>
> Can the attentive listener be moved to pleasure if he is constantly disturbed by the noise of someone beating time, be it with his feet or hands? If he sees a dozen violinists who contort their bodies as if they are ill? If the clavier player writhes his jaw, wrinkles his brow, and contorts his face to such an extent that it could frighten children? If many of the wind instrumentalists contort or inflate their facial features so that they can bring them back to their proper shape and color in half an hour only with difficulty?[16]

[16] ibid., I, vi, 15ff.

Mattheson also provides some interesting national differences which he observed in performance.

> If we turn from playing to singing, oh! that is when the misery really begins. Look at the fervor with which the French men and women singers present their pieces, and how they almost always seem really to feel what they are singing. Hence the reason that they strongly stir the

emotions of the listeners, particularly their countrymen, and replace through gesticulation and mannerisms what they lack in thorough instruction, in strength, or in vocal ability.

The Italians carry this even further than the French; indeed, sometimes they even go a little too far: As in almost all their undertakings they frequently overstep the limits and love the extremes. Meanwhile they frequently have tears in their eyes when they perform something that is melancholy; and on the other hand, their heart is overjoyed when there is something enjoyable: for they are very emotional by nature …

Only the cool Germans, although they have revealed to the Italians their great musical abilities through the three great H's, namely Händel, Heinichen and Hasse, on the one hand place their greatest merit in the fact that they look just as stiff and unemotional with the sad as well as the cheerful affections with which their music deals … they sing very decently and rigidly, as if they had no interest in the content, and are not in the least concerned with the consideration of the proper expression or meaning of the words … as is demonstrated daily by teachers and students. On the other hand, it is quite a favor if they do not gossip with, trifle with or ridicule their neighbors during rests; even if the things of which they sing would be worthy of the highest attention.[17]

[17] ibid., I, vi, 18ff.

The true goal for both church and concert performance, Mattheson summarizes, is 'that gesture, words and music form a three-part braid, and should perfectly harmonize with each other toward the goal that the feeling of the listener be stirred.'

Turning to the theater, here, he says, is 'the real college for all sorts of gesticulations.'[18] *Hypocritica*, communication through gesture, is what an actor does. It is in pretending what he is not, notes Mattheson, that we get the origin of 'hypocrite.' Here also one finds the dance, in which *Hypocritica* 'is as indispensable as the feet themselves.' So closely related are the dancer's gestures and the music, that he finds most dancing masters prefer to write their own melodies. If the composer is to compose the dance music, then he must understand dance and in this regard Mattheson points to Lully who 'personally instructed all his actors, actresses, and male and female dancers in this art of gesticulation.'[19]

[18] ibid., I, vi, 23ff.

[19] ibid., I, vi, 26.

In conclusion, Mattheson points to the importance of gesture in all the arts of ancient Greece and Rome, including mime and pantomime which he says often moved the spectators to tears. The ancient system of notation of gesture, of which he regrets precise knowledge is now lost, was called *Orchesin* in Greek and *Saltationem* in Latin. As a summary of the importance of these relationships in the ancient world, he quotes a contemporary, Charles Rollin, *Histoire ancienne* (Paris, 1730–1738):

> The art of gesticulation also belongs to music, it illustrates and teaches the steps and postures of dance as well as of the common walk, together with the postures which one uses in a public oration. In short, music comprehends all the art of composing and writing public utterances that have nothing to do with singing, through which annotations the sound of the voice is speech as well as the tempo and movement of the gestures would be ordered: which was a very useful art to the ancients but is completely unknown to us.[20]

Because the ancient writers so often made an association between the gestures of music and oratory, perhaps we should pause to consider some of the specific comments on gesture in oratory. The early philosopher whom we most associate with oratory was Cicero. In a discussion centering on the communication with the audience, in which the reader will find many ideas which are also common to musical performance, Cicero focuses on the very important aesthetic topic of Universality. He takes the position that it will always be the masses, and not the experts, who identify the excellent speaker. It is interesting that he begins this discussion with an observation which is almost identical with one Debussy would make twenty centuries later. Debussy noted that an artist is most complimented when he is complimented by the real experts in his field; however, '*fame* is a gift of the masses who know nothing.' Cicero wrote,

> This discussion about the reasons for esteeming an orator good or bad I much prefer should win the approval of you and of Brutus, but as for my oratory I should wish it rather to win the approval of the public. The truth is that the orator who is approved by the multitude must inevitably be approved by the expert …
>
> Now there are three things in my opinion which the orator should effect: instruct his listener, give him pleasure, stir his emotions. By what virtues in the orator each one of these is effected, or from what faults the orator fails to attain the desired effect, or in trying even slips and falls, a master of the art will be able to judge. But whether or not the orator succeeds in conveying to his listeners the emotions which he wishes to convey, can only be judged by the assent of the multitude

[20] ibid., I, vi, 35. Mattheson concludes this chapter with an account of the Imperial composer in Vienna in 1730, Francesco Conti, who, having 'used his art of gesticulation in a most wicked manner,' was placed on bread and water, beaten by a priest and forced to stand before the doors of St. Stefan Cathedral in a long hairy coat holding a black candle for an hour!

Cicero, Musei Capitolini, Rome (Photo by Glauco92) [CC BY-SA]

and the approbation of the people. For that reason, as to the question whether an orator is good or bad, there has never been disagreement between experts and the common people ...

When one hears a real orator he believes what is said, thinks it true, assents and approves; the orator's words win conviction. You, sir, critic and expert, what more do you ask? The listening throng is delighted, is carried along by his words, is in a sense bathed deep in delight. What have you here to cavil with? They feel now joy now sorrow, are moved now to laughter now to tears; they show approbation detestation, scorn aversion; they are drawn to pity to shame to regret; are stirred to anger, wonder, hope fear; and all these come to pass just as the hearers' minds are played upon by word and thought and action. Again, what need to wait for the verdict of some critic? It is plain that what the multitude approves must win the approval of experts.[21]

[21] Cicero, *Brutus*, xlix, 184ff.

In particular, Cicero identified emotion as the universal element which captures the appreciation of the large audience, something which he found similar in both music and oratory.

For just as from the sound of the strings on the harp the skill with which they are struck is readily recognized, so what skill the orator has in playing on the minds of his audience is recognized by the emotion produced.[22]

[22] ibid., liv, 199.

But universality is not the same thing as popularity. Cicero understood this and in his *Tusculan Disputations* he makes it very clear that to actually program at the level of the masses is something quite different and something which the artist does not do.

It must be realized that neither is popular fame to be sought for itself, nor obscurity to be dreaded. 'I came to Athens,' said Democritus, 'and nobody there recognized me.' A steadfast and serious man, to glory in his lack of glory! Or can it be that while the aulos players and those who play the lyre use their own judgment, not that of the crowd, to tune their songs and melodies, the wise man, endowed with a far greater skill, searches out not what is most true, but what the crowd wants? Or is anything more foolish than to think that those whom as individuals one despises as mere hacks and hooligans amount to something when taken all together? He will despise our ambitions and frivolities and spurn the people's honors, even when offered without his seeking them. But we don't know how to despise them until we come to regret our error.[23]

[23] Cicero, *Tusculan Disputations*, V, 104.

On the other hand, Cicero realized that with regard to public speakers the above distinction between what we call universality and popularity are only poles of aesthetic communication. In actual practice other factors make this question somewhat more complicated. First, sometimes the material itself is too complex for the masses to appreciate. He quotes an anecdote in which Demosthenes was reading a long poem and in the midst of his reading all the audience walked out except for Plato. Demosthenes is reported to have said, 'I shall go on reading just the same; for me Plato alone is as good as a hundred thousand.' Quite right, says Cicero,

> for a poem full of obscure allusions can from its nature only win the approbation of the few; an oration meant for a general public must aim to win the assent of the throng.[24]

[24] Cicero, *Brutus*, li, 191.

Second, he had apparently observed that a particularly smooth speaker could win the admiration of the audience even though the speech itself was devoid of content.

> Thus, for example, if the wind instrument when blown upon does not respond with sound, the musician knows that the instrument must be discarded, and so in like manner the popular ear is for the orator a kind of instrument; if it refuses to accept the breath blown into it, or if, as a horse [refuses to move] to the rein, the listener does not respond, there is no use of urging him. There is however this difference, that the crowd sometimes gives its approval to an orator who does not deserve it, but it approves without comparison. When it is pleased by a mediocre or even bad speaker it is content with him; it does not apprehend that there is something better; it approves what is offered, whatever its quality; for even a mediocre orator will hold its attention, if only he amounts to anything at all, since there is nothing that has so potent an effect upon human emotions as well-ordered and embellished speech.[25]

[25] ibid., li, 192.

However, we must believe that Cicero did not object in principle to the idea that the orator, or artist, might aspire to be successful with his audience.

> Ambition is a universal factor in life, and the nobler a man is, the more susceptible is he to the sweets of fame. We should not disclaim this human weakness, which indeed is patent to all; we should rather admit it unabashed. Why, upon the very books in which they bid us scorn ambition philosophers inscribe their names![26]

[26] Cicero, *Academica*, II, xxvi.

Cicero also constantly uses music as a metaphor in discussion of the technique of the orator, beginning with the employment of the emotions. Cicero himself was usually rather distrustful of the emotions, observing in one place, 'emotions, the very sound of which seems to denote something vicious … the Wise Man will always be free from them.'[27] He recognized, however, that there was something universally human about emotions even though in the following it is music itself which he uses as a metaphor to discuss the display of emotions.

[27] ibid., III, x, 35.

> For nature has assigned to every emotion a particular look and tone of voice and bearing of its own; and the whole of a person's frame and every look on his face and utterance of his voice are like the strings of a harp, and sound according as they are struck by each successive emotion. For the tones of the voice are keyed up like the strings of an instrument, so as to answer to every touch, high, low, quick, slow, forte, piano, while between all of these in their several kinds there is a medium note; and there are also the various modifications derived from these, smooth or rough, limited or full in volume, tenuto or staccato, faint or harsh, diminuendo or crescendo. For there are none of these varieties that cannot be regulated by the control of art; they are the colors available for the actor, as for the painter, to secure variety.[28]

[28] Cicero, *De Oratore*, III, lvii, 216.

It is evident that Cicero had observed carefully the practice of music as he reveals in interesting comments where he uses the model of music to explain some point he wishes to make with regard to oratory. For example, he notes that the orator, like the actor, poet and musician, must have a variety of pitch and volume.

> For both poets and composers employ a definite fall in tone and then a rise, a sinking and a swell, variations, pauses.[29]

[29] Cicero, *De Oratore*, III, xxvi, 102.

In particular, Cicero pointed to rhythm as the element which made the orator an 'artist.' The development of this style, he points out, has its origin in music.

> Who then is the man who gives people a thrill? Whom do they stare at in amazement when he speaks? Who is interrupted by applause? Who is thought to be so to say a god among men? It is those whose speeches are clear, explicit and full, perspicuous in matter and in language, and who in the actual delivery achieve a sort of rhythm and cadence—that is, those whose style is what I call artistic.[30]

[30] ibid., III, xiv, 53.

…

After attention to [syntax] comes also the consideration to the rhythm and shape of the words, a point which I am afraid Catulus here may consider childish; for the old Greek masters held the view that in this prose style it is proper for us to use something almost amounting to versification, that is, certain definite rhythms. For they thought that in speeches the close of the period ought to come not when we are tired out but where we may take breath … It is said that Isocrates first introduced the practice … by means of an element of rhythm, designed to give pleasure to the ear. For two contrivances to give pleasure were devised by the musicians, who in the old days were also the poets, verse and melody, with the intention of overcoming satiety in the hearer by delighting the ear with the rhythm of the words and the mode of the notes …

In this matter an extremely important point is, that although it is a fault in oratory if the connection of the words produces verse, nevertheless we at the same time desire the word-order to resemble verse in having a rhythmical cadence … [Nothing] more distinguishes him from an inexperienced and ignorant speaker.[31]

[31] ibid., III, xliv, 173ff.

Of particular interest, in another place Cicero speaks of the aesthetic contribution of rhythm.

There are, speaking generally, two things which lend flavor to prose, pleasing words and agreeable rhythms. Words furnish a certain raw material which it is the business of rhythm to polish …

Wherefore if the question be asked, which rhythms are used in prose, the answer is, 'all, but one is better suited to one part and one to another.' The place? In all parts of a phrase. What is its origin? In the pleasure of the ear … For what purpose is it used? To give pleasure. When? Always. In what place? Throughout the whole period. What produces pleasure? The same phenomena as in verse; theory sets down the exact measure of these, but without theory the ear marks their limits with unconscious intuition.[32]

[32] Cicero, *Orator,* lv, 185 and lx, 203.

Finally, Cicero, mentions rhythm with respect to the accommodations the public performer must make for age, citing the actor Roscius.

As we are taking from a single artist a number of details for our likeness of an orator, that same Roscius is fond of saying, that, the older he grows, the slower he will make the aulos player's rhythms and the lighter the music. Now if he, fettered as he is by a definite system of measures and meters, is none the less thinking out some relief for his old age, how much more easily can we not merely slacken our methods, but change them altogether![33]

[33] Cicero, *De Oratore.,* I, lx, 254.

Cicero also discusses in some detail the use of pitch as an important aspect of vocal delivery, once observing 'that nature herself modulates the voice to gratify the ear of mankind.'[34] In another place he discusses this in more detail with respect to the orator.

34 ibid., III, xlviii, 185.

> Manner of speech falls into two sections, delivery and use of language. For delivery is a sort of language of the body, since it consists of movement or gesture as well as of voice or speech. There are as many variations in the tones of the voice as there are in feelings, which are especially aroused by the voice. Accordingly the perfect orator ... will use certain tones according as he wishes to seem himself to be moved and to sway the minds of his audience ... I might also speak about gestures, which include facial expression. The way in which the orator uses these makes a difference which can scarcely be described.
>
> Demosthenes was right, therefore, in considering delivery to be in the first, second and third in importance ... Therefore the one who seeks supremacy in eloquence will strive to speak intensely with a vehement tone, and gently with lowered voice, and to show dignity in a deep voice, and wretchedness by a plaintive tone. For the voice possesses a marvelous quality, so that from merely three registers, high, low and intermediate, it produces such a rich and pleasing variety in song. There is, moreover, even in speech, a sort of singing ... which Demosthenes and Aeschines mean when they accuse each other of vocal modulations ... Here I ought to emphasize a point which is of importance in attaining an agreeable voice: nature herself, as if to modulate human speech, has placed an accent, and only one, on every word ... Therefore let art follow the leadership of nature in pleasing the ear ... The superior orator will therefore vary and modulate his voice; now raising and now lowering it, he will run through the whole scale of tones.[35]

35 ibid., xvii, 55ff.

Quintilian (30–96 AD) was the first early philosopher who wrote at length on the use of emotions by the orator,[36] believing that the orator must excite the emotions of the listener if he is to be successful. He elaborated his contention in a discussion of the difference between *pathos* and *ethos*. This is a particularly valuable passage, not only for its discussion of various emotions, but for comments on the expression of emotions which apply to musical performance as well. He begins by attempting to convey the meaning of these Greek terms to his Latin readers.

36 Quintilian, *The Education of an Orator* (Institutio Oratoria).

> Emotions however, as we learn from ancient authorities, fall into two classes; the one is called *pathos* by the Greeks and is rightly and correctly expressed in Latin by *adfectus* (emotion): the other is called *ethos*, a word for which in my opinion Latin has no equivalent: it is however rendered by *mores* (morals) and consequently the branch of philosophy known as *ethics* is styled *moral* philosophy by us. But close consideration of the nature of the subject leads me to think that in this connection it is not so much *morals* in general that is meant as certain peculiar aspects; for the term *morals* includes every attitude of the mind. The more cautious writers have preferred to give the sense of the term rather than to translate it into Latin. They therefore explain *pathos* as describing the more violent emotions and *ethos* as designating those which are calm and gentle: in the one case the passions are violent, in the other subdued, the former command and disturb, the latter persuade and induce a feeling of goodwill.[37]

[37] ibid., VI, ii, 8 through 36.

He agrees with some authors who maintain that while the *ethos* is continuous, *pathos* is more momentary in character. On the other hand, *pathos* and *ethos* are sometimes of the same nature, differing only in degree.

> Love for instance comes under the head of *pathos*, affection of *ethos*; sometimes however they differ, a distinction which is important for the peroration, since *ethos* is generally employed to calm the storm aroused by *pathos*.

The orator employs *pathos*, or emotion, when he wishes to create empathy in the listener.

> The aim of appeals to the emotion is not merely to show the bitter and grievous nature of ills that actually are so, but also to make ills which are usually regarded as tolerable seem unendurable, as for instance when we represent insulting words as inflicting more grievous injury than an actual blow or represent disgrace as being worse than death.

But how does the orator do this? Quintilian now tells us that he will reveal to us 'secret principles of this art.' What follows is a precursor of Stanislavsky's 'method acting,' through which one learns to re-experience the emotions one has to convey from the stage. Among the performing arts only musicians are spared such processes, for in music the emotions expressed *are* the real ones. Nevertheless, Quintilian's discussion should remind musicians that true emotional communication must be founded on genuine emotions.

> The prime essential for stirring the emotions of others is, in my opinion, first to feel those emotions oneself. It is sometimes positively ridiculous to counterfeit grief, anger and indignation, if we content ourselves with accommodating our words and looks and make no attempt to adapt our own feelings to the emotions to be expressed. What other reason is there for the eloquence with which mourners express their grief, or for the fluency which anger lends even to the uneducated, save the fact that their minds are stirred to power by the depth and sincerity of their feelings? Consequently, if we wish to give our words the appearance of sincerity, we must assimilate ourselves to the emotions of those who are genuinely so affected, and our eloquence must spring from the same feeling that we desire to produce in the mind of the judge. Will he grieve who can find no trace of grief in the words with which I seek to move him to grief? Will he be angry, if the orator who seeks to kindle his anger shows no sign of laboring under the emotion which he demands from his audience? Will he shed tears if the pleader's eyes are dry? It is utterly impossible ...
>   Accordingly, the first essential is that those feelings should prevail with us that we wish to prevail with the judge, and that we should be moved ourselves before we attempt to move others. But how are we to generate these emotions in ourselves, since emotion is not in our own power? I will try to explain as best I may. There are certain experiences which the Greeks call *øavra_ias*, and the Romans *visions*, whereby things absent are presented to our imagination with such extreme vividness that they seem actually to be before our very eyes. It is the man who is really sensitive to such impressions who will have the greatest power over the emotions ... It is a power which all may readily acquire if they will.

In another place, Quintilian explains that the ability of the orator to communicate emotions to the audience depends on the use of both the voice and the body. Here he recommends to the orator the study of music for learning how this is done.

> Let us discuss the advantages which our future orator may reasonably expect to derive from the study of Music.
>   Music has two modes of expression in the voice and in the body; for both voice and body require to be controlled by appropriate rules. Aristoxenus divides music, in so far as it concerns the voice, into *rhythm* and *melody*, the one consisting in measure, the latter in sound and song. Now I ask you whether it is not absolutely necessary for the orator to be acquainted with all these methods of expression which are concerned firstly with gesture, secondly with the arrangement of words and thirdly with the inflections of the voice, of which a great variety are required for law practice. Otherwise we must assume that structure and the euphonious combination of sounds are necessary only for poetry, lyric and otherwise, but superfluous in law, or that unlike music,

oratory has no interest in the variation of arrangement and sound to suit the demands of the case. But eloquence does vary both tone and rhythm, expressing sublime thoughts with elevation, pleasing thoughts with sweetness, and ordinary with gentle utterance, and in every expression of its art is in sympathy with the emotions of which it is the mouthpiece. It is by the raising, lowering or inflection of the voice that the orator stirs the emotions of his hearers, and the measure, if I may repeat the term, of voice or phrase differs according as we wish to rouse the indignation or the pity of the judge. For, as we know, different emotions are roused even by the various musical instruments, which are incapable of reproducing speech. Further the motion of the body must be suitable and becoming, or as the Greeks call it *eurythmic*, and this can only be secured by the study of music.[38]

[38] ibid., I, x, 22.

Many later writers were to make the point that it is the emotions of the orator which convinces the audience, not the actual words themselves. We will let the Baroque writer, La Rochefoucauld, represent them all.

The passions are the only orators who always persuade. They are like some magically infallible law of nature, and the simplest man, endowed with passion, persuades better than the most eloquent man who lacks it.[39]

[39] *The Maxims of La Rochefoucauld*, Nr. 8, trans., Louis Kronenberger (New York: Random House, 1959).

One of his contemporaries, François Fénelon, in an interesting treatise on eloquence, touches on the obvious correspondence between the orator as a performer before an audience and the performer of music. Oratory also corresponds with music in that much of the meaning is identified through the emotions.

Fenelon, Archbishop of Cambrai, by Joseph Vivien

Eloquence consists not only in proof but also in the ability to arouse the passions. In order to arouse the passions, it is necessary to portray them. Hence, I believe that all eloquence can be reduced to proving, to portraying, and to striking. Every brilliant thought which does not drive towards one of these three things is only a conceit.[40]

[40] *Fénelon's Dialogues on Eloquence*, trans., Wilbur Howell (Princeton: Princeton University Press, 1951), 92.

And again,

[41] ibid., 97.

The manner of saying things makes visible the manner in which one feels them, and it is this which strikes the listeners the more. In such passages as these, not only are sentences completely unnecessary, but one must neglect their order and their interconnections. Otherwise their passion is no longer like real passion; and nothing is so shocking as passion expressed with pomp and in measured periods.[41]

Later, Fénelon discusses physical movement as an expression of emotion.

> A. For what purpose does the action of the body serve? Does it not serve to express the sentiments and the passions which occupy the soul?
> B. I believe that.
> A. The movement of the body is then a painting of the thoughts of the soul.
> B. Yes.
> A. And that painting ought to be a genuine likeness. It is necessary that everything in it represent vividly and naturally the sentiments of him who is speaking and the nature of the things he speaks of. I mean that he must not, of course, go to the point where his representation becomes trivial and ludicrous.[42]

[42] ibid., 99.

Fénelon introduces the analogy of music when he contends that an effective orator must have a vocal range with much variety:

> It is a kind of music: all its beauty consists in the variety of its tones as they rise or fall according to the things which they have to express.[43]

[43] ibid., 102ff.

If this is not the case, if his voice is not naturally melodious, or is badly managed, it fails to please.

> It does not make any striking impression upon the mind such as it would if it had all the inflections which express feeling. His tones are beautiful bells which should be clear, full, sweet, and pleasant; but, after all, bells which carry no meaning, which have no variety, and as a consequence no harmony and no eloquence.

Fénelon also provides some specific details regarding the relationship of orator and listener, a relationship, again, which also corresponds with the performer of music. The orator, he says, must convince the listener that he is speaking directly to him. The style must be natural, familiar, serious and modest. The passions must be expressed with gesture and not by voice alone. Most important, however,

> It is necessary to feel passion in order to paint it well. Art, however great it be, does not speak as does actual passion. Hence, you will always be a very imperfect orator if you are not affected by the feelings which you wish to portray and to inspire in others.[44]

[44] ibid., 104ff.

With respect to the correspondence of the use of gesture among orators, actors and conductors, we find even more interesting detail in the discussion of the use of specific body members, beginning with the hands. In a long discussion on communication, which includes his interesting perception of animal communication, Michel de Montaigne (1533–1592) reminds us of the rather extraordinary possibilities of non-verbal hand-signal communications, which we perceive by sight alone.

> And what about our hands? With them we request, promise, summon, dismiss, menace, pray, supplicate, refuse, question, show astonishment, count, confess, repent, fear, show shame, doubt, teach, command, incite, encourage, make oaths, bear witness, make accusations, condemn, give absolution, insult, despise, defy, provoke, flatter, applaud, bless, humiliate, mock, reconcile, advise, exalt, welcome, rejoice, lament; show sadness, grieve, despair, astonish, cry out, keep silent and what not else, with a variety and multiplicity rivaling the tongue.[45]

[45] ibid., II, xi, 507.

Charles Gildon, in his 1710 biography of the famous English actor, Thomas Betterton, provides an extensive survey of the theory of theater gestures in the late Baroque. Regarding the hands, he begins with a similar list of commonly recognized gestures.

> The lifting of one hand upright, or extending it, expresses force, vigor and power. The right hand is also extended upwards as a token of swearing, or taking a solemn oath; and this extension of the hand sometimes signifies pacification, and desire of silence.
>   The putting of the hand to the mouth is the habit of one, that is silent and acting modestly; of admiration and consideration. The giving the hand is the gesture of striking a bargain, confirming an alliance, or of delivering ones self into the power of another. To take hold of the hand of another expresses admonition, exhortation, and encouragement. The reaching out of a hand to another implies help and assistance. The lifting up both hands on high is the habit of one who implores, and expresses his misery. And the lifting up of both hands sometimes signifies congratulation to Heaven for a deliverance …

> The holding the hands in the bosom is the habit of the idle and negligent. Clapping the hands, among the Hebrews signified deriding, insulting, and exploding; but among the Greeks and the Romans it was, on the contrary, the expression of applause.[46]

Gildon warns that one must avoid all affectation in gesture, which he notes will always appear 'commonly ridiculous and odious.' Rather, all gestures should be true and appropriate to the emotions one intends to express.

> To make these motions of the face and hands easily understood, that is, useful in the moving of the passions of the auditors, or rather spectators, they must be properly adapted to the thing you speak of, your thoughts and design; and always resembling the *passion* you would express or excite.[47]

The gestures of the hands are so powerful, he says, that we are even moved when we see them pictured in a painting. Furthermore, they are so universally understood, as to be a kind of international language.

> Gesture has this advantage above mere speaking, that by this we're only understood by those of our own language, but by action and gesture we make our thoughts and passions intelligible to all nations and tongues.[48]

The most interesting rule given by Gildon regarding the gestures of the hands is a warning that unless a careful distinction is made between left and right hand gestures, the actor (or lawyer, or preacher, he says) may offend the viewer. He pauses to observe that the actor's ear will correct mistakes in his voice, but since he cannot see his own gestures, especially those of his face, some actors practice before a mirror. But this is very dangerous, says Gildon, for everything will appear backwards, that is the left hand will appear as the right, etc. His real concern, in this regard, he expresses in the following rule:

> If an action comes to be used by only one hand, that must be by the right, it being indecent to make a gesture with the left alone.[49]

Indecent?! Why would society consider the use of the left hand alone to be *indecent*? First of all, this brings to mind the fact that throughout the entire history of literature there has

[46] Charles Gildon, *The Life of Mr. Thomas Betterton* [1710] (London: Frank Cass, 1970), 46.

[47] Gildon, ibid., 53.

[48] Gildon, ibid., 50.

[49] Gildon, ibid., 74.

been documented a clear preference for the *right* hand. Familiar to us all are the expressions regarding the favorite sitting on the *right* hand of the king and the *left*-handed compliment. At the direction of Jesus, his disciples catch fish on the right side of the boat, but nothing on the left. Morally we claim to be in the right, but no one is ever said to be 'in the left.'

Physiologically, the explanation for this right hand preference has its roots in the dominance of the left hemisphere of the brain (which controls the right hand), which does our speaking and writing for us and which tends to not even acknowledge the existence of the right hemisphere of the brain. On the social level, however, the explanation lies in an ancient hygienic practice. Before the advent of toilet paper, man traditionally performed this specific daily function with his *left* hand. It is for *this* reason that Gildon considers the use of the left hand alone 'indecent,' and it is for this reason why even today we offer *only* the *right* hand to shake hands and why we hold the baton with the right hand.

With regard to movements of the head, Gildon suggests that moving it from one side to the other, 'wantonly and lightly,' reflects folly and inconstancy.[50] Hanging the head down suggests grief and sorrow, while lifting the head or tossing it up conveys the gesture of pride and arrogance. Carrying the head high is a sign of joy, victory and triumph, but a 'hard and bold' forehead suggests obstinacy, contumacy, perfidiousness and impudence. Hanging the head on the breast he finds 'disagreeable to the eye,' while leaving the head in a position of leaning toward the shoulders is 'rustic, affected, a mark of indifference and languidness.'

The eye-brows should for the most part remain in a natural position, not always raised when speaking in earnest and much less one up and one down. Better, he recommends, to save them for moments of passion, 'to contract themselves and frown in sorrow, to smooth and dilate themselves in joy and to hang down in humility.'

Thrusting out the belly or throwing back the head Gildon finds 'unbecoming and indecent.' Shrugging the shoulders he does not admit in oratory, although he finds it is sometimes appropriate in comedy. He relates how a famous ancient orator cured himself of this habit.

[50] Gildon, ibid., 42–43, 58–59.

> I have read of a pleasant method that Demosthenes took to cure himself of this vice of action, for he at first was mightily given to it. He used to exercise himself in oration in a narrow and straight place, with a dagger hung just over his shoulders, so that as often as he shrugged them up, the point, by pricking his shoulders, put him in mind of his error.[51]

[51] Gildon, ibid., 73.

Of course it is the face in which Gildon finds the most powerful gestures are created. To turn the face toward an object conveys one's attention, to bend the face down suggests consciousness and guilt while lifting it up 'is a sign of good conscience or innocence, hope and confidence.'

> The face is changed into many forms and is commonly the most certain index of the passions of the mind. When it is pale it betrays grief, sorrow, and fear, and envy, when it is very strong. A leering and dark visage is the index of misery, labor and vehement agitations of the soul.[52]

[52] Gildon, ibid., 45.

As the face reveals the emotions, 'the soul is most visible in the eyes.'

> Eyes lifted on high show arrogance and pride, but cast down express humbleness of mind ...
> Denial, aversion, nauseating, dissimulation, and neglect are expressed by a turning away of the eyes.
> A frequent winking, or tremulous motion of the eyes argues malicious manners, and perverse and noxious thought and inclinations.
> Eyes drowned in tears discovers the most vehement and cruel grief.[53]

[53] Gildon, ibid., 44

If, Gildon suggests, one is sincere in his feelings, his eyes will express the correct emotions and with a power that will move the audience.

> For then Nature, if you obey its summons, will alter your looks and gestures. Thus when a man speaks in anger his imagination is inflamed, and kindles a sort of fire in his eyes, which sparkles from them in such a manner, that a stranger who understood not a word of the language, or a deaf man that could not hear the loudest tone of his voice, would not fail to perceive his fury and indignation. And this fire of his eyes will easily strike those of the audience ... and by a strange sympathetic infection, it will set them on fire too with the very same passion.[54]

[54] Gildon, ibid., 66ff.

This reminds us of a charming passage in Wagner's 'Mementos of Spontini,' where he relates that that conductor attributed his success to his eyes.

How important it was to him to suffer not the smallest alteration in his habits I clearly saw when he explained to me his method of conducting, for he directed the orchestra—so he said—by a mere glance of his eye: 'my left eye is for the first violins, my right for the second violins; wherefore, to work by a glance, one must not wear spectacles as bad conductors do, even if one is short-sighted. I,' he admitted confidentially, 'can't see a step before me, and yet I use my eyes in such a way that everything goes as I wish.'

Gildon, in conclusion, suggests that the real secret to facial gesture is to clearly have the specific emotion in mind, which then allows Nature to create the proper expression in the face. No greater advice, we might add, could ever be given a conductor.

Gaspare Spontini

> The orator ought to form in his mind a very strong idea of the subject of his passion, and then the passion itself will not fail to follow, rise into the eyes, and affect both the sense and understanding of the spectators.[55]

55 Gildon, ibid., 70.

Failing this, it is very interesting that he mentions a method by which ancient actors could practice and then produce on demand tears when needed on stage. It turns out again to be the very same method which drama schools today attribute to the nineteenth-century actor, Stanislavsky.

> They kept their own private afflictions in their mind, and bent [their minds] perpetually on real objects, and not on the fable, or fictitious passion of the play which they acted.[56]

56 Gildon, ibid., 68. We might also list the subjects which Gildon states 'the complete actor' must study in the course of his preparation for the stage. They include history, moral philosophy, rhetoric, elocution, painting, sculpture, dance, fencing and the vault.

5 On the Early History of Conducting

A CLAY DOCUMENT FROM 3,000 BC SUMERIA, which describes the music of the temple, identifies several musicians by title, one of whom was responsible for the rehearsal of the choir. A document from Akkad from the same period mentions some temple musicians who 'know the melodies' and are 'masters of the musical movements.' These may well be the earliest descriptions of a conductor.

We first *see* a conductor among the tomb paintings of the Old Kingdom of ancient Egypt (2686–2181 BC). Although little is known of the actual music of ancient Egypt we must presume the possibility of art music for many of the tomb paintings seem to show people listening to the music. In one remarkable painting a female musician plays the trumpet for the god Osiris, who is pictured shedding tears.[1] Frequently there is pictured among these persons who seem to be listening one who is always positioned directly facing one or more musicians and appears to be making some kind of hand gestures or signals. He is called by scholars a *chironomist*, 'one who gestures with his hands,' a definition first given by the rhetorician, Marcus Fabius Quintilinus. The hieroglyph used to describe what this figure is doing means 'singing,' but it is always qualified by another hieroglyph in the form of a human arm, as if the intended meaning were 'singing with the arm.'[2] Given the fact that ancient Egyptian music apparently had no notated form, we are inclined to the theory that he was a kind of conductor who supplied to the player some form of visual notation. In a painting from the eighteenth Dynasty (1580–1320 BC) we see one of these 'conductors' supplying the rhythm as well, with the heel of his foot while snapping a thumb and finger of each hand. The possibility that some chironomists specialized in 'conducting' the rhythm, as in the previous case, and others the melody, etc., may explain one painting which shows five musicians and six chironomists.

Neume notation can be dated from 3,000 BC in Sumeria and our guess is that they also developed from hand signals—the 'tally,' a vertical slash indicating the number one, being an

Harpist and conductor, Tomb of Prince Nikaure, Stela, Necropolis at Saqqara

[1] Lise Manniche, *Music and Musicians in Ancient Egypt* (London: British Museum Press, 1991), 58.

[2] ibid., 30.

obvious example. Our hypothesis is that the later neume notation of music manuscripts of the ninth century in Western Europe have some direct *visual* relationship with the shape in space of the hand motions of the Egyptian chironomist. Willi Apel describes the function, but without making the connection with Egypt.

> In the earliest sources and in many later MSS (9th–11th centuries) the neumes are written in such a manner as to give only the general outline of the melodic motion, but no evidence of the actual intervals … Evidently these signs served only as a mnemonic [memory] aid for the singer who knew the melodies by heart, or for the choir leader who may have interpreted them to this choir by appropriate movements of the hand. These neumes are called cheironomic, staffless, oratorical, or in *campo aperto* ('in the open field,' that is, without clear orientation) … The cheironomic neumes as such cannot be deciphered.[3]

Apel mentions this again under his article on conducting where he mentions Gregorian chant, conducted by,

> a method called cheironomy has been traditionally employed. This consists of motions of the conductor's hand intended to guide the singer's performance, and, in the days when music was orally transmitted (by the so-called cheironomic neumes), to remind him of the direction of the melody.[4]

In medieval literature there are occasional passing comments on this subject. Guido of Arezzo, in his *Mirologus* (1026–1028 AD), in writing of the importance of creating in music emotions which match the emotions of the text, implies some neumes had emotional associations.

> Let the effect of the song express what is going on in the text, so that for sad things the neumes are grave, for serene ones they are cheerful, and for auspicious texts exultant, and so forth.

Regarding the emotions in performance, Guido makes a curious psychological observation.

> We often place an acute or grave accent above the notes, because we often utter them with more or less stress, so much so that the repetition of the same note often seems to be a raising or lowering.

Neume notation

[3] Willi Apel, *Harvard Dictionary of Music* (Cambridge: Harvard University Press, 1953), 488.

[4] ibid., 177. Apel (487) regards the neumes as being an 'outgrowth of grammatical accents of Greek and Latin literature,' while we regard it as the other way around.

For this last phrase, which seems so enigmatic in this context, we are given more information by Roger Bacon (b. ca. 1214 AD). In his discussion of music as one of the Liberal Arts, Bacon contributes the most precise and interesting definition offered by any philosopher of the thirteenth century. He begins by dividing the world of music into two broad categories: 'one part of music deals with what is audible, the other with what is visible.'[5]

Audible Music he recognizes as being of two divisions: vocal music and instrumental music. In vocal music, in turn, Bacon finds four subdivisions.

[5] ibid., XVI, in Burke, op. cit., I, 259, for this entire discussion.

> For one part concerns melody, as in singing; the second concerns meters, and considers the nature and properties of all songs, meters, and feet; the third concerns rhythm, and considers every variety of relations in rhythms; the fourth concerns prose and considers accents and other aforesaid things in prose discourse. For accent is a kind of singing; whence it is called accent from *accino, accinis* [I sing, thou singest], because every syllable has its own proper sound either raised, lowered, or composite, and all syllables of one word are adapted or sung to one syllable on which rests the principal sound. Thus length and shortness and all other things required in correct pronunciation are reduced to music.

This is a very interesting discussion for several reasons. First, these thoughts come at the end of two thousand years, at least, during which poetry was sung. When Bacon says 'every syllable has its own proper sound either raised, lowered, or composite,' we wonder if there was a commonly recognized, but now lost, musical tradition associated with the performance of sung poetry. Did the text, perhaps, 'compose' the music? Is this in fact the key to what the chironomist was signifying with his hand gestures? We also find fascinating his statement, 'For accent is a kind of singing.' This comment, seven hundred years before our age, reminds us that among ancient peoples, singing preceded language. Can we not see a trace here of that distant period when pitch fluctuation preceded, and perhaps turned into, the sounds we call consonants, the first step toward modern language?

We were also struck by a passing comment by that extraordinary twelfth-century woman, Hildegard of Bingen, which seems to suggest some form of hand-symbol conducting was still known.

> ... and they adapted their singing to the bending of the finger-joints.[6]

[6] Quoted in *Hildegard of Bingen*, ed., Fiona Bowie and Oliver Daview (New York: Crossroad, 1993), 151.

Finally, we have mentioned above that Mattheson quoted Cassiodorus as defining the art of gesture as 'silent music,' which is what good conducting is.

Taking everything together, we regard the Egyptian chironomist as the first conductor in the modern sense. Beginning with the Old Kingdom (2686–2181 BC) we can see a testimonial to the importance of individual musicians simply from the fact that they were allowed to have their tombs in the vicinity of the royal ones. We think we see our chironomist–conductor again in those hieroglyphic texts which accompany the tomb paintings which identify the 'royal music director' or 'leader of ritual music.' The discovery of the tombs of Nufer and Kaha at Saqqara introduce us to two men who were 'director of singers,' as well as teachers. Regarding these tombs, Manniche observes,

> Kaha was both 'director' and 'instructor' of singers. He also held a title as priest of the 'southern Merit,' the music goddess, and the inscriptions mention that he was 'unique' among the singers and had a beautiful voice. Nufer, as well as being director of singers, was also instructor in the royal artisans' workshops. Three of his sons were 'instructors of singers,' and a fourth was 'director of singers in the palace.'[7]

[7] Manniche, op. cit., 122.

A New Kingdom (1567–1085 BC) reference to a temple musician as 'Chief of the Singers' may imply a conductor, for in a similar passage[8] in the Old Testament, which describes the temple musicians of the Hebrews, it is specified that,

[8] 1 Chronicles 15:16ff.

> Chenaniah, leader of the Levites in music, should direct the music, for he understood it.

From the extant literature of the ancient Greeks, one reads frequently of the performance of sung poetry, but there are also descriptions of larger concert environments which perhaps employed conductors. There were concert halls, which, according to Plutarch,[9] were called 'Odeum,' with many seats, ranges of pillars and with a roof sloped toward the stage. Xenophon mentions the performance of earlier composed music as well as new works.[10] Later Plato would look back on this period and long for the 'good old days,' when the audience listened in silence to the music.[11]

Actual reference to conductors in the Greek literature is limited to the choral conductor, called *khoregos* (after *Khoros*, the interior civic meeting place of the Spartans). Aristotle considered the importance of the conductor such that he should be elected by the civic authorities.[12] We have a passing reference to the role of the conductor in the *Elements of Rhythm*, a fragment by Aristoxenus (b. 379 BC). In discussing the division of time he seems to suggest the existence of something like the modern conductor, once saying 'signals' are necessary to make the division and in another place, 'Rhythm cannot exist without ... someone to divide the time.'[13]

Finally, in a surviving poem by Theocritus (ca. 315–264 BC), in the form of an epigram intended for a statue of Dionysus, we discover the name of a Greek choral conductor, together with the values which made him a winner in the choral competitions.

> Damomenes the choirmaster put up this tripod,
> Dionysus, and your image, blest and blythest god.
> Measured in all things, he won the victory
> With his male choir, observing beauty and degree.[14]

Ancient Rome also had concert halls, for we know the emperor Trajan (52–117 AD) had one constructed on the Forum. During the same period, the poet Juvenal mentions the concert hall in passing, in a discussion of the disadvantages of the deaf.

> What does it matter to them where they sit in the concert hall
> When a wind band blowing its guts out is barely audible?[15]

---

[9] *Lives*, 'Pericles.'

[10] 'Cyropaedia,' I.

[11] *Laws*, 700ff.

[12] *Politica*, 1299a.17.

[13] Michael Psellus, *Introduction to the Study of Rhythm*, quoted in Aristoxenus, Ibid., 23, 25. Psellus is a later author who seems to have copied his material from portions of the Aristoxenus books which are now lost.

[14] Theocritus, 'Epigram XII.'

[15] Juvenal, *Satire X*.

While we have no mention of conductors in the extant Roman literature, we may presume they were necessary for the performances of the great pantomimes, which sometimes included as many as three thousand singers. The leading scholar of the music practice of this period, Sendrey, also observes,

> From all parts of the empire musicians converged on Rome, attracted by the gold of the capital of the world. The huge number of musically educated slaves made it possible for their masters to maintain large choirs and orchestras with almost no expense.[16]

Extant literature does suggest that secular concerts continued at the beginning of the Christian Era. In fact, the first century philosopher, Philodemus of Gadara, wonders why there is any need for one to actually learn to perform music when there are already so many concerts available. The fifth-century poet, Sidonius, documents that choral performances with their ancient movements still existed, but he criticizes them for making bad compositions sound good through their good singing.[17] The fifth-century Church Father, Salvian, mentions concert halls, but includes them in a list of 'monstrosities' together with games, parades and pantomimes.[18]

References to conductors are quite rare during the Middle Ages, in fact we know of only four. There is attributed to Athenaeus (fourth century AD) a description of,

> a band of Syrbenaens in which every individual plays or sings what he thinks fit, and pays no attention to the instructions of the conductor of the band, who tells them how they ought to play.[19]

A passing mention of secular choral performance by St. Gregory Nazianzus (b. ca. 329 AD) is particularly interesting in its details which throw light on the role of the conductor and the placement of the singers.

> I thought, in my vain imaginings, that once I had control of this throne (outward show carries great weight) I could act like a chorus leader between two choruses. Putting the two groups chorus-fashion, one on this side of me, the other on that, I could blend them with myself and thus weld into a unity what had been so badly divided.[20]

---

[16] Painting, however, was reserved for those of noble birth. Pliny the Elder, in *Natural History*, XXXV, xxxvi, 78, says slaves were forbidden to be instructed in it and he observes that in both painting and sculpture there were no famous works executed by a slave.

[17] *Sidonius Poems and Letters*, trans., W. B. Anderson (Cambridge: Harvard University Press, 1965), II, 445.

[18] Salvian, *On the Government of God*, trans., Eva Sanford (New York: Columbia University Press, 1930), 162.

[19] We did not find this in the modern translations of Athenaeus, but rather quoted by Erasmus, in his 'Adages.' in *The Collected Works of Erasmus* (Toronto: University of Toronto Press, 1992), XXXIV, 29.

[20] Saint Gregory of Nazianzus, 'Concerning his own Life,' trans., Denis Meehan (Washington, DC: The Catholic University of America Press), 119. Gregory was born in 329 or 330 AD.

The famous Saint Augustine (354–430 AD), in his discussion of rhythm in music, seems to suggest a modern concept of meter in his implication that a conductor was responsible for the control of this aspect of time.

> Now, fix your ears on the sound and your eyes on the beats. For the hand beating time is not to be heard but seen, and note must be taken of the amount of time given to the arsis and to the thesis.[21]

[21] *On Music*, II, xiii.

Sidonius mentions a conductor in passing, when he describes the preferred dinner music of Theodoric, the fifth-century king of the Goths. While Roman literature always refers to the Goths as 'barbarians,' here we have the description of a highly discerning taste in music.

> Withal there is no noise of hydraulic organ, or choir with its conductor intoning a set piece; you will hear no players of lyre or flute, no master of the music, no girls with cithara or tabor; the king cares for no strains but those which no less charm the mind with virtue than the ear with melody.[22]

[22] Sidonius, op. cit., I, 6.

By this time the Church had won its victory and secular literature virtually came to an end. We are confident secular concerts continued, but we will not read of them again until the Renaissance, when suddenly the descriptions of conductors seem quite modern. How vivid is a letter of Fontanelli, in 1594, in which he speaks of Gesualdo attacking a conductor!

> On Monday the prince was invited to dine by the patriarch, and there was music. But in Venice they sing badly, and His Excellency has a taste difficult to satisfy, as Your Highness knows. Thus he could not restrain himself from withdrawing from the room, summoning the director and cembalist and reproving them in such a manner that I felt sorry for them.[23]

[23] Quoted in Glenn Watkins, *Gesualdo, The Man and His Music* (Chapel Hill: The University of North Carolina Press, 1973), 64.

One of the most valuable sources for descriptions of musical performance in the Renaissance is Hercole Bottrigari's *Il Desiderio* of 1594. Among other things, in his account of the famous orchestra of the nuns of S. Vito, in Ferrara, he clearly documents the use of the modern baton—and writes nothing to suggest it was a new idea. Nearly all modern books on conducting state that the baton was first used in the nineteenth century, but as the reader will see, the baton was clearly in evidence in the sixteenth century.

> They are indubitably women; and when you watch them come…to the place where a long table has been prepared, at one end of which is found a large clavicembalo, you would see them enter one by one, quietly bringing their instruments, either stringed or wind. They all enter quietly and approach the table without making the least noise and place themselves in their proper place, and some sit, who must do so in order to use their instruments, and others remain standing. Finally the Maestra of the concert sits down at one end of the table and with a long, slender and well-polished baton, and when all the other sisters clearly are ready, gives them without noise several signs to begin, and then continues by beating the measure of the time which they must obey in singing and playing.

The description of the function of the conductor here, with preparatory motions and the giving of metric beats, seems quite modern. Perhaps some will find familiar, as well, a description by Praetorius. He is discussing proportional notation and he worries that the conductor might end up beating so fast that,

> we make the spectators laugh and offend the listeners with incessant hand and arm movements and give the crowd an opportunity for raillery and mockery.

Civic wind bands, of course, were well established by the Renaissance and these ensembles had conductors. The most musically distinguished was no doubt Girolamo Dalla Casa of the sixteenth century, whose title was Leader of the Venetian Civic Wind Band [*Capo de Concerti delli stromenti di fiato della Illustriss. Signoria di Venetia*].

There is also extant a remarkable contract for the 'Musica di Palazzo' of Lucca in 1557, which provides interesting detail on the duties of the conductor.

> Nicolao Dorati is to be the director and head of said musicians, and they must obey him in performing whatever music in whatever manner he may choose. When playing at the city hall, before and after the dinner of the *Signoria*, Maestro Bernardino de Padova is to play the first soprano, and Vincenzo di Pasquino Bastini the second soprano; but

when playing in the hall or the chambers of the *Signoria*, each one is to play and sing the part assigned to him by said Nicolao, their director. However, outside the city hall, in church, on the public square, at weddings, feasts, serenades, or other events, where they will number at least six, Maestro Giulio is to play the first soprano, Maestro Bernardino, his father, the second, and Maestro Vincenzo the third, that is, contralto. And if by chance, which God forbid, there should arise among them a quarrel, ill-will, or other trouble, Maestro Nicolao is to intervene and restore peace, and if anyone should refuse to listen to reason, he is to be reported to the *Signoria* in office at the time, so that steps can be taken accordingly. And since beautiful music and perfect harmony are the result of constant practice, there should be assigned to them for this purpose a room ... equipped with tables and benches in which they are to meet for practice twice a week for two hours, namely, Wednesdays and Saturdays. From the first of February to the last of September they shall meet in the morning, two hours before dinner, and from the first of October to the last of January, in the afternoon, two hours before supper. In order to enforce these rules, the *maestro di casa* shall take the attendance, and those who are absent, shall be fined one *carlino* for each time, except in case of illness or other legitimate excuse.[24]

[24] Carl Anthon, 'Some Aspects of the Social Status of Italian Musicians during the Sixteenth Century,' in *Journal of Renaissance and Baroque Music* (New Haven, 1946), II, 225.

Although one would scarcely know it from reading traditional music history books which deal with the Baroque, the true story of the Baroque was a passion for the expression of the emotions through music. We must assume conductors were beginning to get caught up in this as well, as we think one can sense in a rare eye-witness description of Bach's enthusiastic conducting of a rehearsal in 1738.

> If you could see him ... singing with one voice and playing his own parts, but watching over everything and bringing back to the rhythm and the beat, out of thirty or even forty musicians, the one with a nod, another by tapping with his foot, the third with a warning finger, giving the right note to one from the top of his voice, to another from the bottom, and to a third from the middle of it—all alone, in the midst of the greatest din made by all the participants, and, although he is executing the most difficult parts himself, noticing at once whenever and wherever a mistake occurs, holding everyone together, taking precautions everywhere, and repairing any unsteadiness, full of rhythm in every part of his body.[25]

[25] Quoted in Hans T. David and Arthur Mendel, *The Bach Reader* (New York: Norton, 1966), 231.

One of Bach's sons mentioned that the father usually conducted an orchestra with his violin while he played.[26] The wind ensemble of the Baroque, the Hautboisten, followed the same tradition, with the solo oboe player acting as a conductor.

[26] ibid., 277.

There was one brief moment during the Baroque when even Catholic Church music shared in the excitement of the new ideas. This occurred during the reign of Pope Urban VIII (1623–1644), a man who happened to love music. A French musician, André Maugars, visiting Rome in 1639, describes hearing a performance in the church of a work, in the new large church concerto style, by ten choirs, using one principal conductor and eight sub-conductors!

Immediately after this pope, however, the Church regressed to the older styles of the Renaissance. Papal edicts in 1657, 1662, 1678 and 1692 were issued in an attempt to prevent secular influences from entering the service. In the 'Edict on Music' of 1665, the pope demands that the music be 'grave, ecclesiastical and devout' in character. The rather dark character of this attack can be seen in the following provisions which hold the conductor responsible for seeing that the singers not become more than background music.

Pope Urban VIII, by Gianlorenzo Bernini

> Eighth, that within a period of twenty days from the publication of the present edict by the Fathers Superior and others whose duty it is, that shutters or narrow grilles be placed in the choirs, be the latter temporary or permanent, and that the said shutters be of such a height as the singers will not be seen, under pain of privation of office and other penalties at the discretion of the Holy Visitation.
>
> Ninth, that no maestro di cappella or other person entrusted with ordering the music or giving the beat contravene the aforesaid prescriptions under pain of privation of office and perpetual disqualification from the exercise of this office and the right to make music; and, moreover, that he be punished with a fine of 100 scudi, of which one quarter be given the denouncer (whose name will be held secret), three quarters to the holy places at the discretion of the Holy Visitation, and with other penalties—including corporal punishment—at the discretion of the said Holy Visitation.

There are two very famous music treatises of the Baroque which include a discussion of conducting. The first, by the mathematician, philosopher and priest, Marin Mersenne (1588–1648), is a work of encyclopedia proportions called *Harmonie universelle.* Mersenne represents the ancient Scholastic, Catholic university tradition in which all of music was discussed in relationship with mathematics. Thus, when he comes to the topic of the conductor, he begins with a mathematical definition of the 'beat.'

Marin Mersenne

> The *beat* is the space of time used to lift and lower the hand. Since we can make these two opposing movements swifter or slower, he who conducts the ensemble determines the swiftness according to the kind of music and the material it employs, or according to his wish. I shall, however, henceforth take one beat, whether it is binary or ternary, for one second, that is, for 1/3600 of an hour, inasmuch as the slowest vibration of the pulse of the heart which I have been able to encounter lasts exactly one second and beats 3600 times in an hour. Thus the systole, or the contraction of the heart, will correspond to the lifting, and the diastole, or the dilation, to the lowering of the hand, so that the masters of music speak truly when singing the praises of God, *My heart and my body will rejoice in the living God.*[27]

Second, he offers a few comments on conducting technique.

> The semibrevis ordinarily lasts one lifting and one lowering of the hand, which can be made as well with the foot.[28]

In the case of conducting a ternary beat, Mersenne recommends the one pattern that never works, 'two white notes in striking, and a single one in lifting.' And he notices that where there are those singers who 'have a delicate and exact ears and a well-ruled imagination,' they can keep the beat even without a conductor.

Quite different is the German treatise, *Der vollkommene Capellmeister*, by Johann Mattheson (1681–1764), which is dedicated to performance practice rather than academic theory. We find here the earliest important description of the qualities needed in a good conductor.[29] He begins by placing the greatest emphasis on the integrity and character of the conductor and points to examples he has known of conductors who had cheated their singers out of money due them. But in general,

> He should in no way be offensive or scandalous in his living and conduct, for commonly the greatest contempt arises from that. A good reputation and esteem are such delicate things that with a single false step everything one has gained for oneself in many years through great assiduousness can be destroyed.

A central challenge for the conductor, in Mattheson's view, is the need to balance being friendly as a person with the necessary authority in rehearsal.

[27] *Harmonie universelle*, IV, iv, 20.

[28] ibid., IV, v, 11.

[29] *Der vollkommene Capellmeister* (1739), trans., Ernest Harris (Ann Arbor: UMI Research Press, 1981), III, xxvi.

A director of the choir must not be lazy with unconstrained words of praise, but must copiously employ them, even if he finds only scant cause for them among his students. But if he is to and must admonish and contradict someone, then he should do it quite seriously, yet as gently and politely as is possible. Affability is considered a most favored and rewarding virtue by people in all ranks: a director then should of course also strive for it, and should be very gregarious, sociable and obliging: especially when he is not performing his official tasks. In his official duties, becoming seriousness and precise observation of them probably does more service than too great familiarity.[30]

As for conducting itself, while some 'pound with sticks, keys and feet,' he has found 'that a little sign, not only with the hand but merely with the eyes and gestures, could accomplish most of this; if only the performers would assiduously keep their eyes on the director.'

The personal accomplishments which Mattheson believed were important for a conductor included ability to sing, to play the clavier, knowledge of tuning, knowledge of principles of seating plans and 'the greatest difficulty' of all: having the discernment required to succeed in divining the sense and meaning of another composer's thoughts.

He stresses the importance of rehearsals and points out that the conductor often needs the rehearsal as much as the players.[31] Reminding us that most Baroque performances were also premieres, Mattheson adds that one important purpose of the rehearsal is to make the necessary corrections.

> It is no disgrace but rather an honor to improve that which has not turned out well. How then can one know or perceive it without rehearsal?

With regard to the rehearsal, he cannot help but add that some responsibility lies with the attitudes of the individual musicians as well.

> The director as well as the performers should set their heart and soul on nothing other than the service of God ... [they] must certainly put away all other, dissolute thoughts, and must direct their mind, from reverence, only on the holy work at hand. If this occurs, then the execution will proceed well: for all mistakes which are made derive from inattentiveness and from such a disposition wherewith one is at another place with his thoughts.[32]

---

[30] ibid., III, xxvi, 7. He points to the ideal example of J. S. Cousser, formerly Kapellmeister at Wolffenbüttel, who so charmed and helped his singers cordially in his home that they all loved him. However, in rehearsal, the musicians,
> almost all had fear and trembling before him, not only in the orchestra but also on the stage: for he knew how to reproach a person for his errors in such a sharp manner that often the eyes of the latter filled with tears. On the other hand, he calmed down again immediately, and diligently sought an opportunity to bind the thus-produced wounds through extraordinary politeness.

[31] ibid., III, xxvi, 23.

[32] ibid., III, xxvi, 25.

A final requirement for the successful conductor contains some timeless advice.

> A composer and director of music must be of a vigorous, high-spirited, indefatigable, diligent, and energetic nature; yet also orderly: yet most often the most active are deficient in this last. Idleness must be hated as a devil, because it is his place of repose ...
>
> Neither impatience nor a sudden flush of emotion serves any purpose here. If one does not have enough desire or deep-felt love for the thing so that he can suppress many a displeasure over it and so that adversity cannot alienate him from his noble plan; then he is not well suited for the exercise of this discipline and its sphere of duties.
>
> Indeed, with music and its pursuit very few roses are strewn in the path; moreover persons of authority and in high esteem seek, though it is unfair, to suppress and disparage everything about it as much as possible ... A master must have the heart in such circumstances to set a cheerful example for others, and must know how to create in himself so many pleasures from this noble pursuit that he would always be in the position, all obstacles notwithstanding, of finding his greatest peace in harmony and of reviving his spirit.[33]

33 ibid., II, ii, 55ff.

Mattheson was also the first to call for the study of conducting to be included in music education. In a list of topics which should be studied if the 'essence of music' is to be understood,[34] he includes,

34 ibid., I, i, 9ff.

> The special qualities of a conductor.
> How to direct, produce and execute music.

In another place,[35] Mattheson focuses specifically on the education and skills needed by the conductor. Without education, he says, a musician can exercise his trade, but he cannot be an artist. This education need not be found at a university, but can be gained at home under 'clever leadership.' The specific requirements of this education begin with languages: Greek, Latin, French and Italian, the language of the theater. Without these languages, how can the conductor ever be a *galant homme*? He must also have considerable knowledge in poetry and, in an emergency, be able to write good verse himself.

35 ibid., II, iiff.

The reinstitution of standing armies during the Baroque made possible the first permanent military bands of Western Europe and the first positions for military conductors. By 1768 an English book on the subject of the military includes a description of the desired qualities of a military conductor.

> The music directors should be men whose regularity, sobriety, good conduct and honesty can most strictly be depended upon; that are most remarkably clean and neat in their dress; that have an approved ear and taste for music, and a good method of teaching; without speaking harshly to the youths, or hurrying them on too fast.[36]

[36] Thomas Simes, *Military Medley*.

During the early years of the nineteenth century there began in Europe a tremendous expansion of civic bands, choirs and orchestras. Following the traditions of the civic music guilds, dating to the fourteenth century, these organizations often developed carefully worded constitutions which spell out the duties of both members and conductors. A document for the small town of Stühlingen in 1806 is a typical example. Regarding the conductor, we first find:

> A. Organization. Each society must choose, for the maintenance of order, a chairman, who should be concerned with the leadership of the whole. In music, this person is called the Kapellmeister. [This is not the] place to comment on the duties of the Kapellmeister in so far as they are concerned with musical talent and the art itself, however in so far as he is the leader of a society, it is necessary for him to determine when and where the musical appearances will be held—and who should attend—and the repertoire. The Kapellmeister should be elected through a majority of the votes to a one year term of office.
>
> B. Suborganization. If the Kapellmeister is the leader of a society, then I believe the members should be required to give him not only the necessary attention, but also obedience. Obedience, however, is limited to matters of music.[37]

[37] Quoted in Wolfgang Suppan, *Blasmusik in Baden* (Freiburg, 1983), 140ff.

Subsequent concerns are that everyone must appear when the conductor commands it, but not to assemble on their own without the conductor being given the reasons. No member will be required to remain longer than one hour at a rehearsal and no excuses will be allowed for missing performances.

The constitution of a German civic militia band in Oppenauer for 1824 include the following concerns:

> Each member is required to give the conductor his most respectful attention.
> Everyone must attend rehearsals.
> All conversation is forbidden during the time music is being played.
> The conductor will determine the repertoire.
> Talking about the society is forbidden.
> No one is allowed to take offense at the directions of the conductor.[38]

Anton Friedrich Justus Thibaut (1772–1840), founder of the Heidelberg Choral Society and mentor of Schumann, wrote a treatise, *Purity in Music* (London: W Reeves, 1822), which established guidelines for the establishment of choral societies. On the requirements for a conductor, he recommended that conductors be chosen on the basis of their expertise in classical music, their ability to grasp a score, and humility and humbleness.

Beginning in 1840 Austria set a new standard for military bands by employing conservatory trained civilian conductors for their leading bands. This brought into the service some very talented musicians and conductors, whose names are still familiar today: Fahrbach, Gungl, Komzák, Fucik, Czibulka and J. F. Wagner. As a result the great military bands in Austria, as well as those representing other countries, reached a very high artistic level, playing important music before vast audiences. The famous critic Eduard Hanslick wrote that no civic orchestra could reach these high performance standards, an accomplishment he attributed to the combination of an artistic conductor and military discipline.[39]

Orchestra programs for the first half of the nineteenth century often look rather like vaudeville programs—even the premiere of Beethoven's Seventh Symphony had to share the program with a mechanical trumpet player! The development of the modern repertoire orchestras, after mid-century,[40] offered the first competition to the famous military bands. In their attempt to preserve their audience, the band conductors made the wrong choice, turning to ever more 'popular' repertoire. Thus, while the orchestras flourished, the bands of the nineteenth century disappeared from the art scene. Their long fall is symbolized by a sign before a hall in England, which read, 'There is no concert today. The band will play.'

[38] ibid., 113ff.

[39] His review is quoted in Eugen Brixel, *Das ist Österreichs Militär-Musik* (Graz, 1982), 107.

[40] Surprisingly late. The St. Louis Symphony is older than the Berlin Philharmonic!

Regarding orchestras, the most significant influence on the development of the conductor's art during the nineteenth century was the first appearance of published scores, even though some conductors, such as Habeneck in Paris, continued to conduct from a violin part. Equally significant was the advent of rehearsal numbers, which made modern style rehearsals possible for the first time. Wagner preserved a charming story of one of the early nineteenth-century conductors, Spontini, who only agreed to guest conduct when assured that Wagner would produce a specific style of baton for him to use.

> It was no easy matter for me to elicit from him what plan I must adopt, to move him to accept the direction of this rehearsal. After a little reflection, he asked me what sort of baton we used for conducting. With my hand I indicated, as near as possible, the length and thickness of a moderate-sized stick of ordinary wood, which the orchestra attendant served out to us each day wrapped round with fresh white paper. He sighed, and asked me if I thought it feasible to get made for him by next day a baton of black ebony, of the most portentous length and thickness, which he outlined for me by his arm and hollow hand, and bearing at each end a fairly large white knob of ivory. I promised to see to his having at any rate an instrument that should look just like it, for the very next rehearsal, and another made of the precise material he desired, for the performance itself. Surprisingly calmed, he wiped his forehead, gave me permission to announce his acceptance of the direction for the morrow, and departed to his hotel after once more stamping on my memory his requirements in the matter of the baton.[41]

[41] 'Mementos of Spontini.'

By the second half of the century a new type of conductor emerged, the conductor who makes the performance so personal that the spotlight is focused on him rather than the music itself or the composer. The conductor most criticized during his lifetime, in this regard, was Hans von Bülow. Although he achieved a level of ensemble perfection unknown before, which included making the entire orchestra memorize their music, he took drastic freedom with the music. Felix Weingartner recalled, as an example, a performance of the *Egmont Overture* of Beethoven in which von Bülow, without any indication in the score, would suddenly change the tempo from allegro to andante grave![42]

On the other hand, during the nineteenth century there also emerged conductors who must be considered great conductors in every modern sense of the word, and one thinks in

[42] Felix Weingartner, *On Conducting* (New York: Kalmus), 14.

particular of Berlioz and Wagner. We should like to concentrate on Berlioz here, primarily because of his vivid powers of expression. Although Berlioz himself often complained about his lack of experience as a conductor, judging from objective eye-witnesses we would have to conclude that he was actually quite proficient. One of these eyewitnesses was the English conductor, Hallé, who had the unusual opportunity to not only see Berlioz conduct his own *Roman Carnival Overture*, but also, due to an oversight, saw him perform it in public without a rehearsal!

> But to see Berlioz during that performance was a sight never to be forgotten. He watched over every single member of the huge orchestra; his beat was so decisive, his indication of all the nuances so clear and so unmistakable, that the overture went smoothly, and no uninitiated person could guess at the absence of a rehearsal.[43]

[43] Quoted in *The Memoirs of Hector Berlioz*, ed., David Cairns (London: Gollancz, 1969), 597.

The journal, *Musical World*, for 17 February 1847, reported on Berlioz as a conductor as follows:

> His manner of beating the measure is generous and easy to follow—and the mass of instruments follows the slightest indication of his baton, rendering even more wonderful the exactitude and delicate nuances of expression that he wishes to obtain.

A Concert of Hector Berlioz, by Andreas Geiger, 1846

In his own words, Berlioz has left some very valuable comments on what he considered the paramount qualities of a good conductor. He first commented on this subject when he reflected on one of his own early conducting experiences in 1827.

> Apart from a few slips due to excitement, I did not do too badly. Yet how far I was from possessing the many varied qualities—precision, flexibility, sensitivity, intensity, presence of mind, combined with an indefinable instinct—that go to make a really good conductor, and how much time and experience and heart-searching have I since put into acquiring two or three of them![44]

[44] *Memoirs*, 58.

In another description of the essential qualities of the good conductor, Berlioz points to Nicolai, conductor of the Vienna Kärntnerthor Orchestra, as an outstanding example.

> I regard him as one of the finest orchestral conductors I have ever encountered, and one of those men whose presence in a town can give it a position of unchallengeable musical ascendancy when they enjoy conditions which provide full scope for their powers. Nicolai has to my mind the three indispensable qualities of a good conductor. He is a skilled, experienced and at times inspired composer; he has a thorough sense of rhythm and its complexities, and an impeccably clear and precise technique; and he is a shrewd and tireless organizer who grudges neither time nor trouble spent on rehearsal and knows exactly what he is doing because he does only what he knows how to do.[45]

[45] *Memoirs*, 374.

Similarly, in an article in the *Revue et Gazette Musicale* for 15 October 1848, Berlioz points to Georges Hainl, of Lyon, as another man with the qualities of a fine conductor.

> He brings together all of the qualities necessary in a good conductor—he has a clear, direct, precise, expressive and warm way of conducting. He knows how to remedy problems using the musical strengths at this disposal.

Berlioz also commented on the qualities which prevented a man from being a good conductor. In this regard, he seems to have been most distressed by conductors whose great age prevented their having the energy to keep the music moving.

> Most to be dreaded are those whom high age has deprived of their energy and skill. The maintenance of any somewhat rapid tempo is impossible to them. However fast the initial tempo of a piece entrusted to their direction, little by little they slacken its pace until they have reached a certain degree of moderate slowness which corresponds with the blood circulation of their enfeebled organism. It must be added, however, that old men are not the only ones with whom composers run this risk. There are men in the prime of life, but with a sluggish temperament, whose blood seems to circulate *moderato* ... These people are the born enemies of all characteristic music and the greatest destroyers of style.[46]

[46] Berlioz, *Grand Traite d'instrumentation* (New York: Kalmus, 1948), 417.

He was also doubtful of the advisability of composers attempting to conduct their own works when they lack good conducting skills.

> No one will accuse a composer of conspiring against the success of his own work, and yet there are many composers who unknowingly ruin their best scores because they fancy themselves to be great conductors.

Beethoven, it is said, more than once spoiled performances of his symphonies, which he liked to conduct even at the time when his deafness had become almost complete.[47]

Berlioz has also left some very charming accounts of his own frustration in rehearsal while conducting. One of the most vivid accounts is his pseudonymous publication found in the *Revue et Gazette Musicale de Paris*, for 20 February 1859. This is an extraordinary self-portrait of Berlioz as conductor of an opera chorus rehearsal in Paris, which he wrote under the title, 'Letter from a member of the Opera Chorus.'

[47] ibid., 410.

> Dear Master,
> You have dedicated a book (*Orchestral Evenings*) *to your good friends, the artists of 'X,' a civilized city*. This German city (we know it) is not more civilized than many others, very probably, despite the malicious intention that you had in giving it this epithet. That its arts may be superior to those of Paris, it is permitted to doubt, and as for their affection for you, it cannot be, certainly, either as lively or as old as ours. The Parisian choristers, in general, and those of the Opera in particular, are devoted to you body and soul; they have proved it to you many times in every way. Did they murmur about the length of the rehearsals, about the rigor of your musical requirements, about your violent interruptions, about your fits of anger, even, during the studies of your *Requiem*, the *Te Deum*, the *Romeo and Juliette*, the *Damnation of Faust*, the *Childhood of Christ*, etc.? Never, never. They always, to the contrary, fulfilled their task with unalterable zeal and patience. However, you are not very flattering to men, nor gallant to the ladies, during these terrible rehearsals.
> When the hour to begin approaches, if the personnel of the chorus is not totally complete, if anyone is missing, you stride around the piano as a lion in his cage at the Zoo; you grumble, biting your lower lip, your eyes darting wild lightening; someone speaks to you, you turn away your head; you strike from time to time violently on the piano dissonant chords which indicate your interior rage, and which tell us clearly that you would be capable of tearing apart the late ones, the absent ones—if they were present.
> Then you always reproach us for not singing *piano* enough in the soft nuances, of not attacking together the *fortes*; you want us to pronounce the two 'ss' in the word *angoisse* and the 'r' in the second syllable of the word *traitre*. And, if an unfortunate illiterate, one alone, lost in our ranks, forgets your grammatical observation, and dares to still say *angoise* or *traite*, you hold it against everyone, you pour on us *en masse* cruel pleasantries, calling us porters, loge-attendants, etc.!! Very well, we take all of that, nevertheless, and we love you just the same, because you love us, one sees it, and that you adore music, one feels it …

> But why don't you now write a book, a book of the same kind, less philosophic and more gay perhaps, to conjure away the boredom that gnaws on us in the Opera?
>
> You know it, during the acts or the fragments of an act that do not contain choruses, we are prisoners in the vestibules. There it is as dark as the ship's store; we smell the lamp oil; we are badly seated; we hear old, moldy stories retold in bad language, rancid words repeated; or rather the silence and inaction at the same time crush us, up until the moment when the call-boy comes to make us enter on stage again … Ah! the profession is not beautiful.

As if we would not recognize who this is, he admits this is a description of himself in a similar paragraph in his *Memoirs*.

> I have often been accused by the ladies of the Opera of a want of gallantry; I have a terrible reputation in this respect, and I admit I deserve it. The moment there is a question of taking a large chorus, before rehearsals have even begun, a sort of anticipatory rage possesses me, my throat tightens, and although nothing has yet occurred to make me lose my temper, I glare at the singers in a manner reminiscent of the Gascon who kicked an inoffensive small boy passing near him, and on the latter's protesting that he had not 'done anything,' replied, 'Just think if you had!'[48]

[48] *Memoirs*, 297.

Berlioz has also left some graphic accounts of his frustration during orchestra rehearsals. What conductor would not identify with his despair in attempting to achieve simple accuracy by the trombones in one of his rehearsals of the four brass bands in the 'Tuba Mirum,' of his *Requiem*.

> In the middle of the *Tuba mirum* is found a passage where four groups of trombones sound the four notes of the G major chord successively. The time is very lengthy; the first group must sound the G on the first beat; the second, the B, on the second; the third, the D, on the third; and the fourth, the octave G, on the fourth. Nothing is easier to conceive than such a succession, nothing is easier to play, also, than each of these notes. Well!! when this *Requiem* was presented for the first time in the Invalides, it was impossible to obtain the performance of that passage. When I then had excerpts played at the Opera, after having uselessly rehearsed for a quarter of an hour that single measure, I was obliged to abandon it. There were always one or two groups that would not attack; it was invariably those on B, or those on D, or both. On casting my eyes, in Berlin, on that spot in the score, I thought immediately of the disobedient trombones in Paris: 'Ah! Let's see,' I said to myself, 'if the Prussian artists will succeed in crashing through that open door!' Alas, no! Vain efforts! Neither rage or patience accomplished anything!

Impossible to obtain the entrance of the second or third groups; the fourth, even, not hearing its phrase, which was to be given by the others, did not start either. I take them individually and I ask number 2 to sound the B—they do it very well. Addressing myself to number 3, I ask of them the D—they sound it effortlessly. Let's see now: the four notes, one after the other, in the order in which they are written!—Impossible! Completely impossible! I had to give up! Can you understand that? Doesn't that make you want to go smash your head against a wall?[49]

Berlioz describes the helpless frustration of the conductor in rehearsal again in a letter to Franz Liszt. How lucky, he says, is the great solo artist who controls every aspect of his performance, compared to the composer who must depend on other performers.

> For the composer who would attempt, as I have done, to travel in order to perform his works, how different! The never-ending, thankless toil he must be ready to endure, the sheer torture that rehearsals can be—no one can know what it is like who has not experienced it. To begin with he has to face the chilly looks of the whole orchestra, who resent being put to all this unexpected inconvenience and extra work on his account. The looks say plainly, 'What does he want, this Frenchman? Why can't he stay where he belongs?' However, each man takes his place; but the moment the composer glances round the assembled company he is aware of alarming gaps. He asks the Kapellmeister to explain. 'The first clarinet is ill, the oboe's wife is in labor, the first violin's child has the croup, the trombones are on parade, they forgot to ask for exemption from their military duties, the timpanist has sprained his wrist, the harp isn't coming, he needs time to study his part,' etc., etc. None the less one begins. The notes are read after a fashion, at a tempo more than twice too slow (nothing is so dreadful as this devitalizing of the rhythm!). Gradually your instinct gets the better of you, your blood begins to glow, you get carried away and involuntarily quicken the beat until you are giving the correct tempo. The result: chaos, a raucous confusion to split your ears and break your spirit. You have to stop and resume the original pace and work your way laboriously, piecemeal, through the long phrases that so often before, with other orchestras, you were wont to sail through swiftly and without hindrance. Even then it is not enough; despite the slow tempo, strange discords are discernible among the wind instruments. You try to discover the reason. 'Let me hear the trumpets by themselves ... What are you doing? I should be hearing a third, you're playing a second. The second trumpet in C has a D, give me your D ... Good. Now, the first trumpet has a C which sounds F. Let me hear your C ... Hey! What the devil! You've given me an E♭.'
>
> 'Excuse me, I'm playing what's written.'

[49] *Journal des Debats*, November 8, 1843.

'But you're not, you are a tone out.'
'I'm sorry, I'm playing a C.'
'What key is your trumpet in?'
'E♭.'
'Ah, that's what it is—you should be playing an F trumpet.'
'Oh yes, I hadn't looked properly. Sorry, you're quite right.'
'Timpani, why are you making such a frightful din over there?'
'I have a fortissimo, sir.'
'You haven't, it's mezzo forte—*mf*, not *ff*. In any case you're playing with wooden sticks when you should be using sponge-headed ones. It's the difference between black and white.'

'We don't know them,' the Kapellmeister interposes. 'What do you mean by sponge-headed sticks? We only know the one kind.'

'I suspected as much, so I brought some with me from Paris. Take the pair on the table there. Now, are we all ready? ... For Heaven's sake—it's ten times too loud. And why aren't you using mutes?'

'The orchestral attendant forgot to put them out on the desks. We will have them tomorrow,' etc., etc.

After three or four hours of this antimusical tug of war they have not been able to make sense of a single piece. Everything is fragmentary, disjointed, out of tune, cold, flat, loud, discordant, detestable! And this is the impression you leave on sixty or eighty musicians, who finish the rehearsal exhausted and disgruntled and go round saying that they have no idea what it's all about, it's a chaotic, heathenish music, they have never had to put up with anything like it before. Next day little progress is visible. It is only on the third day that the thing takes shape. Only then does the poor composer begin to breathe. The harmonies, correctly pitched, become clear, the rhythms leap to life, the melodies sigh and smile; the whole ensemble acquires cohesion, confidence, attack. The stumbling and stammering is forgotten: the orchestra has grown up. With comprehension, courage returns to the astonished players. The composer asks for a fourth trial of skill, and his interpreters—who when all is said are the best fellows in the world—grant it with alacrity. This time, *fiat lux!* 'Watch for the expression. You're not afraid now?'

'No. Give us the right tempo.'

Via! And there is light! Art is born, the whole conception becomes manifest; the work is understood! And the orchestra rises to its feet, applauding and acclaiming the composer, the Kapellmeister congratulates him, the inquisitive people lurking in the hall emerge and come up onto the platform and exchange exclamations of pleasure and surprise with the players, with many a wondering glance at the foreign maestro whom at first they took for a madman or a barbarian. At this point you feel the need to relax. Do no such thing! It is now that you must intensify your vigilance. You have to return before the concert to supervise the arrangement of the desks and inspect the orchestral parts so as to make sure none of them have got misplaced. You must go meticulously along the ranks, red pencil in hand, writing German key-indications for

French in the wind parts, altering *ut, re, re bemol, fa diese*, to *C, D, Des, Fis*. You have to transpose a cor anglais solo for the oboe; the orchestra does not possess the instrument in question and the oboist is inclined to be nervous about transposing it himself. If the chorus or the soloists are still unsure of themselves, you must rehearse them separately. But the audience is arriving, it is time; and shattered in body and mind, you stagger to the conductor's desk, a wreck, weary, stale, flat and unprofitable, scarcely able to stand—until that magical moment when the applause of the audience, the zest of the players, and your own love for the work transform you in an instant into a dynamo of energy, radiating invisible, irresistible rays of light and power. And then the recompense begins. Then, I grant you, the composer-conductor lives on a plane of existence unknown to the virtuoso. With what ecstasy he abandons himself to the delight of 'playing' the orchestra! How he hugs and clasps and sways this immense and fiery instrument! Once more he is all vigilance. His eyes are everywhere. He indicates with a glance each vocal and orchestral entry. His right arm unleashes tremendous chords which go off like explosions. At the pauses he brings the whole accumulated impetus to a sudden halt, rivets every eye, arrests every arm, every breath; listens for an instant to the silence—then gives freer rein than ever to the harnessed whirlwind:

> *Luctantes ventos tempestatesque sonoras*
> *Imperio premit, ac vinclis et carcere frenat.*
> [*The rearing winds and roaring tempests*
> *He subdues to his dominion, and curbs and confines them*] (*Aeneid*, I, 53–54)

And in the long adagios, the bliss of floating cradled on a lake of serene harmony while a hundred soft voices intertwined chant his love songs, or seem to confide his present sorrows and past regrets to solitude and the stillness of the night! Then often, though only then, the composer–conductor becomes oblivious of the public. He listens to himself and judges his own handiwork; and if he is moved and the same emotion shared by the artists around him, he takes no further heed of the reaction of the audience: they are remote from him. If he has felt his heart thrill to the touch of the poetry and melody of the music and has sensed within him the secret fire which is the flame of the soul's incandescence, his goal is attained, the heaven of art is opened to him, and what signifies earth?

When the concert is over and he has triumphed, his joy is multiplied a hundred times, shared as it is with the gratified pride of every member of his army. You, the great virtuosos, are princes and kings by the grace of God; you are born on the steps of the throne. We composers must fight and overcome and conquer to reign. But the very dangers and hardships of the struggle make our victories the more intoxicating, and we would perhaps be more fortunate than you—if we always had soldiers.

In recounting his experiences guest conducting in Berlin, Berlioz gives us yet another vivid rehearsal description, this time in the role of the guest conductor of a foreign orchestra.

> For sheer ludicrous ferocity there is nothing to compare with a fanatical German nationalist fully roused. This time, too, I had a section of the Opera orchestra against me, having forfeited their good will by my letters on Berlin, which had been translated by M. Gathy and published in Hamburg a few years before. The letters contained nothing offensive to the Berlin players, as the reader of these memoirs may see for himself. On the contrary, I had praised them comprehensively, merely adding a few carefully qualified criticisms of minor points of detail. I called the orchestra magnificent and declared it exceptional in point of precision, unanimity, power and delicacy. But—and there lay my crime—I made a comparison between some of its principal players and those of Paris, and actually stated (perish the thought!) that where the flautists were concerned, ours were superior. These innocent words had planted a rancorous animosity against me in the breast of the Berlin first flute; and as far as I could make out, he had persuaded many of his colleagues to believe that I had wantonly traduced the entire orchestra. Fresh proof of the risks you run in writing about players, and of the advisability of not standing to leeward of their self-esteem when one has had the misfortune to wound it in the slightest degree. When you criticize a singer, you do not have his colleagues up in arms against you. Indeed, they generally feel that you have not been severe enough. But the virtuoso instrumentalist who belongs to a well-known musical organization always claims that in criticizing him you insult the whole institution, and though the contention is absurd, he sometimes succeeds in making the other players believe it. Once during the rehearsals of *Benvenuto Cellini* I had the occasion to point out to the second horn a mistake in an important passage. I did so in the mildest and politest manner; but the player, Meifred, though an intelligent man, rose in wrath and, losing his head completely, shouted, 'I'm playing what is there. Why do you suspect the orchestra like this?' To which I replied, even more mildly, that it had nothing to do with the orchestra but only him, and that secondly I suspected nothing, for suspicion implied doubt, and I knew he had made a mistake.
>
> To return to the Berlin orchestra, it did not take me long to notice a certain lack of geniality in its attitude to me during the rehearsals of *Faust*. The glacial reception I was given each day as I came in, the hostile silence which followed the best numbers in the score, and the irate glances, especially from the quarter of the flutes, made it only too obvious, and it was confirmed by what I learned from the players who had remained friendly to me. They were too much intimidated by their comrades' antagonism to applaud me.[50]

[50] *Memoirs*, 440ff.

Finally, surely every good conductor today can sympathize with Berlioz's description of his physical state following a concert in Berlin.

> At the conclusion of the concert a great many people spoke to me and congratulated me and wrung me by the hand, but I could only stand there dazed, not comprehending, feeling nothing. My brain and nervous system had over-taxed themselves and craved rest, I was stupid with fatigue.[51]

[51] ibid., 339.

Berlioz conducting the choir, by Gustave Doré, published in *Journal pour rire,* 27 June 1850

Part III
On The Nature And Purpose Of Score Study

6 *The Four Paramount Enigmas of the Score*

SURELY, EVERY THOUGHTFUL AND SERIOUS CONDUCTOR would conclude that it is the duty of the conductor to reproduce in performance the authentic musical idea of the composer. But where is, and how does one find, the composer's authentic musical idea?

Standing between the composer and the conductor are four significant enigmatic obstacles with respect to the nature of the score. These are very complicated philosophical issues and at their roots lie fundamental distinctions between music and the other arts.

Score Enigma Number One

Is the authentic form of the composer's musical ideas in the composer's head, or in his written score?

What do we mean by 'Art?' Is 'art' that which is the artist's original idea, or is 'art' his craft or is 'art' the finished art object itself? Or, we might ask, is the 'art' the composer's original idea, or the finished score, or the performance?

This fundamental aesthetic question has been discussed and debated for a very long time. In general, the philosophers of the ancient civilizations tended to call 'Art' that which was in the artist's mind. Cicero (106–43 BC), for example, believed that the goal of the artist was not merely to imitate, but through his imitation to suggest to the observer something even more beautiful.

> This ideal cannot be perceived by the eye or ear, nor by any of the senses, but we can nevertheless grasp it by the mind and the imagination. For example, in the case of the statues of Phidias, the most perfect of their kind that we have ever seen, and in the case of painting … , we can, in spite of their beauty, imagine something more beautiful. Surely that great sculptor, while making the image of Jupiter or Minerva, did not look at any person whom he was using as a model, but in his own mind there dwelt a surpassing vision of beauty; at this he gazed and all intent on this he guided his artist's hand to produce the likeness of the god.[1]

[1] Cicero, *Orator*, ii, 8.

Plotinus (204–270 AD), the last great philosopher of antiquity, also argued that the finished work of art can never be as beautiful as the original vision within the artist himself.

> Suppose two blocks of stone lying side by side: one is unpatterned, quite untouched by art; the other has been minutely wrought by the craftsman's hands into some statue of god or man, A Grace or a Muse, or if a human being, not a portrait but a creation in which the sculptor's art has concentrated all loveliness.
>
> Now it must be seen that the stone thus brought under the artist's hand to the beauty of form is beautiful not as stone ... but in virtue of the Form or Idea introduced by the art. This form is not in the material; it is in the designer before ever it enters the stone; and the artificer holds it not by his equipment of eyes and hands but by his participation in his art. The beauty, therefore, exists in a far higher state in the art; for it does not come over integrally into the work; that original beauty is not transferred; what comes over is a derivative and a minor: and even that shows itself upon the statue not integrally and with entire realization of intention but only in so far as it has subdued the resistance of the material ...
>
> Every prime cause must be, within itself, more powerful than its effect can be: the musical does not derive from an unmusical source but from music; and so the art exhibited in the material work derives from an art yet higher.[2]

[2] Plotinus, *The Enneads*, trans., Stephen MacKenna (London: Faber and Faber, 1962), 422.

Plotinus, date and artist unknown

With the beginning of the Christian Era, the Church philosophers gave the same answer, but for a different reason. Their reasoning went something like this: the artist made the art object, but God made the artist. It follows that God must be capable of making something greater than the artist could make, hence God's work (the artist) must be ranked above the art object. This rationale was faithfully maintained by all major medieval church figures, as we can see in the example of Saint Augustine (fourth century), who states very clearly that by 'Art' we mean not the art object itself but the artistic impression in the mind of the artist.

> A human artisan, for example, a woodworker, though he is almost nothing in comparison with the wisdom and power of God, nonetheless cuts and handles the wood for a long while, turning, sawing, planing, or shaping and polishing it, until it is brought, as far as possible, in conformity with the norms of the art and pleases the artisan. Did he, therefore, not know what was good, just because he is pleased by what he made? Of course, he knew it interiorly in his mind, where the art itself is more beautiful than the things which are produced by the art. What the artist sees interiorly in the art, he tests externally in his work, and it is finished when it pleases the artisan.[3]

[3] *On Genesis*, trans., Roland Teske (Washington, D.C.: The Catholic University of America Press), 61.

Since the art object is, therefore, of secondary importance, Augustine believed that the observer of art should focus not on the art object, but on the artist.

> The artist through the beauty of his work, intimates in a way to the viewer of it that he should not fasten his attention there completely but should so scan the beauty of the artistic work that he will turn his thoughts back fondly upon him who made it. Those who love the things you make instead of yourself are like the men who listen to the eloquence of a wise man. In their overeagerness to hear his beautiful voice and the skillful cadence of his words, they neglect the primary importance of his thoughts for which the spoken words were to serve as signs.[4]

For Augustine, even the technical skills of the artist are a gift from God.

> Those numbers and the harmony of lines which they impress upon matter with material tools are received in their minds from that supreme Wisdom, which has impressed the very numbers and harmony itself in a far more artistic way upon the whole physical universe.[5]

Similarly, the most influential medieval philosopher of music, Boethius (475–524 AD), in speaking of predestination, uses an analogy which reveals that his definition of art is that it exists first in the mind, and then in the art object.

> As every artist considers and marks out his work in his mind before he executes it, and afterwards executes it all.[6]

With the arrival of the Renaissance, a new perspective presents itself. Some philosophers now contend that it is the art object that is to be valued. Giordano Bruno (b. 1548) goes so far as to suggest that in seeing the art object we do not even see the artist's original idea, a notion he arrived at from the idea that the glory and credit for Art belongs to Nature, and not to the artist.

> Because from the cognition of all dependent things we cannot infer other notions of the first principle and cause than by the rather inadequate method of vestiges: all things being derived from the will or goodness [of the first cause], which is the principle of its operation and from which proceeds the universal effect. The same situation can be made out in our relation to works of art, insomuch as the man who sees the statue does not see the sculptor.[7]

[4] *The Free Choice of the Will*, trans., Robert P. Russell (Washington, DC: The Catholic University of America Press), xvi.

[5] *Eighty-Three Different Questions*, trans., David L. Mosher (Washington, DC: The Catholic University of America Press), 45, 78.

[6] Boethius, *Consolatione Philosophiae*, trans., Samuel Fox (London: George Bell, 1895), XXXIX, vi.

[7] Giordano Bruno, *Cause, Principle and Unity*, trans., Jack Lindsay (New York: International Publishers, 1962), 78.

Bronze statue of Giordano Bruno by Ettore Ferrari, Rome

Even the exceptional Erasmus found the value of art in the more practical considerations of the art object.

> The best picture is not that which displays by its material the wealth of the man who paid for it or the skill of the artist, but the most faithful likeness of the subject.[8]

[8] 'Parallels,' [1514] in *The Collected Works of Erasmus* (Toronto: University of Toronto Press, 1992), XXIII, 226.

For the great artists of the Renaissance, however, it was quite a different story. As might be expected, they were unequivocal in stating that the credit goes to the artist, and not the art object! The great Leonardo da Vinci (1452–1519) defended his view from an ancient prejudice that he was extremely sensitive to, the fact that painting had not been traditionally included in the medieval Liberal Arts, and hence the suggestion that painting was to be considered as something less than science. He answered this by first pointing out that all sciences, because they entail writing with the hand, are also mechanical. He expressed this once in the following way.

> Words are of less account than performances. But you, oh writer on the sciences, do you not, like the painter, copy by hand that which is in the mind?[9]

A statue of Leonardo da Vinci outside the Uffizi Gallery, Florence, Italy

[9] Quoted in Jean Paul Richter, ed., *The Literary Works of Leonardo da Vinci* (London: Phaidon, 1970), I, 78.

Second, since everything the artist understands about painting is understood first in the mind, before it is enacted manually, Art is as much of the domain of the mind as is science. Finally, since Art is in the mind of the artist, it is of a higher level of understanding than that of the observer or of the several disciplines which must be learned prior to engaging in painting.

> These are understood by the mind alone and entail no manual operation; and they constitute the science of painting which remains in the mind of its contemplators; and from it is then born the actual creation, which is far superior in dignity to the contemplation or science which precedes it.[10]

[10] ibid., I, 34.

In another place, he emphasized his belief that the artist is not merely a scientist who copies Nature, but is a creator. Through imitation the artist's mind takes on, that divine power, which lies in the knowledge of the painter, transforms the mind of the painter into the likeness of the divine mind, for with a free hand he can produce [that which does not actually exist, including] different beings, animals, plants, fruits, landscapes, open fields, abysses, terrifying and fearful places.[11]

On no aspect of aesthetics did the great Michelangelo write and speak more frequently than of his conviction that Art is that which is within the mind of the artist, and not in that which he accomplishes with his hands. An early letter in which Michelangelo addresses this distinction between mind and hand is a complaint regarding his treatment at the time he was working on the tomb for Julius II.

> I'll always go on working for Pope Clement with such powers as I have, which are slight, as I'm an old man—with this proviso, that the taunts, to which I see I am being subjected, cease, because they very much upset me and prevented me from doing the work I want to do for several months now. For one cannot work at one thing with the hands and at another with the head, particularly in the case of marble.[12]

Michelangelo states this principle very clearly in some of his poems, one of which reads,

> The greatest artist has no conception
> Which a single block of marble does not
> Potentially contain within its mass,
> But only a hand obedient to the mind
> Can penetrate to this image.[13]

Another, a sonnet for Tommaso Cavalieri, has the same meaning.

> In the same way that pen and ink embrace
> The high and the low style and the middle,
> And rich pictures or crude are in the marble,
> Whichever our wits are able to express.[14]

Nothing testifies to this more clearly than Michelangelo's unfinished sculptures. Anyone who sees one of these pieces is struck by the illusion of the mind's vision of a work already finished within the marble, just waiting for the unneeded stone to be struck away.

[11] Quoted in Anthony Blunt, *Artistic Theory in Italy, 1450-1600* (Oxford: Clarendon Press, 1959), 37.

A statue of Michaelangelo outside the Uffizi Gallery, Florence, Italy

[12] Letter to Giovan Francesco Fattucci, October 24, 1525.

[13] Quoted in Blunt, op. cit., 73.

[14] Creighton Gilbert, trans., *Complete Poems of Michelangelo* (Princeton: Princeton University Press, 1963), 58.

Unfinished slave, Michelangelo, Accademia, Florence

Perhaps the fact that there is relatively little commentary on his finished pieces in his letters is due to his awareness that the version in his mind was more beautiful than that which he completed. A contemporary, Condivi, who recalls Michelangelo having discussed this very point with him, described him as having had,

> a most powerful imagination, whence it comes, chiefly, that he is little contented with his works and has always underrated them, his hand not appearing to carry out the ideas he has conceived in his mind.[15]

[15] Quoted in Blunt, op. cit., 72.

With respect to the composer and his score, we must view this ancient question first and foremost from the perspective of one of the most significant distinctions between music and the other arts. Among all the arts, music *alone* is not a representational art. That is to say, a painting is a representation of something else, but music is not a representation of something—it is the real thing itself.

It is for this reason that, with respect to the art of painting, it is the finished canvas that we pay millions of dollars for. In music, however, it is obviously not the printed score we value, but rather the experience of the music itself—the performance. If the conductor fulfills his duty to the composer, this live experience–performance form of the music will ideally correspond with that in the composer's mind. But, of course, as valid as this principle is, it does not answer the question: how does the conductor *find* this authentic form of the music.

For now, we will simply suggest that the conductor must place his faith in the fact that he is capable of finding this authentic form of the music. The fact that he *can* lies in the universality of music and emotions. Let us examine this question further by considering the quality of the composer's inner idea.

Does only the 'genius' have the ideas from which great music is constructed? When Mozart died, his wife immediately sold all his completed works, thinking she would get the best price while he was still remembered. But, interestingly enough, she *saved* his incomplete works and sketches for her two children, reasoning that if one of them wanted to be a composer he would be guaranteed success by having Mozart's melodies to use! It certainly would be a good place to begin, but unfortunately it is the working out of the material, not just the material itself, which results in great music. One only has to see the sketches of Beethoven to observe how a composer can begin with a rather mundane idea and gradually shape it into something special. So the answer to this question is, No!

It does seem that the Mozarts and the Einsteins are born with their genius and no amount, or absence, of education seems to contribute to the quality of their genius, but this may only be because we cannot know fully their individual histories in gaining left and right brain information. But if we accept the idea that some men are simply born with different potentialities, born with genius, how do they differ from us? They probably have much more in common with the rest of us than we might suppose. For, as the most important contemporary philosopher of aesthetics, Benedetto Croce, points out, it is only because we have so much in common that we are able to recognize their genius.

> Nor can we admit that the word *genius* or artistic genius, as distinct from the non-genius of the ordinary man, possesses more than a quantitative signification. Great artists are said to reveal us to ourselves. But how could this be possible, unless there were identity of nature between their imagination and ours, and unless the difference were only one of quantity? It were better to change *poets are born* into *men are born poets*, some men are born great poets, some small … It has been forgotten that genius is not something that has fallen from heaven, but humanity itself.[16]

[16] Benedetto Croce, *Aesthetic* (New York: Noonday), 14.

We recognize a part of ourselves in every composer and in every composition and this is because of the common emotional characteristics which are passed down to us genetically. We differ, both in ordinary life and in art, in the quality of the expression and individual meaning of these emotions.

The idea that the greatest composers are 'born and not made' should not disturb us. With regard to the world of the left hemisphere, we accept without concern the fact that the wheel of fortune allots to each of us a different level of 'intelligence,' which we most inadequately measure as IQ but perhaps it is more accurate to suppose we are born with differing abilities to absorb the extra-self data we are presented with over time. In the case of the right hemisphere, the experiential side of ourselves, clearly it is the differing exposure to non-rational experiences which differentiate us. Indeed, there is no stronger justification in performing only the best music than that of permitting ourselves the opportunity to communicate with great minds.

In any case, music begins with an *inner* idea; art begins with thought. In both music and in painting, this is 'thought' in the right hemisphere. Here language fails us, because 'thought' normally is associated with reason, hence the left hemisphere. The word most often substituted is 'intuitive,' but this seems vague to us and we prefer just 'thought,' with the understanding that we mean non-rational thought.

That art begins in the mind is perfectly illustrated in an engaging anecdote of Leonardo and his famous painting, the *Last Supper*. He had, apparently, by this time of this anecdote, finished everything except the head of Judas when he apparently stopped. Two friars complained to the duke who was paying for the painting that Leonardo was not working. When the duke inquired, Leonardo answered that it was not true, that in fact he devoted two hours a day to the painting of the head of Judas. By this he meant, of course, that he had been *thinking* two hours a day. In another version of this anecdote, Leonardo responds,

> The minds of men of lofty genius are most active in invention when they are doing the least external work.[17]

[17] Quoted in Croce, op. cit., 10.

In this regard, Croce takes the very rigid position that this inner thought is everything. He maintains that the formulation of this inner idea is synonymous with the finished art work, that if the idea is not perfectly defined it cannot be expressed in art.

> One often hears people say that they have many great thoughts in their minds, but that they are not able to express them. But if they really had them, they would have coined them into just so many beautiful, sounding words, and thus have expressed them. If these thoughts seem to vanish or to become few and meager in the act of expressing them, the reason is that they did not exist or really were few and meager. People think that all of us ordinary men imagine and intuit countries, figures and scenes like painters, and bodies like sculptors; save that painters and sculptors know how to paint and carve such images, while we bear them unexpressed in our souls. They believe that any one could have imagined a Madonna of Raphael; but that Raphael was Raphael owing to his technical ability in putting the Madonna on canvas. Nothing can be more false than this view.[18]

[18] ibid., 9.

With a little reflection, the reader will see that this is nonsense. Have we, for example, never had thoughts and feelings more beautiful than our speech? Any lover who has ever tried to write a love letter can answer this question, for these feelings, which can be very profound and precise, are never satisfactorily communicated in words. Croce is certainly wrong in this viewpoint with respect to music, for music is of the right hemisphere and musical notation, a symbolic language just like English, can never satisfactorily communicate the composer's complete inner idea—which brings us to the second score problem.

Score Enigma Number Two

Isidore, Bishop of Seville (560–636 AD), is the only writer known today representing Gothic Spain. His twenty-volume *Etymologiarum*, which is really the first encyclopedia, has the goal of presenting all the information a Christian needs to know. Its practical importance lies in the fact that it treats the seven liberal arts, including music, and thus was one more powerful weapon for preserving traditional knowledge throughout the Dark Ages.

In his initial definition of music, Isidore mentions a notion which many early writers seemed to find a particularly significant characteristic of music, that once a performance is finished the music is gone, it has disappeared and does not exist anymore except in the memory. This is probably one of the reasons the ancient writers could not accept music as a rational discipline. That is, since the music cannot be seen and disappears after the performance, it is as if they considered it as almost an illusion.

Isidore, Bishop of Seville, by Bartolomé Esteban Murillo, 1655

> The sound of [music], since it is an impression upon the sense, flows by into the past and is imprinted upon the memory ... Unless sounds are remembered by man, they perish, for they cannot be written down.[19]

[19] *Etymologiarum*, III, xv, trans., W. M. Linsay, quoted in Oliver Strunk, Source Readings in Music History (New York: Norton, 1950).

Isidore was writing before the introduction of notation in Western European music, so in that sense, of course, music could not be 'written down.' But now that we have notation, one *still* has to say 'music cannot be written down.' This is because musical notation does not notate *music*; musical notation is only a *symbol* of the music. As a symbolic notation it is particularly ineffective in the fact that it makes no attempt to notate feeling. Thus Carl Maria von Weber once observed of emotions in music,

> We have in music no signs for all this. They exist only *in the sentient human soul.*[20]

[20] Letter to Praeger, music director at Leipzig.

Carl Maria von Weber

And to this very day, we have not a single notational symbol which represents feeling.

Then you must add to this the fact that many of the symbols we do have are of an indefinite nature, left to the performer, not the composer, to define. The fundamental problem which lies at the heart of the indefinite quality of our music notation is wonderfully summarized by Carlo Maria Giulini.

> Music has this problem. We have a note in music with the value of one; we know the quarter-note is double the eighth-note. But we don't know how much one is. What does a quarter-note mean? Nothing. Nothing. Absolutely nothing, because a quarter-note can be long, can be short; and what does adagio mean? Piano? Forte?[21]

[21] Gerald Stein, 'Giulini: On Preparation, Rehearsal, and Performance,' *The Instrumentalist*, October, 1980.

All in all, Isidore remains correct—music 'cannot be written down.'

Let us state this problem in the form of a Proposition.

Score Enigma Number Two

Music notation is incapable of notating music.

Because of the enormous obstacle a symbolic notational system represents to a conductor intent on discovering the composer's original, authentic idea, we must pause to reflect on symbolic languages in general.

The earliest writing we know of early man are the pictures in the caves of France, dating from the last Ice Age. In a written language composed of pictures, as one also finds in the Egyptian tomb paintings, and in the ancient Asian languages, you have a language in which the written symbol is synonymous with one's experience (the symbol for 'cat' is a picture of a cat). Let us emphasize this, these early pictorial written languages were very effective for the reason that they combined as one both the symbol *and* the experience.

Early man had no written pictorial equivalent for his music. His music was a means of *directly* communicating his feelings. This was a sufficiently effective system of communication that no further 'improvements' were needed over a great period of time. This is very much worthy of reflection, the fact that music existed quite effectively for many thousands of years without any need for notation at all.

A very fundamental change in the culture of man occurred with the invention of the much more efficient phonetic writing. Now language became only a *symbol* of the experience itself, for example, now 'c–a–t' is a word which now only phonetically represents a cat, but does not look like a cat. But more than that, if we recall that spoken language predates the written language, then with phonetic writing the written word is a symbol of the spoken word, which in turn is a symbol of the real thing or experience. So, as Aristotle reminds us, a written word is a symbol of a symbol and that in the case of emotions the symbols change while the experience remains universal.

> Words spoken are symbols or signs of affections or impressions of the soul; written words are the symbols of words spoken. As writing, so also is speech not the same for all races of men. But the affections themselves, of which these words are primarily signs, are the same for the whole of mankind.[22]

[22] 'On Interpretation,' I, trans., Harold P. Cook (Cambridge: Harvard University Press, 1962).

Because of this, this new phonetic writing had the negative effect of putting a barrier between man's experience and his language, as explained by Marshall McLuhan.

> The phonetic alphabet did not change or extend man so drastically just because it enabled him to read. Tribal culture had already coexisted with other written languages for thousands of years. But the phonetic alphabet was radically different from the older and richer hieroglyphic or ideogrammic cultures. The writing of Egyptian, Babylonian, Mayan and Chinese cultures were an extension of the senses in that they gave pictorial expression to reality, and they demanded many signs to cover the wide range of data in their societies—unlike phonetic writing which uses semantically meaningless letters to correspond to semantically meaningless sounds and is able, with only a handful of letters, to encompass all meanings and all languages. This achievement demanded the separation of both sights and sounds from their semantic and dramatic meanings in order to render visible the actual sound of speech, thus placing a barrier between men and objects and creating a dualism between sight and sound.[23]

[23] Marshall McLuhan, 'An Interview,' *Playboy*, March, 1969.

Once man turned to this new kind of writing, where the language–picture no longer corresponded with experience, things in our rational world became confusing.

> Verbal identifications and confused abstractions begin at a tender age … Language is no more than crudely acquired before children begin to suffer from it, and to misinterpret the world by reason of it.[24]

[24] Stuart Chase, *The Tyranny of Words* (New York: Harcourt, Brace, 1938), 56.

Another very important point is that from that moment we needed an intermediary, a teacher, to connect us with our language. Someone has to answer our questions, 'Why isn't *gnat* spelled with an *n*?' or 'When do we use *to, too,* or *two*?'

In modern Europe the development of our *right* hemisphere language, music, followed much the same course. The 'improvement' which came was music's equivalent of a phonetic alphabet, and we call it music notation. As with left hemisphere language, once notation arrived it also required an intermediary to connect the musician's experience with the notation, to show him how you really play what is on paper. It is no surprise, therefore, that soon after the modern conductor appeared. But as Wagner points out, until the nineteenth century the composer was also present to tell the players how the music should *really* be played, a role now given over almost entirely to the conductor.

Even today, although we have accustomed ourselves to a most minute notation of the nuances of phrasing, the more talented conductor often finds himself obliged to teach his musicians very weighty, but delicate shadings of expression by *viva voce* explanation; and these communications, as a rule, are better understood and heeded, than the written signs.[25]

[25] William Ashton Ellis, ed., *Wagner's Prose Works* (New York: Broude), IV, 192.

In another place,[26] Wagner reminds us of an additional complication. In the case of music we have the original symbol in the right hemisphere while the notation is in the left hemisphere and, medically speaking, the hemispheres do not converse much but tend to act separately. This, notes Wagner, leads to a separation of man from his feelings, in terms remarkably similar to McLuhan. 'Understanding,' by which he means what we call today the rational left hemisphere,

[26] ibid., II, 230ff.

> through the process of imagination acquired a language by which it would make itself intelligible *alone* and in a direct ratio: as the rational man became more intelligible the feeling man became less. In modern Prose we speak a language which we do not understand as being related to Feeling, since its connection with the objects, whose impression on our faculties first generated the roots of speech (pictures), has become lost to us.

Since our feelings cannot communicate in traditional language,

> it was altogether consequent that Feeling should have sought a refuge from absolute intellectual-speech by fleeing to absolute tone-speech, our Music of today.

The most essential thing to remember about musical notation is that it is only a *symbol* of something else, a symbol of the real thing.[27] This was accurately recognized by the ancient Greeks, who had the earliest music notation we know of. Aristoxenus (b. 379 BC), a student of Aristotle, was careful to make this very point.

[27] Ravel, who suffered from aphasia late in life, was no longer able to express his musical ideas in symbols (musical notation).

> [Just because] a man notes down the Phrygian scale it does not follow that he must know the *essence* of the Phrygian scale. Plainly then notation is not the ultimate limit of our science.[28]

[28] Aristoxenus, *The Elements of Harmony*, 16, trans., Henry S. Macran (Hildesheim: Georg Olms Verlag, 1974), 39.

When modern music notation first appeared in Western Europe it is very clear that it was considered to be only a symbolic notation, not an exact one. In fact, Franchino Gaffurio (1451–1518), in his very important music treatise, *Practica Musicae*, not only mentions the symbolic nature of notation, but goes further in making the fascinating suggestion that singers were regularly singing things 'which cannot be written down!'

> An interval, or space, can be understood to be the distance between a high and a low sound. Moreover, the mental concept of sound is symbolized in given notes. One must express the fixed, raised and lowered pitches of these notes arranged on a variety of lines and spaces vocally. Consequently, these notes are called vocal symbols. Further, sounds which cannot be written down are committed to memory by usage and practice so that they will not be lost, for their delivery flows imperceptibly into the past.[29]

But there is yet another problem with symbolic languages, alike in both English and music. That is that the symbols inevitably have some limited meaning of their own. An English word, for example, standing by itself has a dictionary meaning. This we might call its universal meaning. But the same word may have a different meaning in common usage, or perhaps according to geography. This we might call a more individualized meaning. Thus, when a speaker uses the word 'cat,' he is using the universal definition, but the listener will usually hear instead an individual definition, reflecting some actual cat he has owned or known. Thus everyone in the audience is actually thinking of a *different* cat, each differing with the single word of the speaker!

The same is true for our symbolic language of music. In musical notation we have a very limited, yet universally, agreed upon understanding of, let us say, the difference intended between *piano* and *forte*. On the other hand, we have no agreed upon meaning at all regarding the precise measurement of *piano*. It is simply left to the individual performer's perspective. The development of a symbolic language in both English and music has the advantage of bringing literacy to a broader range of people. The danger is that we will tend to fixate on the symbol and not what it represents experientially.

[29] Irwin Young, trans., *The Practica musicae of Franchinus Gafurius* (Madison: University of Wisconsin Press, 1969), 18.

Thus we have inherited a symbolic musical notation which is incapable of expressing the composer's original, authentic musical ideas, which alone is a significant obstacle to the conductor. But in addition to this there are a host of additional, peripheral problems related to musical notation. One is that we can never be quite sure if what we see on paper is what the composer wrote. Here we are not thinking so much of copyist and publisher errors, which are a real enough problem by themselves, but rather the work of that unseen person whose name often never appears on the page, the editor. Here we speak from experience, having once been employed by a major United States publisher as the unseen, anonymous person in the basement who was paid to edit. In one case it was an orchestral score by an important living composer, to which the unseen person was paid to add slurs and articulation markings unknown to the composer. In another case, involving a famous European publishing house, the present writer was paid to prepare an urtext edition of a number of Mozart piano sonatas. But when the present person took the finished manuscripts in to the editor, the editor picked up a pencil and immediately began to draw slurs, change articulations, etc. 'But,' we cried, 'our purpose is to make an urtext edition, just the way Mozart wrote it!' 'Yes,' said the editor, 'but everyone knows this should be slurred.' So a generation of pianists bought an urtext edition which was not really an urtext edition. So can we ever really know what the composer wrote?

Another interesting problem is represented by Verdi, as reported by Toscanini,[30] who believed that no matter what he put on paper, in terms of dynamics, an Italian orchestra would play *mezzoforte* at all times. So, in his operas, Verdi would write '*ppp*' in the hopes of getting '*p*.' Can we ever know what Verdi *really* wanted?

In summary, neither our present notational system, nor any other system of notation that could ever be invented, can precisely communicate, by itself, the composer's original idea. Rational symbolic language can never be the real thing when it comes to the experiential. Berlioz once wrote,

It is said that a Greek was once asked to go and hear a man whistle like a nightingale. 'Not I,' replied the Greek, 'I have heard the actual bird.'[31]

[30] Related in Erich Leinsdorf, *The Composer's Advocate* (New Haven: Yale University Press, 1981), 200.

[31] 'On Imitation in Music '(1837).

Score Enigmas Number Three and Four

For most of music history, composers never expected a performance to only reproduce what was notated.

We have seen that the form of music notation developed in Western European music during the late Middle Ages was an indefinite, symbolic one and not a literal one. But, perhaps the notation of music has never intended to be a precise written record of the actual music.

The very important early Renaissance theorist, Jean de Muris (1290–1350), began his book, *Ars nove musice*, which became a standard university text, with a discussion of the notation of earlier music. He makes a very significant observation, for which, unfortunately, he offers no further details.

> For reasons which we shall pass over, their symbols did not adequately represent what they sang.[32]

More to the point is that admonition by Galilei, in 1584, that players not aspire to simply play what is on the page.

> And let it not come into your mind to try to defend yourself with the silly excuse of some who say they did not feel called upon to do more than that which they found written or printed.[33]

A passage by François Couperin is particularly interesting, in view of what has been discussed above, for it also draws an analogy between language and music as symbolic languages. He seems to suggest that, in the case of both language and music, the performance form does not follow the written form.

> In my opinion, there are faults in our way of writing music, which correspond to the way in which we write our language. The fact is we write a thing differently from the way in which we execute it.[34]

We must also remember that the accumulated experience of many centuries of improvised music before the adoption of a standardized notation continued on as part of performance practice long after the advent of notation. Nowhere is this

[32] Quoted in Oliver Strunk, *Source Readings in Music History* (New York: Norton, 1950), 175.

[33] Vincenzo Galilei, *Fronimo* (1584), trans., Carol MacClintock (Neuhasen-Stuttgart: Hänssler-Verlag, 1985), 83.

[34] François Couperin, *L'Art de toucher* (Paris, 1717, reprinted Wiesbaden: Breitkopf & Härtel, 1933), 23.

François Couperin, etching by Jean-Jacques Flipart after a painting by André Boüys, 1735

more evident than in the performance practice of the Baroque. Jacopo Peri (1561–1633), one of the midwives of opera, felt much of the music he heard could not be notated.

> This lady, who has always made my compositions seem worthy of her singing, adorns them not only with those groups and those long windings of the voice, simple and double, which the liveliness of her talent can invent at any moment (more to comply with the usage of our times than because she considers the beauty and force of our singing to lie in them), but also with those elegances and graces that cannot be written or, if written, cannot be learned from writing.[35]

Charles Avison (1709–1770) agreed that ornamentation was 'impossible to be expressed' in notation. His chief concern was that since every performer viewed this practice individually, the result was that the student became 'discouraged in the progress of his study.'[36]

The English philosopher, John Donne (1573–1631), in a letter of circa 1600, is speaking of the importance of not depending on books for one's education, but on personal observation and experience. Then, in analogy, he adds his very interesting observation that everyone would rather hear the performance of improvised music than that which was notated.

> For both listeners and players are more delighted with voluntary than with sett musicke.[37]

The famous English philosopher Thomas Hobbs (1588–1679) suggests in one place that music 'with often hearing become insipid,'[38] by which he means repeated identical performances. This appears to be the meaning, also, when Charles Burney recalled Henry Purcell complaining that writing everything out robs music of its special quality of being performed in the present tense ['modernized by a judicious performer']. When one plays written music, it is automatically music of the past ['obsolete and old fashioned'].[39]

Most readers who have not followed revelations in early performance practice during recent years would be surprised to learn how much music performance during the Classic Period did not 'follow the page.' In a remarkable example, Mozart's sister writes to him about a passage he has written questioning whether he really intended it to be performed as written.

[35] Quoted in Oliver Strunk, op. cit., 375.

[36] Charles Avison, *An Essay on Musical Expression* [London, 1753] (New York: Broude Reprint, 1967), 126.

John Donne, by Wenzel Hollar

[37] John Donne, 'Paradoxes and Problems,' in *Selected Prose*, ed., Helen Gardner (Oxford: Clarendon Press, 1967), 109.

[38] 'The Answer of Mr. Hobbes to Sir William Davenant's Preface before *Gondibert*,' in *The English Works of Thomas Hobbes*, ed., William Molesworth (London: Bohn, 1839), IV, 455.

[39] Charles Burney, *A General History of Music* [1776] (London, 1935), II, 443.

Mozart writes back saying, essentially, 'Oh no, of course you would not perform it as written, but rather like the following,' whereupon he writes out some florid melodic material which is fairly remote from what he actually wrote on paper.

With regard to the nineteenth century, there is that wonderful anecdote which Berlioz tells of his pleading (to no avail!) with an oboist in Frankfurt to please just play what he has written at the beginning of the second movement of the *Symphonie fantastique*. And there is an extant piano roll of Mahler playing, on piano, the first movement of his Fifth Symphony, with tempi and rubato found nowhere in the actual score. Strauss once asked a conductor, 'But why do you want it so exact?'[40]

In a letter to his parents, Strauss concludes that no conductor could ever perform a work 'the way one imagines it oneself.'[41] And Tchaikovsky, in a letter to von Meck, said exactly the same thing.

> Ah, how difficult it is to make anyone else see and feel in music what we see and feel ourselves![42]

This is the real issue: can a composer, given the indefinite nature of our symbolic notation, reasonably assume that a different person will reproduce exactly what he, the composer, has imagined in his head? Carlo Maria Giulini goes further, believing that even the finest composer cannot predict in advance how something will really sound.

> After many years I have arrived at this opinion: the composers themselves do not know exactly what they want from their music. They write music, of course, but the sound is always a mystery. Take Mahler, who was not only a great composer, but also a great conductor. He had an experience of sound, of balance, of everything. Yet he changed the score after the first performance.[43]

We think it is reasonable to conclude that, because of the limited and indefinite nature of our symbolic notation system, most composers place their trust in the performer to see 'through' the symbols to discover what the composer really meant by the notation. This seems to be the point of a story which Giulini relates about Verdi.

[40] Related in Erich Leinsdorf, *The Composer's Advocate* (New Haven: Yale University Press, 1981), 48.

[41] Letter to his parents, February 3, 1890.

[42] March 16, 1878.

[43] Gerald Stein, 'Giulini: On Preparation, Rehearsal, and Performance,' in *The Instrumentalist*, October, 1980.

You know, Toscanini once told me that he wanted to do the *Four Sacred Pieces* by Verdi. And he had the feeling that at one point he had to do a small ritardando that wasn't written. So he got an appointment with Verdi though he was very young and very afraid of going to this old man. Verdi asked Toscanini to play the piano and when he arrived at this point he did a small rallentando expecting an explosion from Verdi. Nothing happened.

At the end, Verdi said, 'All right. Good.' So Toscanini said, 'But I did this small rallentando which is not in the score,' and then Verdi became angry. He said, 'We can't write everything—the composer can write a few things, but not everything. The musician has to understand and do it.'[44]

44 ibid.

What Verdi recommends seems so evident, not only in view of our indefinite symbolic notational system, but in view of the relationship between performer and composer over the whole of music history.

But, in fact, it is not evident to everyone. Gunther Schuller's recent book on conducting, *The Compleat Conductor* (New York: Oxford University Press, 1997), seems to have sprung from years of accumulated anger dating from his years as an orchestral player. He seems to have been obsessed with wondering why these famous conductors were doing things which did not correspond with what he saw in his horn part. 'Nobody Gives a Damn About the Composer,' he was tempted to title his book, and he accuses the most beloved conductors of the century of disloyalty to the composer. If conductors actually did what Schuller would have them do, it might be the biggest disservice to the composer of all.

If the composer did not expect the performer or conductor to reproduce exactly what is on the page, what did he expect the performer or conductor to reproduce?

Giuseppe Verdi, by Théobald Chartran, *Vanity Fair,* 15 February 1879

What is best in music is not to be found in the notes.
    Gustav Mahler

Nothing so perfectly symbolizes the fourth enigma of scores than this phrase which Mahler was in the habit of saying.[45] What did he mean? He was referring to the fact that although the paramount purpose of music is to express emotions, there

45 According to colleague Bruno Walter, in *Gustav Mahler* (New York: Greystone Press, 1941), 83.

are no specific symbols by which emotions can be expressed. The supreme challenge to the conductor in studying a score is to find this 'the best of music.'

How does the conductor do this? Some routes will lead him there and some will not, as will be discussed in the following chapters.

7 How Not to Study a Score

Wolfgang von Goethe
It is always a sign of the unproductivity of an age when it loses itself in petty technicalities, and in the same way it is a sign of the unproductivity of an individual when he occupies himself with that sort of thing.[1]

Heinrich Heine
Nothing is more futile than theorizing about music.[2]

Tchaikovsky
I do not understand how to analyze music.[3]

Wagner
If one needs a science for it, then Art is useless.[4]

Ned Rorem
Meditation more than analysis will take us toward the heart of music.[5]

René Descartes
The music of the ancients was more moving than ours, not because they were more learned, but because they were less.[6]

What are these people talking about? They are referring to the problem that music notation is both a *sign* and a *symbol*. When a composer writes an F♯ on paper it is a sign which designates a specific pitch and, as a sign, observes the understood conceptual and mathematical relationships with other signs—this is what we mean by music theory. But this same F♯, and the context in which it is placed, is also a *symbol*, a symbol of something beyond music theory and in a sense beyond notation. The problem is that musicians often error by placing their emphasis on the sign (theory) rather than on the symbol (the *meaning* of music).[7]

Deryck Cooke, in his *The Language of Music*, reminds us that literary critics who analyze fine works of literature do not make this mistake.

[1] J. P. Eckermann, *Conversations with Goethe*, trans., Gisela C. O'Brien (New York: Frederick Ungar Publishing Co.,), 201.

[2] *Letters on the French Stage* (1837)

[3] Tchaikovsky, *Diary* (1886).

[4] William Ellis, *Wagner's Prose Works* (New York: Broude), VIII, 392.

[5] *The Final Diary* (1974).

[6] Letter to Mersenne, quoted in Nat Shapiro, *An Encyclopedia of Quotations About Music* (New York, Da Capo, 1977), 45.

[7] This is one of the central themes of the writings on Western civilization by Joseph Campbell, who finds most religions of the world place their emphasis on the myth, or sign, rather than on its symbolic significance. You don't have to go to Israel, he assures his readers, to find the 'Promised Land.' Joseph Campbell, *Transformations of Myth Through Time* (New York: Harper & Row, 1990), 96.

> When we try to assess the achievement of a great literary artist, one of the chief ways in which we approach his work is to examine it as a report on human experience. We feel that, in his art, he has said something significant in relation to life as it is lived; and that what he has said—whether we call this a 'criticism of life' or a *Weltanschauung* or something else—is as important as the purely formal aspect of his writing. Or rather, these two main aspects of his art—'content' and 'form'—are realized to be ultimately inseparable: what he has said is inextricably bound up with how he has said it; and how he has said it clearly cannot be considered separately from what he has said.[8]

[8] Deryck Cooke, *The Language of Music* (Oxford: Oxford University Press, 1959), Preface.

Cooke then points out that we do not do this in the analysis of music—we analyze only the 'form' and not the 'content.' He uses the word 'form,' of course, to include all the grammar of music, including harmony, rhythm, etc. He concludes,

> By regarding form as an end in itself, instead of as a means of expression, we make evaluations of composers' achievements which are largely irrelevant and worthless.

He also reminds us of the unfortunate cultural consequence of our traditional approach to the analysis of music.

> But there is another, more serious consequence of our attitude: one whole side of our culture is impoverished, since we deny ourselves the possibility of enlarging our understanding of human experience by a specifically musical view of it. After all, if man is ever to fulfill the mission he undertook at the very start—when he first began to philosophize, as a Greek, and evolved the slogan 'Know thyself'—he will have to understand his unconscious [non-rational] self; and the most articulate language of the unconscious is music. But we musicians, instead of trying to understand this language, preach the virtues of refusing to consider it a language at all; when we should be attempting, as literary critics do, to expound and interpret the great masterpieces of our art for the benefit of humanity at large, we concern ourselves more and more with parochial affairs—technical analyses and musicological *minutiae*—and pride ourselves on our detached, dehumanized approach.

The fundamental problem here is one that had been clearly recognized since at least the late Baroque Period. One of the greatest of French philosophers on aesthetics, Charles Batteux (1713–1780), correctly pointed out that we do not understand music, as listeners, in anything remotely near the 'rules,' or conceptual aspects of it we study in school.

> If I were to say that I could derive no pleasure from a lecture that I did not understand, my confession would in no way seem strange. But if I ventured to say the same of a piece of music, people would ask whether I considered myself enough of a connoisseur to appreciate the merits of so carefully constructed and fine a composition. I would dare to reply yes, for it is a matter of feeling [and not conceptual knowledge]. I do not [while listening to music] pretend in any way to calculate the sounds, their interrelationships or their connection with the ear. I am speaking here neither of oscillations, string vibrations, nor mathematical proportions. I leave such speculations to learned theorists; these are akin to the grammar and dialectic of a lecture which I can appreciate without going into such details. Music speaks to me in tones: this language is natural to me.[9]

[9] Charles Batteux, *Les beaux-arts réduits à un même principe* [Paris, 1746], quoted in Peter le Huray and James Day, *Music and Aesthetics in the Eighteenth and Early-Nineteenth Centuries* (Cambridge: Cambridge University Press, 1981), 48ff.

Berlioz adds that the public judges music on the basis of emotions, and not by 'ridiculous theories.' He continues,

> The public does not ask whether such and such a modulation bears a due relation to some other one; whether certain harmonies are admitted by the teachers of theory; or whether *it is permitted* to employ certain rhythms, previously unknown. It simply perceives that these rhythms, these harmonies and modulations, set off by a noble and passionate melody, and clothed in powerful instrumentation, make a strong impression upon it, and in an entirely new way. Could anything further be necessary to excite its applause?[10]

[10] *A Travers Chant* (1862).

Wagner had also expressed the concern that we analyze only half of the music, and the unimportant half. He wrote, 'the art of Music has taken a development which has exposed her to so great a misapprehension of her veritable character.' In subjecting music to only the analysis of theoretical details, we are 'asked to wholly repress her own nature for the mere sake of turning her outmost side to our delectation.'[11]

[11] 'Beethoven,' in William Ellis, *Wagner's Prose Works* (New York: Broude), V, 77.

The point all these writers make is absolutely valid and germane to the modern experience. What we do in traditional analysis of music is study only the grammar of music. It is a shortcoming no less significant than studying only the grammar of *Hamlet* and missing its great themes altogether.

We observed a conducting clinic some years ago when the clinician passed out a four-page, single-spaced, outline entitled 'The Technique of Musical Style Analysis.' Under one caption alone, 'Melody', the conductor was encouraged to analyze melody by subjecting it to the following points of investigation:

Prominence of melodic element
Relationship to texture
    Monophonic
    Homophonic
    Polyphonic
General qualities
    Lyric or dramatic?
    Cantabile or instrumental?
    'Tunefulness'—folk-song quality?
Dimensions
    Vertical: narrow or wide range?
    Horizontal: long, continuous lines or short, motival fragment
Scale Basis
    Major
    Minor: natural, melodic, harmonic
    Modal
    Pentatonic
    Chromatic
    Whole-tone
    Other scale systems (Hungarian, pseudo-Oriental, Etc.)
    Unconventional division of the octave
Progression
    Diatonic or chromatic?
    Conjunct or disjunct?
    Tonal or atonal?
    Repeated notes
    Prominence of certain intervals
    Characteristic patters or clichés
Contour
    Direction: ascending, descending, combinations
    Contour patterns
Emphasis on certain scale degrees
    Repetition
    Recurrence
    Rhythmic stress
    Contour
Ornamentation
    Embellishment
    Coloration
    Figuration
Use of melodic material
    Repetition
    Modification
    Variation
    Development
    As cantus firmus
    Sequence
    Ostinato
    Leitmotif

Suffice to say, one *can* do all this—but such an analysis will not reveal the meaning and true nature of the melody because it does not address at all the fundamental role of melody, to communicate feeling. Consequently, when the conductor finishes all this analysis, he will discover he has gained no insights whatsoever regarding how to *perform* the melody. This is what Couperin meant when he observed,

> Just as there is a difference between grammar and declamation, so there is an infinitely greater one between musical theory and the art of fine playing.[12]

[12] François Couperin, *L'Art de toucher*, Preface.

Equally distressing are the numerous dissertations which propose to study some major band composition, but in fact study only the theoretical grammar and report to us nothing of the meaning or emotional purpose of the music. One recent dissertation studied a work by Husa and presented, in parallel sections, discussions of the theoretical grammar followed by 'challenges to the conductor.' In one telling place the author analyzed some music which the composer had spoken of as being the outgrowth of his pain and sorrow following the death of his father. The 'challenges for the conductor,' for this passage speaks of the difficulty which the trumpets will have getting their mutes in place in time, an exposed note in the E♭ clarinet, etc. But *this* is not the challenge for the conductor. The challenge for the conductor is to express the composer's pain and sorrow!

This entire process of how we analyze music is really a kind of deception we are introduced to in school by teachers who can discuss music in no other way than as concepts and math. We are led to believe that through this kind of analysis we will understand the composition—but it is not true. What we will learn is only the grammar, a kind of data that has no practical application in performance. As Fuchs observes,

Peter Paul Fuchs

[13] Peter Paul Fuchs, *The Psychology of Conducting* (New York: MCA, 1969), 27.

> To be able to say whether, in a diminished seventh chord, F-sharp–A–C–Eb, voiced in twelve wind instruments, that the note of the third horn is C or Eb may be very gratifying to the conductor's ego, but it will hardly make a difference in the quality of his performance.[13]

The fact is that the knowledge of this kind of musical grammar is vitally important to the composer, but not to anyone else. Consider the first two chords of Beethoven's Third Symphony, chords which are certainly a greater instance of 'fate knocking on the door' than the beginning of the Fifth Symphony. Do we learn anything about the meaning of these chords or about how to conduct them by discovering they are Eb major chords? Would we conduct them differently if they were F chords? Is our understanding of the meaning of these chords influenced by discovering which chord tone the third horn plays? And yet, which note the third horn plays was very important to the composer, who was following the distribution and doubling necessitated by the overtone series. These kinds of details are the composer's private business, not the conductor's business and certainly not the business of the listener. Even Schönberg understood that this theoretical grammar is only the means and not the end of notation.

> Evenness, regularity, symmetry, subdivision, repetition, unity, relationship in rhythm and harmony and even logic—none of these elements produces or even contributes to beauty. But all of them contribute to an organization which makes the presentation of the musical idea intelligible.[14]

[14] *Style and Idea.*

To this Schumann added that in the best music 'the artistic root-work, like a flower, is so beautifully concealed that we only perceive the flower.'[15]

[15] 'Museum,' in *Neue Zeitschrift für Musik*, 1837.

But how did this tradition of so limited an analysis of music begin? Surely the blame must lie with the early Church controlled universities, where music was considered only as concepts and as math. Therefore it is no surprise that we find in the Jesuit-trained Marin Mersenne's *Harmonie universelle* (1636), a work whose purpose was an attempt to prove mathematically the ancient Greek thought that music must be related to a great harmony of nature created by God, what may represent the birth of the rationale for modern analysis. Again, this reflects the fact that the birth of modern analysis lay in the Church's placement of music in the realm of mathematics.

> Since the *goodness* of composition consists in the natural order of the consonances, in their succession, and in the harmony which they make, we can say that the examination of this order is the idea of all the examinations which can be made of all the other kinds of compositions.[16]

[16] Marin Mersenne: *Fourth Treatise of the Harmonie Universelle*, ed., Robert Williams (Rochester: Eastman School of Music, unpublished dissertation, 1972), IV, iv, 24.

But in the later Baroque, with its enthusiasm for the expression of feeling in music, we find the tide has turned. Johann Heinichen (1683–1729) ridiculed the old-fashioned theorists as having wasted their entire life in pursuit of *rudera antiquitatis*.

> All will be sheer Greek to those steeped in prejudices when nowadays they hear that a moving music composed for the ears requires even more subtle and skillful rules—to say nothing of lengthy practice—than the heavily oppressive music composed for the eyes which the cantors of even the tiniest towns maltreat on innocent paper according to all the venerable rules of counterpoint … And we Germans alone are such fools as to jog on in the old groove and, absurdly and ridiculously, to make the appearance of the composition on paper, rather than the hearing of it, the aim of music.[17]

[17] Quoted in Beekman Cannon, *Johann Mattheson, Spectator in Music* (Archon Books, 1968), 141ff.

In his *Der vollkommene Capellmeister* of 1739, Johann Mattheson also discusses the nature of analysis.[18] Here he begins with the basic point that mathematics is an aid to music, as it is to most disciplines. However, 'they are wrong who believe or want to teach others that mathematics is the heart and soul of music' or that it is responsible for changes in emotion in the music. From this he concludes mathematics can measure, but not determine the essence of a thing. 'Everything that goes on in music is based on mathematical relationships of intervals just about as much as seamanship is based on anchors and cables.'

[18] Johann Mattheson, *Der vollkommene Capellmeister* (1739), trans., Ernest Harris (Ann Arbor: UMI Research Press, 1981), Foreword, VI.

> However one defines the mathematical relationships of sounds and their quantities, no real connection with the passions of the soul can ever be drawn from this alone.

Mathematics is only the 'science, theory and scholarship' of music. To introduce what exists beyond this he quotes Andreas Papius.

> 'The mere *cognition of the ratio* of a step, a half step, a comma, the consonances, etc., will bring the name virtuoso or artistic prince to no one, but rather the minute examination *according to the laws of nature* of the various works which are produced by great artists: from this we can understand the composer's *soul*, in regard to how and to what extent, in his particular work, one thing more than another masters the *human mind and emotions*, which is the *highest pinnacle of the discipline of music*.'

Again, his point here is that mathematics can describe the elements of music, but not how these elements are used.

> A perfect understanding of the human emotions, which certainly are not to be measured by the mathematical yardstick, is of much greater importance to melody and its composition than the understanding of tones ... This is certain: it is not so much good *proportion*, but rather the apt *usage* of the intervals and keys, which establishes the beautiful, moving and natural quality in melody and harmony. Sounds, in themselves, are neither good nor bad; but they become good and bad according to the way in which they are used. No measuring or calculating art teaches this.

This problem is not much discussed during the Classic Period and the nineteenth century, no doubt because the importance of music communicating feeling was clearly understood. Nevertheless, it is interesting to find Schumann returning to this problem, presenting it from the perspective of the composer. In a review of a composition of a trio by a composer named Fesca, Schumann seems determined to make the point that music is for the ear, not the eye.

> Fesca does not trouble himself much about grammar, or even octaves and fifths (at least as regards the eye); he writes down what sounds well to him, and considers the ear the highest court of appeal. We have nothing to say against this principle. Whatever sounds well mocks all grammar, and whatever is beautiful may scoff at aesthetics.[19]

[19] 'Trios,' in *Neue Zeitschrift für Musik*, 1840.

Arthur Schopenhauer (1788–1860), suggested that even the composer may not completely understand the 'theory' of what he has written down on paper.

> The composer reveals the innermost being of the world and expresses the deepest wisdom in a language which his own reason does not understand; like a somnambulist, who tells things of which he has no clear knowledge in his waking state.[20]

[20] *The World as Will and Idea* (1818).

In spite of all the preceding advice regarding the value and futility in the analysis of theoretical grammar in the score, the conductor can, of course, engage in this kind of analysis and, indeed, at times will feel a need to do so. The important thing, however, is to keep the results of this labor in proper perspective. Berlioz was one who had his priorities straight.

> Tone and sound are subordinate to ideas. Ideas are subordinate to feelings and passions.[21]

[21] *A travers chants* (1862).

Gounod warns the conductor on getting these priorities backward.

> It is not necessary that the rule of the conductor should amount to an unyielding and mechanical rigidity, which would be the absurd triumph of the *letter* over the *spirit*.[22]

[22] Charles Gounod, *Memoires d'un Artiste* (Paris, 1896).

Charles Gounod, 1863, artist unknown

And it was in this regard that Schönberg, in his discussion of Mahler as a conductor, recalls Mahler saying,

> I consider it my greatest service that I force musicians to play exactly what is in the notes.[23]

[23] *Style and Idea*.

But please observe he did not say 'play exactly the notes,' but rather 'what is *in* the notes.' This, in fact, is what Mahler meant by his famous maxim, 'The best things in music are not found in the notes.'

The important thing for the conductor to remember is that everything having to do with 'theory' is only the *means* to expressing something above, and more important, than theory. The danger is that the more you focus the eye on the musical grammar, the less likely you are to find 'the best things.'

Regarding this aspect of score study, we are reminded that Schumann once observed, 'mastership is finally lost, through excess of study.'[24] And this was surely the concern of Pablo Casals when he wrote,

[24] 'Etudes for the Pianoforte,' in *Neue Zeitschrift für Musik*, 1839.

> The written note is like a strait-jacket, whereas music, like life itself, is constant movement, continuous spontaneity, free from any restriction.[25]

[25] *Conversations with Casals* (1956).

Pablo Casals

Wagner, in his essay on Beethoven, quotes Schopenhauer as suggesting the real 'Idea' of music is only dimly expressed in the objective character of the notation. He then continues, still paraphrasing Schopenhauer,

> We should not understand this character itself were not the inner essence of things confessed to us elsewhere, dimly at least and in our Feeling. For that essence cannot be gathered from the Ideas, nor understood through any mere *objective* knowledge.[26]

[26] 'Beethoven,' in *Wagner's Prose Works*, op. cit., V, 66.

In closing, it is the emotional content that the artist looks for in music, and not the abstracted grammar of music we were all taught, under the name '*music* education,' in school. We believe conductors who wish to study scores for the purpose of finding the true meaning of the music might well reflect on the process which Wagner himself used once in studying a new work for the first time, in this case the C♯ Minor Quartet, op. 131, of Beethoven. In an unpublished diary, one finds some notes Wagner made in 1864, after this study. In these private notes written for himself, he did not write of the beginning key and where it modulated to, nor of the elements of melody, harmony, or rhythm, nor of counterpoint, scoring, articulations, dynamics nor grammar of any kind.

Here were the results of *his* analysis:

> (Adagio) Melancholy morning-prayer of a deeply suffering heart: (Allegro) graceful apparition, rousing fresh desire of life. (Andante and variations). Charm, sweetness, longing, love. (Scherzo) Whim, humor, high spirits. (Finale) Passing over to resignation. Most sorrowful renunciation.[27]

[27] ibid., VIII, 386.

8 *How to Study a Score, I*
The Paramount Object of Score Study

Music is Truth

> Music Educators National Conference:
>   Music is a form of beauty.[1]

[1] *The Report of the National Commission of Music Education* (Reston: MENC, 1991), 4.

> Distinguished Conductor, Sergiu Celibadache:
>   Anyone who still hasn't got past the stage of the beauty of music still knows nothing about music. Music is not beautiful. It has beauty as well, but the beauty is only the bait. Music is true.[2]

[2] Quoted in *Los Angeles Philharmonic Notes*, April, 1989.

It is interesting that we find in Plato the very same observation which Celibadache made.

> Music ought not to seek for that which is pleasant, but for that which is true.[3]

[3] *Laws*, 668b.

A century before Plato, Confucius (551–479 BC), in a treatise on music, appears to confirm that this most fundamental value of music was well known at a very distant age: We say Music is Truth because the right hemisphere of the brain cannot lie and has no equivalent of 'no.'[4] Confucius observed,

[4] Robert Ornstein, *The Right Mind* (New York: Harcourt Brace, 1997), 93.

> Music is the one thing in which there is no use trying to deceive others or make false pretenses.[5]

[5] Quoted in Nat Shapiro, *An Encyclopedia of Quotations About Music* (New York: Da Capo, 1977), 244.

Cicero (106–43 BC) noticed this distinction between the two hemispheres, the two 'sides' of ourselves, when he compared the performance of the musician to the orator. The musician ignores the wishes of the crowd and performs his own form of truth. The orator is not interested in truth, but only in what appeals to the crowd.

> Can it be that while the aulos players and those who play the lyre use their own judgment, not that of the crowd, to tune their songs and melodies, the [orator], endowed with a far greater skill, searches out not what is most true, but what the crowd wants?[6]

[6] Cicero, *Tusculan Disputations*, V, 104.

Machaut, speaking of one of his love songs, tells the lady in effect, 'ignore the words, it is the music which will tell you my true feelings.'

> And if it please you, my dear lady, to consider the last little song I sang, of which I composed both words and music, you can easily tell whether I'm lying or speaking the truth.[7]

The fourth century AD poet, Ausonius, says of one of the Greek gods of music, 'Phoebus bids us speak truth.'[8] And sixteen hundred years later we find artists of our own time still associating music with Truth. The great pianist, Arthur Rubinstein, remarked that 'A concert is ... the moment of truth.'[9]

The Baroque French philosopher, Jean-Baptiste Du Bos (1670–1742), contended that music was truth because the sounds came from Nature herself, while spoken words are only symbols of emotional truth.

> All these sounds, as we have already shown, have a wonderful power to move us because they are the signs of the passions that are the work of nature herself, from whence they have derived their energy. Spoken words, on the other hand are only arbitrary symbols of the passions.[10]

A passage in Calderón's *Life is a Dream* (act 2, scene 1) makes the same point. In this case, Astolfo observes,

> Tell the eyes
> In their music to keep better
> Concert with the voice, because
> Any instrument whatever
> Would be out of tune that sought
> To combine and blend together
> The true feelings of the heart.
> With the false words speech expresses.[11]

What do all these writers mean when they say music is 'Truth?' The *Truth* in music is not a conceptional form of Truth, but an experiental one. It is the deepest form of personal knowing by feeling.[12] The importance and validity of music as a form of emotional truth is based on two facts. First, as we have seen in Chapter One, modern clinical research has established that music itself has universal characteristics which are genetic to the species.

---

[7] Guillaume de Machaut, 'Remede de Fortune,' trans., James Wimsatt and William Kibler (Athens: The University of Georgia Press, 1988), 374.

[8] *Ausonius*, trans., Hugh G. Evelyn White (London: Heinemann, 1921), II, 17.

[9] Quoted in Robert Jacobson, *Reverberations* (1974).

[10] Jean-Baptiste Du Bos, *Réflexions critiques sur la poësie et sur la peinture* [Paris, 1719], quoted in Peter le Huray and James Day, *Music and Aesthetics in the Eighteenth and Early-Nineteenth Centuries* (Cambridge: Cambridge University Press, 1981), 18.

[11] Don Pedro Calderón (1600–1681) represents the final chapter of the 'Golden Age' of Spanish literature.

[12] There is an expression, 'Seeing is believing.' But this would be better expressed, 'Seeing is knowing; *feeling* is believing.'

Second, the emotions which music expresses are themselves both genetic and universal, as has been firmly established by modern clinical research. But this is evident to anyone who has noticed that the fetus already shows all the various emotional facial expressions—which it obviously could never have seen and imitated. Likewise, children born blind have the same facial expressions relative to emotions as normal children.[13] This universality of emotions has been long recognized. Aristotle points to this in the interesting context of symbolic language.

> Words spoken are symbols or signs of affections or impressions of the soul; written words are the symbols of words spoken. As writing, so also is speech not the same for all races of men. But the affections themselves, of which these words are primarily signs, are the same for the whole of mankind.[14]

Thomas Aquinas speaks of the temperamental constitution of the individual man being genetic in origin.[15] Descartes agreed that we are born with prenatal emotions. In a letter to Pierre Chanut, French ambassador to Sweden, Descartes acknowledges the genetic nature of the emotions, but contends that the prenatal fetus has only four 'passions,' joy, love, sadness and hatred. It was the unconscious retention of the confused prenatal emotions which complicated our judgments of the passions in later life.[16] The important seventeenth-century English philosopher of aesthetics, Anthony Cooper, Earl of Shaftesbury (1671–1713), also believed the emotions are genetic. Referring to an anonymous philosopher, Shaftesbury adds,

> Perhaps if the philosopher would accordingly examine himself and consider his natural passions, he would find there were such belonged to him as Nature had premeditated in his behalf, and for which she had furnished him with ideas long before any particular practice or experience of his own.[17]

The great philosopher, Spinoza (1632–1677), very much to his credit, recognized that all individual men seemed to be ruled by their emotions in their daily life, and not by Reason. Medical research only confirmed this physically in the past few years.

[13] See also Ornstein, op. cit., 34, fn. If you ask people from widely differing cultures to judge emotions, no matter their words, they judge them the same.

[14] 'On Interpretation,' I, trans., Harold P. Cook (Cambridge: Harvard University Press, 1962).

[15] *Summa Theologiae.*, XXI, 99.

[16] Letter to Chanut, February 1, 1647.

[17] *Characteristics of Men, Manners, Opinions, Times*, 'Miscellaneous Reflections,' IV, ii, fn.

> Every one shapes his actions according to his emotion, those who are assailed by conflicting emotions know not what they wish; those who are not attacked by any emotion are readily swayed this way or that.[18]

[18] Spinoza, *The Ethics*, 'Of the Origin and Nature of the Emotions,' Proposition II.

Finally, the important eighteenth-century French philosopher, Charles Batteux (1730–1780), reminds us that the emotions experienced in music are real, even if they cannot be identified by name.

> It is true, you may say, that a melodic line can express certain passions: love, for instance, or joy, or sadness. But for every passion that can be identified there are a thousand others that cannot be put into words.
>
> That is indeed so, but does it follow that these are pointless? It is enough that they are felt; they do not have to be named. The heart has its own understanding that is independent of words. When it is touched it has understood everything. Moreover, just as there are great things that words cannot reach, so there are subtle things that words cannot capture, above all things that concern the feelings.[19]

[19] Charles Batteux, *Les beaux-arts réduits à un même principe* [Paris,1746], quoted in Peter le Huray and James Day, op. cit., 50

The composer's purpose

That the paramount purpose of music is to express feelings, is documented throughout the history of both ancient and modern Europe. With respect to our present discussion, the struggle of the composer is one of trying to express genuine feeling through a limited notational system. We certainly sense this struggle in Guillaume de Machaut (1300–1377), in 'Remede de Fortune,' where at the end of a song, he observes,

> But I composed it to her praise in accord with the skill I possessed, and as near to my feelings as I well could.[20]

[20] Guillaume de Machaut, 'Remede de Fortune,' op. cit., 206.

We gain some insight into what 'feeling' meant to Machaut in the following passage. While the thirteenth-century troubadour also mentioned the pain of love, one does not find in that literature the emphasis on the feelings themselves that we read here—it is a distinction of the Renaissance.

> Then, like one accustomed to sighing, I uttered a lament and sigh from the depths of my heart, accompanied by weeping and washed in tears; and with great effort I turned toward her my flushed, pale, sad, sorrowful, and weeping face, full of suffering.[21]

[21] ibid., 254.

Charles Butler, in 1636, recalled the ancient Greek poet's reference to 'divine frenzy' when he wrote of the composer's struggle.

> [Good composing is impossible] unless the Author, at the time of Composing, be transported as it were with some Musical fury; so that himself scarce knoweth what he doth, nor can presently give a reason for his doing.[22]

[22] Charles Butler, *The Principles of Musik in Singing and Setting* [1636] (New York: Da Capo Press, 1970), 92.

Johann Mattheson (1681–1764) observed that although the emotions are like a bottomless sea, one can *write* very little about them. We get some idea what he meant by 'emotions are like a bottomless sea' in his reference to some of the emotions available to the composer of opera.

> [Opera is the best medium of all for expressing] each and every *Affectus* since there the composer has the grand opportunity to give free rein to his invention. With many surprises and with as much grace he there can, most naturally and diversely, portray love, jealousy, hatred, gentleness, impatience, lust, indifference, fear, vengeance, fortitude, timidity, magnanimity, horror, dignity, baseness, splendor, indigence, pride, humility, joy, laughter, weeping, mirth, pain, happiness, despair, storm, tranquility, even heaven and earth, sea and hell, together with all the actions in which men participate ...
> Through the skill of composer and singer each and every *Affectus* can be expressed beautifully and naturally ... by heart-moving music.[23]

[23] Johann Mattheson, *Das Neu-Eröffnete Orchestre* (Hamburg, 1713), 167ff.

The conductor's duty, then, is to seek something much more fundamental than mere notes or 'theory,' because music is *felt* before it is ever notated. Wagner made this same point in observing that the importance of music lies in what we feel, not what we think.

> An artist addresses himself to Feeling, and not to Understanding. If his work is discussed in terms of Understanding, then it might as well be said he has been misunderstood.[24]

[24] 'Eine Mitteilung an meine Freunde,' William Ellis, *Wagner's Prose Works* (New York: Broude), I, 271.

In another place, Wagner explains this process in music. The important points he makes here are that [1] music is the form of communication by the *feeling* (experiential) side of us, which can not otherwise speak; [2] unlike painting, in which we must contemplate a canvas as a prerequisite to finding the 'art,' music speaks directly to us; [3] music allows us to 'gaze into the inmost essence of ourselves'; and [4] the quality of a composition is determined by the degree to which it helps us do this.

> Music, who speaks to us solely through quickening into articulate life the most universal concept of the inherently speechless Feeling, in all imaginable gradations, can once and for all be judged by nothing but the category of the *sublime*; for, as soon as she engrosses us, she transports us to the highest ecstasy of consciousness of our infinitude. On the other hand what enters only *as a sequel* to our contemplation of a work of plastic art ... the required effect of *beauty* on the mind, is brought about by Music by her very *first entry*; inasmuch as she withdraws us at once from any concern with the relation of things outside us, and—as pure Form set free from Matter—shuts us off from the outer world, as it were, to let us gaze into the inmost Essence of ourselves and all things. Consequently our verdict on any piece of music should be based upon a knowledge of those laws whereby the effect of Beauty, the very first effect of Music's mere appearance, advances the most directly to a revelation of her truest character through the agency of the Sublime. It would be the stamp of an absolutely empty piece of music, on the contrary, that it never got beyond a mere prismatic toying with the effect of its first entry, and consequently kept us bound to the relations presented by Music's outermost side to the world of vision.[25]

[25] ibid.,V, 77.

Relative to Wagner's point that art allows us to 'gaze into the inmost Essence of ourselves,' Blaise Pascal (1623–1662) once observed that this is the real value of art, that the artist reveals not his emotional richness, but our own.

> When a natural discourse paints a passion or an effect, one feels within oneself the truth of what one reads, which was there before, although one did not know it. Hence one is inclined to love him who makes us feel it, for he has not shown us his own riches, but ours.[26]

[26] Blaise Pascal, *Pensées* (New York: Modern Library, 1941), I, xiv.

The conductor's purpose: to find the musical truth, the *melos* of music

Music has this great characteristic, that it communicates on both a general level and, as Pascal observed, on an individual level. Thus a composer may have in mind a general form of, let us say, 'sadness,' which is communicated by the performance to the audience. But each member of the audience sifts this general form of the emotion through the experiential side of himself and subsequently perceives it as an *individual* understanding of sadness.

The conductor, of course, cannot assign himself the obligation of attempting to forecast in advance a thousand forms of sadness among a thousand listeners. His obligation is to attempt to understand the *general* form of the emotion, as found in the music itself. This was a fundamental concern of Richard Wagner and it was he who gave a name to this general form of emotion. He called it the *melos*.

Richard Wagner, by Franz Hanfstaengl, ca. 1860

It is well known, both from his writings and his correspondence, that Wagner was much influenced by the ideas about music published by the great philosopher, Arthur Schopenhauer (1788–1860)—whom, we might add, is the only nineteenth-century philosopher whose explanation of the nature of music corresponds with modern clinical findings. It seems clear that the core idea for what Wagner meant by *melos* was inspired by this passage in Schopenhauer's *The World as Will and Idea* (1819).

> Music stands quite alone. It is cut off from all the other arts … It does not express a particular and definite joy, sorrow, anguish, horror, delight or mood of peace, but joy, sorrow, anguish, horror, delight, peace of mind themselves, in the abstract, in their essential nature, without their customary motives. Yet it enables us to grasp and share them fully in this quintessence.

Arthur Schopenhauer, 1859, artist unknown

What Schopenhauer calls the 'quintessence' of emotion is precisely what Wagner meant by *melos*. The evidence that this passage was of fundamental significance to Wagner is documented by his paraphrase of it in his prose essay, 'A Happy Evening.'

> What Music expresses is eternal, infinite and ideal; she expresses not the passion, love, desire, of this or that individual in this or that condition, but Passion, Love Desire itself, and in such infinitely varied phases as lie in her unique possession and are foreign and unknown to any other tongue.[27]

[27] *Wagner's Prose Works*, op. cit., VII, 81.

It is Schopenhauer's 'quintessence' of emotion, and Wagner's *melos*, which form the universal aspect of the communication of music. In this regard, in his essay on Beethoven, Wagner again cites Schopenhauer's 'wonder at Music's speaking a language immediately intelligible by everyone.'[28] Wagner mentions this universality in his 'Art Work of the Future':

[28] ibid., V, 65.

> Through the sense of hearing, [music] urges forth from the feeling of one heart to the feeling of its fellow.[29]

[29] ibid., I, 91.

He was probably recalling the fact that when Beethoven finished his great *Missa Solemnis* he wrote on the score, 'From the heart, may it go to the heart.'

The challenge for the composer is to condense his feelings into this quintessence form, in order to make it universal. Wagner discusses this by way of contrast with the poet, who must do the opposite by enlarging his description in order to achieve correct understanding. That is, the poet cannot just say 'cat' but must elaborate by adding a black cat, with white paws, a crooked tail, etc., in order for the observer to be able to picture the cat in question.

> To address the Feeling at all seizably, the poet wandered into that vague diffuseness in which he became the delineator of a thousand details, intended to set a definite shape ... On the other hand, the [composer] saw himself driven, in his shapings, to condense an endless element of Feeling into a definite point such as the understanding best might apprehend.[30]

[30] 'Opera and Drama,' in ibid., II, 277ff.

Wagner's discussion of the importance of the conductor finding the *melos* is found in his essay 'On Conducting,' in the course of a description of Habeneck's performance of Beethoven's Ninth Symphony with the Paris Conservatory Orchestra.

> The French musician is so far influenced by the Italian School, to which he primarily belongs, that music to him is unseizable except through Song: to play an instrument well, in his eyes, means to be able to make it sing. And that glorious orchestra really *sang* this symphony. To be able to 'sing' it correctly, however, the right tempo had to be found for its every beat[31]: and that was the second point impressed upon my mind on this occasion. Old Habeneck ... *found the proper tempo, while diligently leading on his orchestra to grasp the symphony's melos.*
>
> But a correct conception of the melos alone can give the proper tempo: the two are indivisible; one conditions the other. And if I do not scruple to declare that by far the most performances of our classic instrumental works are seriously inadequate, I propose to substantiate my verdict by pointing out that our conductors know nothing of proper Tempo, because of their understanding nothing about Song. I have never met a single German Kapellmeister or musical conductor who could really *sing* a melody, let his voice be good or bad.[32]

François-Antoine Habeneck, by Lange. P. C. Van Geel, Paris, date unknown

[31] While several nineteenth-century composers, including Beethoven, questioned whether a metronome marking should be thought of as referring to an entire movement, or just the beginning measures, here Wagner suggests tempo being determined beat by beat!

[32] ibid., IV, 303.

Wagner's emphasis on singing in this passage has led many writers to associate 'melos' only with 'melody.' But when Wagner says of the orchestra, here, 'to be able to "sing" it,' not to mention his reference to the French desiring to make instruments 'sing,' it is clear he is thinking of the expressive style of the entire performance. This would also seem to be the meaning of the German soprano, Berta Morena, who observed on seeing Mahler conduct in New York.

> He makes the orchestra sing.[33]

[33] Berta Morena, in *The Sun*, March 15, 1908.

It seems clear that both Wagner and Morena were also using instrumental 'singing' as a synonym for 'feeling.' Certainly, it was feeling in music to which Wagner constantly addressed himself, even with respect to something like tonality.

> The Key of a melody is that which presents to Feeling its various included tones in their earliest bond of kinship.[34]

[34] 'Opera and Drama,' in *Wagner's Prose Works*, op. cit., II, 291.

One also finds the emphasis on feeling in almost every account by one of his contemporary references to him. Berlioz considered the prime characteristic of Wagner to be 'that he possesses the rare intensity of feeling.'[35] And Weingartner, interviewing orchestral players to find out what it was like to play under Wagner as a conductor, found that the players were under the impression that they were freely following their own feelings.[36]

[35] *Journal des Débats*, February 9, 1860.

[36] Felix Weingartner, *On Conducting* [1895], trans., Ernest Newman (New York: Kalmus), 11.

In our view, it was Weingartner, following his discussions with Wagner on the subject of conducting, and his independent investigation of Wagner's work as a conductor, who best explained what Wagner's concept of *melos* was understood to mean at that time. We might add that this could also be taken as an ideal goal for the conductor.

> From all we have learned of him as conductor, from himself and from others, he obviously aimed in his own performances not only at correctness but at bringing out that to which the sounds and notes are only the means. He sought for the unifying thread, the psychological line, the revelation of which suddenly transforms, as if by magic, a more or less indefinite sound-picture into a beautifully shaped, heart-moving vision, making people ask themselves in astonishment how it is that this work, which they had long thought they knew, should have all at once become quite another thing, and the unprejudiced mind joyfully confesses, 'Yes, thus, thus, must it really be.'
>
> Out of the garment of tones there emerges the spirit of the artwork; its noble countenance, formerly only confusedly visible, is not unveiled, and enraptures those who are privileged to behold it. Wagner calls this form, this quintessence, this spirit of the artwork its melos.[37]

[37] ibid., 9.

We prefer, and will use henceforth, Wagner's term, *melos*, but the same idea has been expressed by others with different phrases. F. W. Marpurg, in 1749, called it 'the distilled essence' of emotion.[38] Serge Koussevitzky called it the 'elan vital' of the composition.[39] Bruno Walter called it the 'soul,' as opposed to the 'body' of a composition.[40] And this is what Weingartner meant when he observed that while 'some conductors see only the notes, others see what is behind the notes.'[41]

If the student conductor can understand what these distinguished musicians are describing, and take up this idea as his standard, no further study of conducting will be necessary.

To find and communicate the *melos*, then, is the conductor's supreme challenge. Johann Mattheson referred to this problem as,

> the greatest difficulty of all: having the discernment required to succeed in divining the sense and meaning of another composer's thoughts.[42]

Leinsdorf described this challenge as one of attempting to recreate 'each work as it sounded and was experienced when it was first heard.'[43] We would rephrase this to say the goal is to recreate the music the way the composer *felt it* in his mind before he put pen to paper. It is the essential honesty of this search which prevents the pitfalls which worried Weingartner.

> It is this homogeneous conception of the essential nature of a musical work that constitutes what there is of specially artistic in its interpretation; it originates in a deep feeling that is not dependent on the intellect, that cannot, indeed even be influenced by this, while it itself must dominate everything that pertains to the intellect—such as routine, technique, and calculation of effects. If this feeling is not strong enough, then the intellect usurps the foremost place and leads, as was often the case with Bülow, to a propensity to ingenious analysis. In the contrary case the feeling becomes unwholesomely powerful and leads to unclearness, false sentimentality and emotional vagueness. If neither feeling nor intellect is strong enough, then we get, according to the prevailing [19th century] fashion, either mere metronomic time-beating or a senseless mania for *nuance*.[44]

---

[38] F. W. Marpurg, *Der critische Musicus an der Spree* (Berlin), September 2, 1749.

[39] Quoted in Carl Bamberger, *The Conductor's Art* (New York: McGraw-Hill, 1965), 144.

[40] ibid., 159.

[41] Weingartner, op. cit., 43.

[42] Johann Mattheson, *Der vollkommene Capellmeister* (1739), trans., Ernest Harris (Ann Arbor: UMI Research Press, 1981), III, xxvi, 7 ff.

[43] Erich Leinsdorf, *The Composer's Advocate* (New Haven: Yale University Press, 1981), 59.

[44] Felix Weingartner, op. cit., 17.

9 *How to Study a Score, II*
The Five Steps of Musical Score Study

FIRST OF ALL, LET'S BE HONEST. Conducting is very easy to fake—at the first rehearsal. By the second rehearsal, even student musicians are perfectly aware if you know your score and they can no longer be fooled. We might go further and say that by the second rehearsal the highest goals of performance have already been lost beyond retrieval, because even if the conductor suddenly decided to learn his scores, too many poor impressions have already been implanted in the minds of the players. Conductors who desire to perform at the highest musical level accept that score study is a given—slow, difficult and concentrated score study. The enemy, says Georg Solti, 'is laziness and self-complacency.'[1] We would propose, as a rule of thumb, that a serious conductor will average two hours of study for each hour of rehearsal, with much of it occurring before the first rehearsal.

Score study is simply part of the job and any form of 'not having time' is indefensible. If you are lucky, you convince your administration that study is part of the job and receive time to do it. If not, you do it anyway. I was once for six weeks in the company of a major young conductor who had (encouraged) a reputation for amazing photographic memory. But he confided to me that he had to stay up all night, almost every night, studying scores in order to maintain this impression—an impression to which he attributed his entire success at that time. By the end of six weeks, he had great black circles under his eyes, but he did very impressive things on the podium.

This task of studying scores has been no easier for famous conductors. Consider the fact that Claudio Abbado took a six-month sabbatical to learn the score of Mahler's Ninth Symphony.[2] Von Karajan once observed that he spent more than six months studying the *Symphonie liturgique* of Honegger before he felt he was ready to conduct it.[3] Wagner claimed he actually copied out the entire score of Beethoven's Ninth Symphony as a means of studying it.[4] Carlo Maria Giulini made the interesting observation that 'it took Mozart two days

[1] Sir Georg Solti, *Memoirs* (New York: Alfred A. Knopf, 1997), 143.

[2] Norman Lebrecht, *The Maestro Myth* (New York: Citadel, 1993), 220.

[3] Richard Osborne, *Conversations with Von Karajan* (New York: Harper & Row, 1989), 66.

[4] William Ashton Ellis, *Wagner's Prose Works* (New York: Broude), IV, 300.

to write the Linz Symphony, but it takes me two weeks to get ready to rehearse it.'[5] Hermann Scherchen summarized the problem as follows:

> Only when a work has come to absolute perfection within him can the conductor undertake to materialize it by means of the orchestra.[6]

There have also been some exceptions. Eugene Ormandy had an exceptional subjective facility based on little apparent traditional study. I have seen him read with the orchestra a new score which he had never seen. He would then begin at the beginning and read it again, but in this second reading one could hear important architectural details taking shape which most of us would have discovered only by study. But, at this time he was doing two hundred concerts per year and had been conducting the Philadelphia Orchestra for thirty years—he had more experience than most of us. For the rest of us, to say that we can learn a score in rehearsal is to say we are not serious about conducting.

[5] Gerald Stein, 'Giulini on Preparation, Rehearsal, and Performance' in *The Instrumentalist*, October, 1980.

[6] Quoted in Carl Bamberger, *The Conductor's Art* (New York: McGraw-Hill, 1965), 223.

The Philadelphia Orchestra, conducted by Eugene Ormandy, and the Valley Forge Military Academy Band under the leadership of Colonel D. Keith Feltham, 18 January 1970, at the Academy of Music in Philadelphia, PA.

We hasten to add that even in the professional world there are always a few who manage to perform without really knowing what they are doing. Solti recalled that Knappertsbusch, although extremely popular with the audience, never 'thoroughly mastered a score's details.'[7]

[7] Sir Georg Solti, op. cit., 88.

Step Number One

Begin with the thought clearly in mind that the goal is to discover the **melos**, *the emotional meaning of the composition.*

It is very important, in the first stage of score study, to remember that the paramount goal is to discover the *melos*, the emotional meaning communicated by the music. All traditional analysis must occur later. Johann Mattheson addressed this already during the eighteenth century:

> The proper goal of all music can be nothing other than the sort of diversion of the hearing through which the passions of the soul are stirred: thus no one at all will obtain this goal who is not aiming at it, who feels no affection, indeed who scarcely thinks at all of a passion.[8]

[8] Johann Mattheson, *Der vollkommene Capellmeister* (1739), trans., Ernest Harris (Ann Arbor: UMI Research Press, 1981), II, xii, 31.

This priority was also expressed by the great contemporary pianist, Alfred Brendel.

> Although I find it necessary and refreshing to *think* about music, I am always conscious of the fact that *feeling* must remain the Alpha and Omega of a musician; therefore my remarks proceed from feeling and return to it.[9]

[9] Quoted in *The New Yorker*, May 30, 1977.

What most conductors worry about, according to Wagner, is only the 'How,' and not the 'What.'

> For the absolute musician it seemed necessary only to identify the 'How?': but it was impossible for him to identify even this correctly, chiefly because he did not understand the 'What' that ought to be expressed by this 'How.' As a result, all contact between conductor and orchestra floundered on a complete lack of understanding between them: the conductor strove solely to articulate musical phrases which he himself did not understand and which he had made his own rather as one learns melodious verses by heart according to their sound alone when the verses in question are written in a foreign language unknown to the person reciting the poem.

...

In the case of present-day conductors (many of whom do not even understand the music), the situation at best is as follows:—they can identify the key, the theme, the part-writing, the instrumentation, etc., and with that they think they have identified everything that is present in the piece of music.

Interestingly enough, Wagner says it was the non-musicians who first encouraged attention to the *melos*, the central emotional meaning of a composition, by wanting to know more about what the composer had in mind in writing the music. Wagner's practice as a conductor, as we shall see below, was to actually discuss the *melos* with the orchestral players in rehearsal to insure proper understanding of the music.

Stokowski summarized well what we have called the paramount duty of the conductor, to understand the *melos* of a composition. The reader will note that there is no reference to the study of grammar.

Leopold Stokowski, Library of Congress

> The conductor must devote and concentrate all his life to conducting and to music. It must mean everything to him. He must have musical intuition—he must know instinctively the inner invisible powers of music—through imagination he must be able to reveal remote, yet intensely stimulating and inspiring, possibilities and moods in music. When a truly great violinist plays ... he not only plays all the notes and rhythms correctly, but he conveys through these notes and rhythms an immense range of profound emotion—he suggests states of feeling and illumines visions we have all experienced and know to be among the highest possibilities of music. With an orchestra these possibilities are sometimes greater, and therefore demand an even wider range of expression. A true conductor must be able to fulfill the creative side of this responsibility. In addition, a conductor must have a complete understanding of the music's emotional content—its range of imagination—the quality and subtlety of its psychic suggestion—because great music has the power of suggesting moods in us which are remote from this life and utterly different from the outer world in which we live. The more a conductor can—through his imagination—intensely evoke these remote and subtle states of feeling, the more is he a worthy collaborator with the composer.[10]

So, how does one begin to discover the *melos*? The first key is to learn to approach a score with a certain passiveness, an absence of prejudice in the sense of predetermined conclusions and expectations. The nineteenth-century Austrian poet, Siegfried Lipiner, once coined a witty phrase in this regard. He said,

[10] Quoted in Carl Bamberger, op. cit., 204.

> One's attitude toward great works of art should be similar to that prescribed by the court ceremonial for intercourse with persons of princely rank: don't speak; wait until they speak to you.

In other words, one must take care not to impose any personal ideas, especially subjective ones, on the score before the score speaks to you.

Eugen Jochum relates just such a process as being the first of three major types of study he undertook *before* rehearsals began, the second being the traditional analysis, and the third memorization.

> I take care first of all to have, so to speak, a passive attitude toward the work; that is, to establish a lack of bias, a receptiveness that will allow the work of art to best develop its own reality. First I abandon myself to the work, which I read through again and again … without my thinking of particulars. What is this tempo? How does it relate to later tempi? What is the nature of the themes? How do they relate to one another? These questions are left for later.
>
> In this manner the tempo focuses 'by itself,' the piece becomes so self-evident that it begins to live its own life, still practically completely withdrawn from my conscious will and shaping impulses. The condition described as passivity now reveals itself as having many layers; only the intellectual layers of consciousness are actually passive. The possessive, forming will is only excluded by the thinking mind. On the other hand, the deeper layers of consciousness are vibrantly awake, straining toward the work, so that an emotional field of tension is formed in which the 'spark leaps over.' This is the decisive point. When it is reached, conscious work of the greatest precision can and must begin. It is only important that the impulse of the will and conscious control do not take over too soon, and that one's own personality is not brought in at the wrong moment. It is thus a question of humble acceptance of a law, of listening to an inner meaning.[11]

[11] ibid., 260.

In other words, as Jochum has pointed out, critical to this process is not getting bogged down in detail in the initial study. There will be time to study detail later. We might make this a Rule: one should not study the detail on paper until one is confident he understands the things not on paper, by which we mean, of course, the essential emotional communication of the score. In this regard, Fuchs quotes the conductor, William Steinberg, as lamenting,

> The trouble with many present-day conductors is that they ... get caught up in a number of trifling details.[12]

[12] Peter Paul Fuchs, *The Psychology of Conducting* (New York: MCA Music, 1969), 21ff.

To say this in a different way, in the initial score study one must have the confidence to put his trust in his own feelings, rather than in his intellect, to understand the score. As Schumann once observed,

> The first concept is always the best and most natural. The intellect can error, the sentiment—never.[13]

[13] Quoted in Nat Shapiro, *An Encyclopedia of Quotations About Music* (New York: Da Capo, 1977), 53.

Similarly, in a letter which refers to his poem, 'To abbé Chaulieu,' Voltaire mentions in passing, 'But though I distrust my head, I am always sure of my heart.'[14]

[14] Letter to abbé Chaulieu, July 26, 1717.

Step Number Two

Study and learn a score by ear, not by eye.

Now it is time to study the details of the score, all the things discussed in theory classes in school. The *musical* conductor, in opposition to the method taught in school, must seek to think of these details as things to be *heard*, not things to be *seen*. Musical Truth is judged by the ear, not the eye. The great organist, Girolamo Frescobaldi, addressed this very point.

> Since it also seems that many may have neglected the practice of studying the score, I wished to point out that ... one must first of all seek *the feeling of the passage* and the aim of the author concerning *the effect on the ear*, and the way in which one should try to play them.[15]

[15] Girolamo Frescobaldi, 'Capricci fatti sopra diversi soggetti,' quoted in Carol MacClintock, *Readings in the History of Music in Performance* (Bloomington: Indiana University Press, 1979), 135.

The most important issue here is that the ear is how we connect with feeling in music. Johann Mattheson (1681–1764) understood this perfectly.

> Numbers in music do not govern but merely instruct. The Hearing is the only channel through which their force is communicated to the inner soul of the attentive listener ... The true aim of music is not its appeal to the eye, nor yet altogether to the so-called 'Reason,' but only to the Hearing, which communicates pleasure, as it is experienced, to the Soul and the 'Reason.'[16]

[16] Johann Mattheson, *Das Neu-Eröffnete Orchestre* (Hamburg, 1713), 126ff.

Wagner had the same concern:

> Man's nature is twofold, an *outer* and an *inner*. The senses to which he offers himself as a subject for Art, are those of *Vision* and of *Hearing*: to the eye appeals the outer man, the inner to the ear.[17]

[17] *Wagner's Prose Works*, op. cit., I, 91.

Because the ear is the musician's world, the conductor may be tempted to try to learn a score by ear during rehearsal. This, of course, is irresponsible and such conductors are described by Fuchs as follows:

> They feel frustrated by the too abstract process of learning, and so they merely go through a few perfunctory motions of preparation and do not really start learning the score until they stand before the orchestra, naturally with dire results.[18]

[18] Fuch, op. cit., 33.

Of course, one *can* learn a great deal about a score from listening to *another* conductor's rehearsal, provided he is a master musician. Von Karajan claimed he learned the whole of Verdi's *Falstaff* by ear while watching Toscanini rehearse it at La Scala—and thereafter never had to open a score![19] On the other hand, Wagner complained already in the nineteenth century that band directors were simply following tempi used by other band directors.[20]

[19] *Conversations with Von Karajan*, op. cit., 69.

[20] *Prose Works of Wagner*, V, 278ff.

Fuchs raises the issue most worried about by beginning conductors: will they hear all the 'wrong notes?' Fuchs answers, yes, if the conductor knows the score he will always hear anything not in accord with the page. Furtwängler made the same point:

> Generally considered, there is no such thing among conductors as a good or bad ear. There is only a greater or lesser mastery of the material, that is, the score and its every detail. One can only hear individual mistakes in the complicated mass of sound when one knows completely just what the composer wanted.[21]

[21] Quoted by Albert Stoessel, *The Technique of the Baton* (New York: Carl Fischer, 1928).

Finally, we must point out that when we speak of the importance of the ear to the conductor, we are by no means limiting the discussion to pitch, for the conductor needs an ear for all the elements of music. We will always hear music quite differently than it appears on paper. Things like texture, or color, and the influence of overtones; the effect of chords heard, rather than seen; the influence of one tone against another, not to mention things like combination tones; these kinds of factors are all quite different 'live' than they are in ink. Hearing the music often reveals what the eye did not see.

Certainly one should not worry if one does not have 'perfect pitch.' All of us were born with perfect pitch and those who happened to be encouraged toward music at an early age usually retain it and the rest of us more or less lose it. But we have seen conductors who used it as a crutch, in substitution for score study and the results were usually unmusical. If the young conductor studies his score, and practices critical listening in rehearsal, he will in time develop listening skills sufficient for distinguished performance.

Step Number Three

Introduce your own experience.

The score is a document in the past tense, yet one of the most significant distinctions of music, in contrast to other arts, is that performance is in the *present* tense. So how does the conductor communicate the score in the present tense? He does this by employing his own musical, emotional and personal experience as a key to help unlock the intentions of the composer. It is like the two keys which are necessary to open a private bank box, in this case the score is one key and the live conductor has the other. This has to do with what we mean when we say we *recreate* music—which, of course, is all you can ever do with music written on paper. Berlioz once gave an illustration of the importance of this addition of the experience of the conductor in a discussion of the imprecision of the notational system, in this case the Italian tempo markings.

> The different degrees of slow movement that may be used for a Largo are very numerous; only the individual feeling of the conductor can be the guide in such a case.[22]

[22] Berlioz, 'On Conducting,' in *Treatise on Instrumentation* (New York: Kalmus, 1948), 411.

This all makes sense if one only remembers that the composer also wrote his score from the departure point of feeling. Speaking of the composer's perspective, Johann Mattheson suggests that it is not necessary, when one composes a dirge or lamentation, to begin to cry, 'yet it is absolutely necessary that he open his mind and heart to the affection at hand.' For how, Mattheson asks, will he be able to excite a passion in other people's feelings if he has not experienced it himself?[23]

The conductor or performer comes from the same perspective, from feeling. F. W. Marpurg, in 1749, wrote of the performer's need to have a breadth of emotional experience, which, together with sensibility, will connect with the feeling of the composer.

> All musical expression has an affect or emotion for its foundation. A philosopher when expounding or demonstrating will try to enlighten our understanding, to bring it lucidity and order. The orator, the poet, the musician attempt rather to inflame than to enlighten. The philosopher deals in combustible matter capable of glowing or yielding a temperate and moderate warmth. But in music there is only the distilled essence of this matter, the most refined part of it, which throws out thousands of the most beautiful flames, always with rapidity, sometimes with violence. The musician has therefore a thousand parts to play, a thousand characters to assume at the composer's bidding. To what extraordinary undertakings our passions carry us! He who has the good fortune at all to experience the inspiration which lends greatness to poets, orators, artists, will be aware how vehemently and diversely our soul responds when it is given over to the emotions. Thus to interpret rightly every composition which is put in front of him a musician needs the utmost sensibility and the most felicitous powers of intuition.[24]

One gains this sensibility and emotional experience primarily from music itself, from performance and from listening.[25] The early Renaissance writer, Henry Agrippa (1486–1536), was struck by the fact, and reminds us as well, that music, unlike other disciplines of the Liberal Arts, has no terminal point of completion, but must be a lifelong study.[26] But if the study of music has no end, we are compensated with continued growth through exposure to great minds. Socrates once observed that he particularly envied the fact that the singer does not merely learn words by rote, but comes to understand the mind of the poet.[27]

Before leaving the subject of musical growth, we must cite another curious conclusion by Gunther Schuller in his book on conducting. The entire book seems to exist for the purpose of expressing his venom toward conductors who do not reproduce what is on the page. Finally he states this proposition:

[23] Johann Mattheson, *Der vollkommene Capellmeister*, op. cit., II, ii, 64ff.

[24] F. W. Marpurg, *Der critische Musicus an der Spree* (Berlin), September 2, 1749.

[25] Rameau, writing in 1726, makes the same point.
> It is often by seeing and hearing musical works (operas and other good musical compositions), rather than by rules, that taste is formed. [Rameau, *Le Nouveau Système de musique théorique* (1726)].

[26] Agrippa, *Of the Vanitie and Vncertaintie of Arts and Sciences*, ed., Catherine Dunn (Northridge: California State University, Northridge Press, 1974), 68.

[27] *Ion*, 530c.

> The more a work is played, the more familiar it is, the more popular it becomes, the more likely it is to be bastardized and vulgarized, and its composer's intentions disregarded.[28]

[28] Gunther Schuller, *The Compleat Conductor* (Oxford: Oxford University Press, 1997), 541.

But Gunther has it backwards. The more a conductor performs and comes to know a score through his own experience, the more he will come to understand that the composer's ideas were much more beautiful than he was able to express on paper with our limited notational system.

And so the conductor grows through experience, which fact contributes to the reality that some of the most inspiring conductors have been rather old men. The great Toscanini, as a mature conductor, observed,

> I shall be satisfied only when every musician in the orchestra feels exactly what I feel … Isn't it sad—I've been conducting for more than a generation, and only now begin to understand how it should be done.[29]

[29] Bamberger, op. cit., 311.

It is also very important that the conductor strive to expand his experiential nature through the pursuit of culture apart from music. Fuchs, after quoting Mahler's famous 'What is best in music is not to be found in the notes,' observes,

> This certain element which starts with style but is really far more than style—call it 'Weltanschauung'—can hardly be done justice to by an interpreter who knows nothing beyond what can be expressed in strictly musical terms. Music is not generally written in ivory towers; it is one of the manifestations of the cultural climate … Can a conductor of serious ambition depend on purely musical knowledge, the way a mason depends on brick and mortar? If he is lucky, he may have been taught some of the essentials of cultural history in college. Just the same, he should never stop adding to his knowledge of art, literature, poetry, psychology and many related subjects.[30]

[30] Peter Paul Fuchs, op. cit., 20.

Fuchs points to Weingartner as a student of Hindu philosophy, Greek drama and Molière; Bruno Walter as well-read in Shakespeare, Goethe and Dostoyevsky and Ansermet in mathematics and physics.[31]

And finally it is probably the case that one's experiential growth cannot be separated from matters of character. As the fifteenth-century Spanish poet, Fernando Rojas, asked, 'How can a man tune a lute who is himself out of tune?'[32]

[31] ibid., 20.

[32] *La Celestina*, act I.

Henry Agrippa found sixteenth-century music degraded in practice by the character of the men who performed it.[33] The Baroque writer, Johann Mattheson, speaks of the conductor in particular:

[33] Agrippa, op. cit., 68.

> The conductor should in no way be offensive or scandalous in his living and conduct, for commonly the greatest contempt arises from that. A good reputation and esteem are such delicate things that with a single false step everything one has gained for oneself in many years through great assiduousness can be destroyed.[34]

[34] Johann Mattheson, op. cit., III, xxvi.

Bruno Walter also wrote of his concern in this regard.

> The value of a conductor's artistic achievements is to a high degree dependent upon his human qualities and capacities; the seriousness of his moral convictions, the richness of his emotional life, the breadth of his mental horizon, in short, his personality, has a decisive effect on his achievements; if his personality is unable to fulfill the spiritual demands of the works he performs, his interpretations will remain unsatisfactory although their musical execution may be exemplary.

Step Number Four

Memorization

A student was walking through the village, whereupon he came to the house of his teacher. There he saw his teacher, on his hands and knees, apparently looking for something in the grass.

'Master, what are you looking for?'

'I am looking for my house key,' his teacher replied, 'Come and help me look for it!'

The student joined his teacher in the grass, but after a time he concluded that there was probably no key in the grass at all and that this was intended to be some sort of lesson.

'OK, Master, where did you actually lose your house key?'

His teacher answered, 'Well, actually I lost it somewhere inside my house.'

'Why then,' said the student, 'are we looking out here in the grass?'

'Because there is more light here,' explained the teacher.

Nothing illustrates the benefit of score memorization more vividly than this famous Sufi parable. Memorization allows us to step way from the score to a place where 'there is more light.' Any conductor who has contemplated a score after memorization will testify that he came to know and understand things which had not been revealed by traditional study, no matter how thorough the prior study had been. These otherwise unobtainable insights generally have to do with the *melos*, but can also involve clarification of all kinds of detail. The value of these insights, with their sense of illumination and compensation, is perhaps the single most important reason why most conductors, singers and pianists undertake the effort to memorize their music.

The fundamental problem lies in the fact that our senses prefer to work one at a time in terms of our concentration. Thus the eye, being our most dominant sense at this point in the development of our species, tends to shut down the ear. Looking at the score seems to limit hearing. Von Karajan refers to this when he recalled a rehearsal when he suggested that the orchestra also memorize their individual parts.

> There is a problem here with the eyes, with the musician being chained to the printed page in front of him. I remember during some very intensive rehearsals we were doing for the *Ring* we came to a passage where the figuration of the accompaniment always comes out too strongly. I said, 'Gentlemen, this will never be right until you have mastered it completely and are free of the page. When we have achieved that, then you will be able to play, not looking at the page all the time, but hearing the woodwinds, which have the melody at this point.'[35]

Sometimes the score can simply be more a hindrance than a help, as Weingartner admitted even though in general he personally placed little value on memorization.[36] We, ourselves, have found this is particularly true with difficult modern scores with constant meter changes—they are simply too difficult to use a score. In such a score, without memorization one might be afraid even to take his eyes from the page for fear of getting lost. But Weingartner says that the conductor who cannot take his eyes off the score, 'is a mere time-beater, a bungler, with no pretension to the title of artist.'

[35] *Conversations with Von Karajan*, op. cit., 103.

[36] Felix Weingartner, *On Conducting* (New York: Kalmus), 42ff.

Weingartner most admired the conductor who placed his score on the stand, yet still conducted from memory. Such a contemporary example which immediately comes to mind is Georg Solti, who always had scores on the stand but almost never looked at them. Fuchs also points out that Bruno Walter, although he always knew his scores from memory, did not begin conducting without them until quite late in his career.[37] This reminds us of a nice phrase by Fuchs, which really touches on the important issue at hand.

> The decision is not 'to memorize or not to memorize,' but to conduct from memory *with* or *without* the use of a score.[38]

Before continuing, we must bring to light the truth about a myth regarding memorization which has been perpetuated for the purpose of impressing boards of directors and ticket buyers (the reader should understand that all famous conductors of history have been *personally* involved in controlling what was written about them in programs, etc.). The myth is that some conductors, especially favored by the gods, have a photographic memory which retains forever even the smallest details of the score.

This myth began with Toscanini, of whom it was said he could merely glance at a score and then years later, upon request, sit down and play it at the piano. And of course in all photos approved for release showing Toscanini conducting one never sees a score. But, in a book by his intimate admirer, Marcia Davenport (one of few persons permitted to watch him rehearse) we find the following report of an incident during a rehearsal of Mozart's G Minor Symphony with the NBC Symphony.

> There followed one of the worst Toscanini rages I ever saw. He tore the place apart, he threw the score at the first violins, he screamed ... and finally, kicking his music stand in an arc right out into the empty hall.[39]

Score? Music stand? A score and music stand for a Mozart symphony?

Felix Weingartner, by Julius Cornelius Schaarwächter, ca. 1900

[37] Fuchs, op. cit., 25, fn.

[38] ibid., 31.

[39] Marcia Davenport, *Too Strong for Fantasy* (New York: Scribner's, 1967), 193.

Another hero-worshiper who was allowed to watch Toscanini rehearse, B. H. Haggin, reports that sometimes in rehearsal Toscanini would begin without saying a word to the orchestra.

> But more often I saw him do what he did on March 2, 1950, when, after his good morning, he picked up the score of Tchaikovsky's *Pathétique*, found the fourth measure after letter M in the third movement, explained to the flutes and clarinets that in this measure he wanted them to break off the held G-sharp.[40]

Picked up the score? Wait a minute! Why did Toscanini need a score for another standard repertoire work, which he had conducted for decades, if he had photographic memory?

The other conductor most associated with this myth was Dimitri Mitropoulos (1896–1960), who astounded all by his ability to rehearse new contemporary scores from memory. Von Karajan recalled,

> My great friend Mitropoulos had a photographic memory; the players would watch him and say 'Now he turns the page!'[41]

By chance, we once had the opportunity to get to know a retired man who had been a household servant of Mitropoulos. He reported that the conductor, exactly as in the case of the young conductor we mentioned at the beginning of this chapter, stayed up all night studying scores in order to be able to sustain this myth.

As the reader can see, there are some evident questions regarding the claims of the two most famous examples of conductors with 'photographic' memory. Fuchs, whose own powers of memorization are documented by his having conducted *Tristan* at the Met without a score, very tactfully questions these same claims and concludes with a very important observation.

> Hans von Bülow, who according to all reports must have been a mental giant, is said to have made the statement that if by some ghastly catastrophe all documented knowledge of Beethoven's nine symphonies were lost, he could rewrite their orchestral scores from memory, 'probably with complete accuracy.' Bülow's undoubtedly honest claim was also a most remarkably unusual one ... Just the same, anyone

Arturo Toscanini, by Arnold Genthe, 1934

[40] B. H. Haggin, *Conversations with Toscanini* (Garden City: Dolphin Books, 1959), 83.

[41] *Conversations with Von Karajan,* op. cit., 131.

who is not aware of the enormity of such a potential accomplishment should try to write down from memory one single page of the score of any Beethoven symphony ... and I wager that he will not have to compare his own version with Beethoven's in order to become aware of the inadequacy of his memory! And as far as Bülow's claim is concerned, I doubt whether any living musician could match it with a clear conscience.

    I am mentioning this because I have heard it said not only of Toscanini but also of some much lesser lights among conductors that they could write down from memory any score they conducted. Perhaps in the case of Toscanini this was often true, although we have no way of ascertaining it. Possibly it was also true of Mitropoulos. But in many other cases I would consider the claim most irresponsible ... and I think it is time that the truth of the matter be faced with honesty. To be able to write down from memory the score of, say, *Le sacre du printemps* would be an achievement of truly legendary proportions. However, it would be as legendary as it would be unnecessary. A conductor can do a most workmanlike job of conducting a score from memory without being able to write down accurately every artificial harmonic in the second violins, or every thirty-second-note in a run of the third flute which is merely part of a coloristic effect.[42]

[42] Fuchs, op. cit., 26ff.

    The final thought in the above quotation is a very important and honest one by Fuchs. We suspect that no conductor has ever had truly 'photographic' memory and that no conductor who has conducted without scores knew *all* the notes. You may study details, but you need not memorize them. As Fuchs points out, it is simply not necessary. We return to the example we have previously mentioned, the first two chords of the Third Symphony of Beethoven. One needs to know nothing whatsoever of a theoretical nature, nor the name of a single note, to be able to properly conduct these chords. What we need to know is not the details, but the *melos*. This is the important fact that the Haggin report of Toscanini, quoted above, seems to document. No one would doubt that Toscanini knew the *melos*, but he always had a score available when he needed to refer to details. He had a great memory, but it was not photographic.

    The proper way to memorize a score is to have a system of study by which the memorization follows automatically as a natural development of study. The study system we learned in Vienna, at the Akademie für Musik, has proved to be a very valuable one in this respect. We were taught to think of form not as it is taught in schools, but rather as a continuous, sequential series of short sections. Of course, this is how the composer composed: he wrote something, then something next, then something next, etc. The 'secret' is to analyze the elements of music within each section before going on to the next section. One will find, for example, that harmony within the section becomes something very real and functional, whereas harmony in a larger sense ('the Harmony of Beethoven') will always be purely academic. When one studies this way one remembers the progression of these sections, rather like so many cars of a railroad train. Memorization, over several weeks of study, tends to develop largely on its own like a mental slide show.

We are under the impression that virtually all important European conductors use a system similar, if not identical to this. It is this system Fuchs refers to when he writes,

> I have found pencil marking very useful, particularly when it comes to the periodicity of the melodic and rhythmical line ... Periodicity is the pulsebeat of the music, and only the conductor who has taught himself to think in terms of bar-units can render full justice to every structural detail, and to the rise and fall of its thematic sequence.[43]

[43] ibid., 35.

Von Karajan speaks of the same system.

> When I conduct a symphony or make a film, I have the impression of the complete work in my mind. This is not with me a photographic thing ... With me it is the sound of groups of bars that form a phrase. But, certainly, it is my aim to show the work as it is constructed.[44]

[44] *Conversations with Von Karajan*, op. cit., 131.

Solti described himself as 'an architectural conductor,'[45] and we know of one who has examined his personal scores that reports they were blocked out in the Viennese method.

We recommend it.

[45] Solti, op. cit., 206.

Step Number Five

Assimilation

Von Karajan once recalled the following story told him by a priest who had studied the Buddhist faith in the Far East.

> One day a young man went to the guru to seek his help. The guru sent him into his hut to mediate on his parents. The young man came out again. He couldn't concentrate. The guru suggested he mediate on a rose. Again, failure. So the guru asked him, 'What is the thing that is dearest to you?' And the young man said it was a buffalo that lived on his farm. 'So, go into my hut and meditate on that,' said the guru. After a very long time the young man had not reappeared. Eventually the guru was so worried he called into the hut to see what was happening. The young man said he was fine. 'So why do you not come out?' asked the guru. 'I have the problem,' the young man replied, 'that I cannot maneuver my horns through your narrow door.'[46]

This story of the young man who felt he had become the buffalo illustrates the final step of score study. After one has sought the *melos*, absorbed the score by ear, applied the insight of one's own experience and memorized the score, the final step is an assimilation in which the music and the conductor become one.

The conductor who has discussed this idea at the greatest length was Bruno Walter. In his study of Gustav Mahler, Walter uses Mahler's work as a conductor to illustrate how the personalities of composer and conductor merge to create the highest level of performance.

> 'What is best in music is not to be found in the notes,' Mahler was in the habit of saying. And this best and soulful element which surged with eloquent force from the music he performed produced so elemental an effect and one of so personal an avowal that doubts were entertained at times whether it was still the composer himself who spoke or whether Mahler's impetuous soul had not perhaps seized upon the musical language of the other man as a means of pouring out his own feelings. That Mahler desired nothing but to disclose to his very depths 'the other man,' that is to say, the work to be performed, is beyond any doubt. The question, however, whether, from such a performance of music, the soul of the composer spoke, whether it was that of the interpreter, or a mixture of both, touches upon the real secret of musical recreation.[47]

[46] *Conversations with Von Karajan*, op. cit., 103.

[47] Bruno Walter, *Gustav Mahler* (New York: Da Capo Press, 1970), 83ff.

It is this merging of music and conductor which Walter associates with what he calls the 'inspired interpreter.'

Bruno Walter, George Grantham Bain Collection, Library of Congress

> Ecstasy loosens within him the fetters of individualization and the recreation of the other becomes a co-creation and almost a creation of his own ... Heart and imagination are so filled with 'the other' that, in an excess of fellow-feeling, a kind of amalgamation takes place: the barriers separating the creating and the recreation artist seem to disappear and the conductor now rules as over a work of his own.

Again, it is the merging of man and music which makes it possible for the music to live in the present tense. In this regard, he points to performances by Wagner, and again Mahler, as ideal.

> In musical recreation, serving loyalty and ruling license go hand in hand, and only he who understands that, under Wagner's baton, the Ninth Symphony sounded entirely in the spirit of Beethoven and that yet Wagner's own personality fully lived in it—nay, what is more, that only the unstinted pouring forth of Wagner's substance was able to set free the spirit of Beethoven—comprehends the essence of musical interpretation. And that is how it was with Mahler's conducting. By the full power of his great personality the work of the other man arose pure and strong and received its potent vital glow from the amalgamation of the two souls.

But how does one achieve this 'amalgamation' of composer and performer? In another place, Walter seems to suggest that the essential step is for the performer to align his feelings with those of the composer.

> If a pianist, in Beethoven's E-flat major Concerto, wishes to put himself fully at the service of Beethoven's genius ... this does not imply an act of servile self-negation. On the contrary, he will only be successful in his endeavor if he freely unfolds his own self, to the limits of its capacity. In bringing to life the fire, the grace, the melancholy, the passion of the composer's work, what can he call upon but his own fire, his own grace, melancholy and passions?[48]

[48] Bruno Walter, *Of Music and Music-Making* (New York: Norton, 1957), 23.

Between this emotional assimilation and the concert, Walter finds another stage. He seems to suggest a process at work here which is similar to what the composer had first done in terms compressing his feeling into that which we call the *melos*.

How is the largely spiritual, gradually evolving first stage—the assimilation of the work—converted into the dynamic, time-bound, second stage, the execution? Now, there is such a thing as reproductive inspiration, which compresses the entire, multifarious results of a prolonged study of a work of music by which one approaches a composer, into one spontaneous outpouring. This form of inspiration recreates, in the specifically interpretative talent to which it is bound, the particular sphere in which the erstwhile creative inspiration had taken place. In this way is born what we may well call an authentic performance. It is only when the creative impulse which has engendered a composition reverberates in every detail of a performance, that we can speak of an authentic interpretation.[49]

[49] ibid., 24ff.

This concept of the conductor, or performer, assimilating personally the score is not new. This seems to us to be the intent of a recommendation by the great Baroque violinist, Francesco Geminiani.

> I would advise, as well the composer as the performer, who has ambitions to inspire his audience to be first inspired himself, which he cannot fail to be if he chooses a work of genius, if he makes himself thoroughly acquainted with all its beauties; and if while his imagination is warm and glowing he pours the same exalted spirit into his own performance.[50]

[50] Francesco Geminiani, *A Treatise of Good Taste in the Art of Musick* [1749] (New York: Da Capo Press, 1969), 4.

Charles Gounod, after a discussion of various problems in conducting, wrote of this assimilation as being the highest purpose of the conductor.

> The conductor is the ambassador of the master's thought; he is responsible for it to the artists and to the public, and *ought to be* the living expression, the faithful mirror, the incorruptible depositary of it.[51]

[51] Charles Gounod, *Memoires d'un Artiste* (Paris, 1896).

Felix Weingartner recognized this same high purpose, concluding his book on conducting with these thoughts.

> Not even the most assiduous rehearsing, so necessary a prerequisite as this is, can so stimulate the capacities of the players as the force of imagination of the conductor. It is not the transference of his personal will, but the mysterious act of creation that called the work itself into being takes place again in him, and, transcending the narrow limits of reproduction, he becomes a new creator, a self-creator.

Among the contemporary conductors, Von Karajan observed that the conductor must be able to,

> see yourself in a great work of art. Taking the score out of my briefcase and putting it on the podium: that is not my way.[52]

[52] *Conversations with Von Karajan*, op. cit., 126.

Carlo Maria Giulini goes further, suggesting the conductor become the composer.

> An interpreter, in the moment he is involved in a great expression of art, becomes himself the composer. A great actor, in the moment he is playing Iago, has to be Iago. A great interpreter must live with a deep 100% conviction in what he is doing.[53]

[53] 'Giulini on Preparations,' op. cit.

Leonard Bernstein had the same experience.

> I can at certain points (usually of intense solitary study) feel that I have become whoever is my alter ego that day or week.[54]

[54] Lebrecht, op. cit., 190.

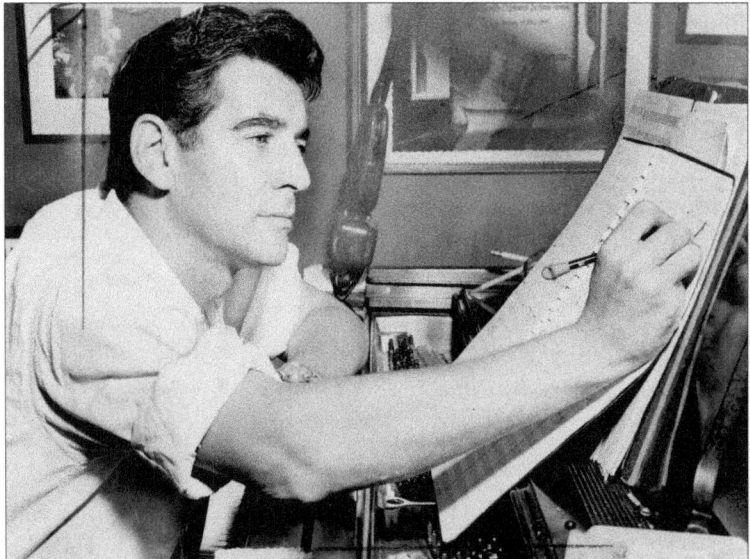

Leonard Bernstein making annotations to a musical score, 1955 (Al Ravenna, World Telegram staff photographer)

With such intense levels of assimilation, is there a danger that the personality of the conductor becomes so dominant in performance that the meaning of the composer is overshadowed? This was a particular worry of Bruno Walter.

> [Music] transmits the ego of the performer more directly to the listener than can any other medium of direct communication from one human being to another. This explains the unequaled personal success of executant musicians of strong individuality, and their breathtaking, though transitory, impact which overwhelms the listeners and makes them oblivious of the work itself.[55]

We believe the serious conductor is very unlikely to fall into this trap. It is always, and only, the universality of the communication which 'overwhelms the listeners.' Further, the listeners can not be oblivious to 'the work itself,' for the work itself is what they hear.

When a conductor responds with strong feelings to what he has found through study of the music, this should never be confused with merely an expression of his own ego. Even this remarkable outburst by Wagner, as he attempts to express the feelings he finds in a single fermata in the Fifth Symphony of Beethoven, should be considered as an example of Wagner's feeling inspired by the smallest details of music, and not as an idiosyncratic anomaly.

> Now let us suppose the voice of Beethoven to have cried from the grave to a conductor: 'Hold thou my fermata long and terribly! I wrote no fermata for jest or from bepuzzlement, haply to think out my further move; but the same full tone I mean to be squeezed dry in my Adagio for utterance of sweltering emotion, I cast among the rushing figures of my passionate Allegro, if need be, a paroxysm of joy or horror. Thus shall its life be drained to the last blood-drop; then do I part the waters of my ocean, and bare the depths of its abyss; or curb the flocking herd of clouds, dispel the whirling web of mist, and open up a glimpse into the pure blue firmament, the sun's irradiate eye. For this I set fermate in my Allegros, notes entering of a sudden, and long held out. And mark thou what a definite thematic aim I had with this sustained E-flat, after a storm of three short notes, and what I mean to say by all the like held notes that follow.'[56]

Even though it is the purpose of each conductor to assimilate the music itself, it follows that no two conductor's views will ever be the same because they differ in the history of their personal experience. As Erich Leinsdorf observed,

> Two different personalities cannot ever produce the same result, no matter how hard they try to mimic one another.[57]

---

[55] Bruno Walter, op. cit., 122ff. See also 24 and 32.

[56] 'On Conducting,' in *Wagner's Prose Works*, op. cit., IV, 312.

[57] Erich Leinsdorf, *The Composer's Advocate* (New Haven: Yale University Press, 1981), 62, fn 12.

In this regard, Von Karajan recalled an embarrassing moment when he was guest conducting the Cleveland Orchestra.

> Szell and I were great friends. I remember, he was always insisting that I conduct the Prokofiev Fifth. I wondered what he wanted, so I did it; and in the interval of the rehearsal he came and said he was suffering from nervous shock because the moment I started he realized I was doing exactly the contrary of all the things he had taught the orchestra.[58]

[58] *Conversations with Von Karajan*, op. cit., 90.

These differing perspectives are part of the richness of the musical experience. As Wagner pointed out, 'the very essence of the human species consists in the diversity of human individuality.'[59]

[59] *Wagner's Prose Works*, op. cit., I, 276.

Even in the example of one individual conductor, he also continually changes experientially and this can sometimes be felt on a daily basis. Thus Bruno Walter justifies the fact that if he conducts the Bach B Minor Mass on three successive evenings, the performances are likely to differ in small details, yet he feels each performance is 'correct.'[60]

[60] Walter, op. cit., 44.

It is this fact, that the individual grows and changes experientially throughout his life, in which lies the explanation why, as is so often remarked, composers are often poor interpreters of their own compositions—in spite of the fact that they should be reasonably expected to more perfectly assimilate their scores. Composers also change experientially and years after they have written a composition they may be quite removed from the feelings they experienced when they composed the work. We saw an example of this in 1975 when we were the host for a performance of Aaron Copland conducting his *Emblems*. At the first rehearsal he appeared to be reading a score with which he was not familiar. He remarked later, that compositions are like children: one is intimately involved with them at their birth, but eventually they leave home and go off to live a life of their own. Thus composers may have no real advantage over the conductor in terms of their original understanding of the *melos* of a composition and at the same time they have the disadvantage of lacking a rich experience and training in conducting itself.

And it is for this same reason, that all musicians differ experientially, that we must question, in general, the notion that any one conductor should feel he must adhere to the 'tradition' of performance for any given score. It is in fact often the case that Mahler's much quoted expression is quite true, 'Tradition is the last bad performance.' We find it interesting that eight hundred years before Mahler, the theorist, John Cotton, writing around 1100 AD, made the same comment about church music.

> We do know most assuredly that a chant is often distorted by the ignorance of men, so that we could now enumerate many corrupted ones. These were really not produced by the composers originally in the way that they are now sung in churches, but wrong pitches, by men who followed the promptings of their own minds, have distorted what was composed correctly and perpetuated what was distorted in an incorrigible tradition, so that by now the worst usage is clung to as authentic.[61]

[61] Quoted in *Hucbald, Guido, and John* on Music, trans., Warren Babb (New Haven: Yale University Press, 1978), 104.

While we hasten to acknowledge that there are certain general stylistic idioms for each period of music which every musician must be expected to know, with regard to the question of emotional communication we believe it is wise for the conductor to assume that the most authentic performance is the one *he* feels is correct.

Finally, assimilation also plays a vital role in helping the audience make a personal connection with the composer. The great conductor, Antal Dorati, explains,

> If you don't feel it completely, then you cannot convey it. You cannot act music. It will always leave the audience cold. They will feel immediately that it is not true. An audience will forgive many technical shortcomings for genuineness. A great polished thing which is not very well felt they will accept as such.[62]

[62] Richard Carter, 'An Interview with Antal Dorati,' in *The Instrumentalist*, December, 1980.

Erich Leinsdorf provides a perfect example of what Dorati meant, when he compares Gennaro Papi, a long time conductor at the Metropolitan Opera with great technical skills, including conducting all rehearsals and performances without scores, yet who 'passed as just another maestro,' with Koussevitzky, a conductor with weak conducting skills and so unskilled in score reading that he required a pianist to play the work to learn, but who nevertheless achieved performances which were 'welcomed into the halls of fame.'[63] One cannot help but recall some advice Horace (65–8 BC) once gave a young singer-poet.

> If you expect me to weep, then first
> You yourself must mourn.[64]

[63] Erich Leinsdorf, op. cit., 169.

[64] *De Arte Poetica liber*, ed., F. Vollmer (Leipzig, 1925), 108–111, 102, 103.

10 *How to Study a Score, III*
On Thinking of Conceptual Detail as Music

WE HAVE QUOTED in several places Mahler's famous observation, 'What is best in music is not to be found in the notes.' Mahler, of course, was talking about what was *symbolized* by the notes. The problem is that since music schools generally only teach notation as *signs*, many performers are reared with the idea that they are only supposed to pay attention to the signs. Consequently, the performer, or conductor, can easily become a stumbling block, for the listener has not the slightest interest in the signs. Rhythm, for example, is taught to the performer as math, but for the listener it is *movement*. Thus, while the conductor may *understand* the elements of music as concepts and math, in searching for the composer's intent, and in performing that intent, he must define the elements of music *experientially*. One must never forget that the composer, of whatever period, first *felt* music and only then, as a later process, attempted to express those feelings using the concepts and math available to him in a symbolic notational language.

Our purpose in this chapter is to encourage the conductor to think of the elements of music as symbols of the *experience* of music, not the grammar of music.

On Rhythm

Rhythm is taught as mathematics. The origin of this tradition clearly lies in the late medieval universities when all music courses were under the mathematics faculty and all music instruction was given by mathematicians. It is no wonder that as modern European notation was developed, the first concern, after pitch, was rhythm and meter. The 'beats' became the 'numbers' needed for a mathematical explanation of time in music, as is evident in the proportional 'meters' expressed by fractions. It was to establish a mathematical definition of 'one' that theorists such as Gafurius began associating the 'beat' with the human pulse as the basic unit of time.[1] This, of course,

[1] See Irwin Young, trans., *The Practica musicae of Franchinus Gafurius* (Madison: University of Wisconsin Press, 1969), 69.

makes no sense if one considers the wide variety of pulse rates which fall into the 'normal' range, not to mention the extreme fluctuation of pulse due to emotional factors.

Aristides Quintilianus, who lived between the first and fourth century AD, was a philosopher who believed you could determine a man's character by the rhythm of his walk.

> We find that people whose steps are of good length and equal, in the manner of the spondee, are stable and manly in character: those whose steps are long but unequal, in the manner of trochees or paions, are excessively passionate: those whose steps are equal but too short, in the manner of the pyrrhic, are spineless and lack nobility: while those whose steps are short and unequal, and approach rhythmical irrationality, are utterly dissipated. As to those who employ all the gaits in no particular order, you will realize that their minds are unstable and erratic.[2]

[2] Andrew Barker, *Greek Musical Writings* (Cambridge: Cambridge University Press, 1989), II, 457ff.]

If matters of time are considered primarily as mathematics, then it follows that the only aesthetic judgment that can apply is *correctness*, the same as in mathematics. Thus in Shakespeare's *Richard II*, following a stage direction reading, 'The music plays,' the king observes,

> Music do I hear?
> Ha, ha! Keep time. How sour sweet music is
> When time is broke and no proportion kept![3]

[3] *Richard II*, act 5, scene 5, lines 41ff.

In our view any association of mathematics with music is in fundamental conflict with the paramount purpose of music, which is to communicate feeling. Nevertheless, some musicians, even distinguished musicians, think about mathematics. We are astonished to find Bruno Walter, whose own performances never exhibited such academic thinking, maintaining that the purpose of rhythm was neither movement, nor feeling, but merely the beats.[4]

One can understand this point of view in the context of the early universities where music was only conceptual, something on paper. But in real music, music heard live, rhythm exists in a state of movement through time and space. We suspect such an association of time with movement was widely understood before modern notation, especially when one recalls the emphasis given movement by the ancient Greek choruses

[4] See Bruno Walter, *Of Music and Music-Making* (New York: Norton, 1957), 45ff.

and the sequential understanding of rhythm based on Greek poetry. In fact, the very word 'rhythm' has as its root the Greek *rhythmos*, from *rheo*, meaning *to flow*!

Martianus Capella, in the fifth century for example, made an important observation when he defined 'a tone' as something 'stretched over a space.'[5] It is also significant that he recognized that rhythm can be 'visual' as well as aural. All rhythm, he says, falls into three categories: visual, auditory, or tactual.

> An example of the visual is in bodily movements; of auditory, in an appraisal of a vocal performance; of tactual, when a doctor looks for symptoms by feeling the pulse.[6]

Wagner addressed this idea of time having to do with space in his discussion of drama.[7] He points out that the words 'time' and 'space' are intellectual concepts representing real physical phenomena. But, he says, the minute you *think* about them they have already lost their meaning, for the true meaning can only be understood in *actual* motion through space.

Emile Jaques-Dalcroze, whose system of music education begins with movement, often wrote of the relationship of rhythm and movement. In an article published in 1907, he explains,

> Muscles were made for movement, and rhythm is movement. It is impossible to conceive a rhythm without thinking of a body in motion. To move, a body requires a quantum of space and a quantum of time. The beginning and end of the movements determine the amount of time and space involved.[8]

In the same article he speaks of the personal relationship of the conductor with rhythm and movement.

> Observe the movements by which a conductor of an orchestra, endowed with temperament, represents and transmits rhythm ... His whole body will be seen to co-operate in his representation of the rhythm: each articulation, each muscle, contribute to render the rhythmic impression more intense; the aspect of his whole person becoming, in short, the reflected image of the movement of the music, and animating the executants—his own representation of the rhythm being transmitted to them.[9]

[5] *Martianus Capella and the Seven Liberal Arts*, trans., William Harris Stahl and Richard Johnson (New York: Columbia University Press, 1977), II, 370.

[6] ibid., 373.

[7] William Ashton Ellis, *Wagner's Prose Works* (New York: Broude), II, 349ff.

[8] Dalcroze, 'The Initiation into Rhythm,' in *Rhythm Music & Education* (London: Dalcroze Society, 1980), 39.

[9] ibid., 42.

We believe Von Karajan was thinking of time as space, rather than as beats, when he observed,

> What you should know is how much tempo passes *overall* in one certain phrase, and this is the most important thing.[10]

[10] Richard Osborne, *Conversations with Von Karajan* (New York: Harper & Row, 1989), 100.

One eyewitness reports that Mahler, in particular, personified the *movement* of time, rather than thinking of beats as mathematical arrival points.

> Conducting, according to Mahler, should be a continual elimination of the bar, so that it retreats behind the melodic and rhythmic content ... On the contrary, the average plodding conductor treats every bar-line as a barrier, and scans the subdivisions of each measure indiscriminately ...
>
> In Mahler's conducting, it is often impossible to distinguish what beat he is using. His baton strokes serve only to emphasize the significant melodic and rhythmic content at any one moment. Consequently, he often guides completely over the first beat of a bar, and stresses instead the second or third beat, or wherever the principal emphasis should be placed.[11]

[11] Natalie Bauer-Lechner, *Recollections of Gustav Mahler*, ed., Peter Franklin, trans., Dika Newlin (Cambridge: Cambridge University Press, 1980), 109.

[12] Note the close relationship of the words themselves: Motion—Emotion.

Although we regard movement the essence of rhythm and time in music, we cannot ignore a relationship with the emotions.[12] Walter wrote about this briefly, but he had it all wrong. He suggests that feeling is an *addition* of 'energy' by the conductor, not a characteristic found in the rhythm itself. A better explanation relates to life, as Jaques-Dalcroze explains.

> Rhythm is to intuition, emotion, and aesthetics what scientific order and logic are to the intellect. One of the essential qualities—if not *the* essential quality—of rhythm is its power of conveying the presence of life.[13]

Here are additional observations by Jaques-Dalcroze on the subject of rhythm and emotions which might be of special interest to conductors.[14]

> The aim of eurhythmics is to enable pupils, at the end of their course, to say, not 'I know,' but 'I have experienced,' and so to create in them the desire to express themselves; for the deep impression of an emotion inspires a longing to communicate it, to the extent of one's powers, to others.

...

Emile Jaques-Dalcroze, 1912

[13] Jaques-Dalcroze, quoting James Shelly's 'Rhythm and Arts,' in 'Rhythm, Time, and Temperament' (1919) op. cit., 186.

[14] ibid., 63, 107, 119, 139.

> Rhythm is the live essence of feeling, the fundamental impulse of a movement in the form impressed on it by the first emotional reaction.
>
> ...
>
> Gesture must define musical emotion and call up its image.
>
> ...
>
> Gesture itself is nothing—its whole value depends on the emotion that inspires it.

It is our view, then, that rhythm should be thought of by the conductor, and taught in schools, not as an abstracted mathematical element of music, but as the emotional expression of melody and harmony in their movement through time.

On Tempo

> How is it that the rubato style adopted by most pianists is generally regarded as a favorable proof of sensibility, whereas it would not be tolerated for a moment in an orchestral performance?[15]

It is certainly true today that conductors are generally much more reserved than individual artists with regard to modification of tempo within a movement. But it was not always so.

Gunther Schuller, in his conducting book, could not be more misinformed when he suggests that Baroque music was so 'steady' that no conductor was needed.[16] Following are some observations, taken from many, by Baroque musicians which reflect much more freedom than performers today would dare.

In 1615, Frescobaldi wrote,

> These pieces should not be played to a strict beat any more than modern madrigals which, though difficult, are made easier by taking the beat now slower, now faster, and by even pausing altogether in accordance with the expression and meaning of the text.[17]

Giovanni Bonachelli, in 1642, also suggested that feeling is the key.

> In accordance with the feeling one must guide the beat, sensing it now fast, now slow, according to the occasion, now liveliness, and now languor, as indeed anyone will easily know immediately who possesses the fine manner of singing.[18]

[15] Emile Jaques-Dalcroze, 'Contradictions and Inconsistencies' (1922), in *Eurhythmics, Art and Education* (New York: Sarnes, 1931), 252.

[16] Gunther Schuller, *The Compleat Conductor* (Oxford: Oxford University Press, 1997), 71.

[17] Girolamo Frescobaldi (1583–1643), *Toccatas and Partitas*, Book I.

[18] Giovanni Bonachelli, *Corona di sacri gigli a una, due, tre, quattro, e cinque voci* (Venice, 1642), preface.

Statue of Gerolamo Frescobaldi above the main door of the Conservatory of Music, Ferrara

Thomas Mace, in 1676, seems to suggest that the freedom in time extended even to form! If, he says, the music falls into sections, these may be played,

> according as they best please your own fancy, some very briskly, and courageously, and some again gently, lovingly, tenderly and smoothly.
> ...
> Beginners must learn strict time; but when we come to be masters, so that we can command all manner of time, at our own pleasures; we then take liberty ... to break time; sometimes faster and sometimes slower, as we perceive, the nature of the thing requires.[19]

During the nineteenth century we still find the same ideals expressed. Weber, in a letter to the music director, Praeger, in Leipzig, wrote of the importance of tempo modification.

> The beat must not be like a tyrannical hammer, impeding or urging on, but must be to the music what the pulse-beat is to the life of man.
> There is no slow tempo in which passages do not occur that demand a quicker motion, so as to obviate the impression of dragging.
> Conversely there is no presto that does not need a quiet delivery in many places, so as not to throw away the chance of expressiveness by hurrying ...
> Neither the quickening nor the slowing of the tempo should ever give the impression of the spasmodic or the violent. The changes, to have a musical-poetic significance, must come in an orderly way in periods and phrases, conditioned by the varying warmth of the expression.[20]

Wagner complained that the 'conductor-guild' of his time held that there should be no tempo modification in the music of Beethoven, a view which Wagner attributes to 'the incapacity and general unfitness of our conductors themselves.' He hastens to add that he does not mean 'the willful introduction of random nuances of tempo.'[21]

When Brahms conducted his Fourth Symphony with the famous Meiningen Orchestra he had difficulty achieving fully expressive performances and afterward wrote Joseph Joachim saying (of things not notated in the score), 'In these concerts I couldn't make enough slowings and accelerations.'[22]

If it is true that we modern conductors are somewhat conservative about tempi modification, we are terrified when we see a Metronome marking.[23] These Metronome numbers are

---

[19] Thomas Mace, *Musick's Monument* [1676] (Paris: Éditions du Centre National de la Recherche Scientifique, 1966), 429, 432.

[20] Quoted in Felix Weingartner, *On Conducting* (New York: Kalmus), 41.

[21] *Wagner's Prose Works*, op. cit., IV, 336. H. A. VanderCook's book, *Expression in Music* (Chicago: Rubank, 1926), 42, gives an illustration of four bars of music with a different tempo in each bar (quarter-note 60, 72, 66 and 60 respectively). Doing this sort of thing, he recommends, will eliminate 'humdrum results.'

[22] Johannes Brahms im Briefwechsel mit Joseph Joachim (Berlin, 1908), II, 205.

[23] William Finn, in *The Conductor Raises his Baton* (London: Dobson, 1944), 84, recommends rehearsing with an amplified metronome so as to induce confidence in the musicians!

Statue of Carl Maria von Weber in front of Dresden Cathedral, photograph by Erich Höhne and Erich Pohl, 1954, Bundesarchiv, Bild 183-27363-0006

taken as direct commandments from the composer and we dare not depart from the number given! But once again, the view of our earlier colleagues was quite different. They seem to have regarded the Metronome marking as only a suggestion for the first few bars. Beethoven, for example, wrote on one of his autograph scores,

> 100 according to Maelzel; but this must be held applicable to only the first measures, for feeling also has its tempo and this cannot entirely be expressed in this figure.[24]

[24] Quoted in Erich Leinsdorf, *The Composer's Advocate* (New Haven: Yale University Press, 1981), 165.

And Berlioz, in his essay on conducting,

> I do not mean to say that it is necessary to imitate the mathematical regularity of the metronome, which would give the music thus executed an icy frigidity; I even doubt whether it would be possible to maintain this rigid uniformity for more than a few bars.

And Brahms, as he attempts to answer a nervous conductor,

> I hardly know what to answer: 'If the indications by figures of the tempi in my Requiem should be strictly adhered to?' Well—just as with all other music. I think ... that the metronome is of no value ... The so-called 'elastic' tempo is moreover not a new invention.[25]

[25] ibid., 129.
[26] ibid., 130.
[27] *Prose Works of Wagner*, op. cit., III, 190.

And Verdi, in a note in his *Te Deum*,

> This entire piece ought to be performed in one tempo as indicated by the metronome. This notwithstanding, it will be appropriate to broaden or accelerate in certain spots for reasons of expression and nuance.[26]

And Wagner, writing of performance suggestions for *Tannhäuser*,

> As to the 'tempi' of the whole work in general, I here can only say that if conductor and singers are to depend for their time-measure on the metronomical marks alone, the spirit of the work must stand indeed in sorry case.[27]

Giuseppe Verdi, lithograph by Etienne Carjat, 1860

Among conductors, Bruno Walter also suggests that the Metronome marking is good only 'for the first few bars, but must needs lose its validity as soon as a change in expression demands a modification of speed.'[28] Erich Leinsdorf pretty much brings the discussion to a close: 'I do not consult the little clock.'[29]

Probably the best advice to the conductor regarding tempi is Beethoven's: 'feeling has its tempo.' Monteverdi made the same observation in his *Madrigali guerrieri et amorosi* (Venice, 1638) when he spoke of the voice following 'her lament, which is sung to the time of the heart's feeling, and not to that of the hand.' Once again, feeling, and not mathematics, is the key.[30]

As the conductor must permit his heart to overrule metronomic markings, so he must allow his heart to translate the familiar Italian tempo terms as they are found in specific compositions. Most musicians today think of these familiar Italian words in terms of rather specific tempi, but earlier musicians

[28] Walter, op. cit., 43.

[29] Leinsdorf, op. cit., 130.

[30] Some anomalies: Von Karajan, in Richard Osborne, *Conversations with Von Karajan* (New York: Harper & Row, 1989), 101, says slow music with intermittent pauses puts such stress on the system as can cause death! He was thinking in particular of two conductors who died while conducting Act III of *Tristan*. The famed choral conductor, William Finn, in op. cit., 62ff, presents a curious discussion on racial aspects of tempo. He finds, for example, that the Nordic character is to be associated with a slower tempo than the Latins.

Claudio Monteverdi, etching by Barberis, ca. 1800s

associated them with the *character* of the music. The views of these earlier writers can seem rather extraordinary today, for example when Johann Mattheson (1681–1764) writes,

> An *Adagio* indicates distress; a *Lamento* lamentation; a *Lento* relief; an *Andante* hope; an *Affetuoso* love; an *Allegro* comfort; a *Presto* eagerness.[31]

And Roger North (1653–1734):

> The *Grave* comes nearer a sober conversation, and the *Allegro* light and chirping. The *Tremolo* is fear and suspicion, the *Andante* is a walking about full of concern, the *Ricercata* is a searching about for somewhat out of the way; the *Affectuoso* is expostulating, or *amour*; and so every other manner, as masters are pleased to title them, are but so many states of humane life, as they have a fancy to represent or imitate.[32]

Perhaps the single most common error with regard to tempo in earlier music, is the interpretation of the '*Andante*' in Mozart, which is usually heard entirely too slow. Even Georg Solti admits he had trouble with this.

> Gradually, however, I found my way. I began to understand that 'andante' means 'moving at a natural tempo,' not 'slow,' and that Mozart must never be heavy or slow.[33]

Consider, for example, the etheral *Ave, verum corpus*, a work one would automatically think of as a 'slow' piece. It is even marked '*Adagio*,' but choirs sing it at a natural tempo of about M.M. half-note = 72 (quarter-note = 144!).

Today only a few of the traditional terms, such as *Grave*, still carry an implication of character as well as speed. But in performing earlier music, one should trust the ear and not the eye.

On Melody

When one reads traditional music history texts one encounters a thousand years or so of linear church music, of one type or another, and then you turn the page, it's the Classic Period and suddenly, without any explanation, melody appears! The truth is there was always melody in popular music,[34] but being outside the church it is not discussed in music history texts.

---

[31] Johann Mattheson, *Der vollkommene Capellmeister* (1739), trans., Ernest Harris (Ann Arbor: UMI Research Press, 1981), II, xii, 34ff.

[32] Quoted in John Wilson, *Roger North on Music* (London: Novello, 1959), 119ff.

[33] Sir Georg Solti, *Memoirs* (New York: Alfred Knopf, 1997), 212.

[34] There are 8,000 year old clay flutes with tone-holes cut for diatonic scales.

It does seem clear that it was the enthusiasm for the emotions, a topic so much discussed during the Baroque (but not in music history texts), with the encouragement offered by the Enlightenment (also not discussed in music history texts), which opened the door for melody in art music and made possible the popularity of late seventeenth-century Italian opera. One of the first theorists to understand this was Johann Mattheson. His entire understanding of the definition of music was centered in his conviction that melody was the primary element in music which communicates feeling.[35]

This fact did not pass unnoticed by Wagner.

> To the musician are explained the laws of harmony, of counterpoint; his learning, without which he can build no musical structure, is an abstract, scientific system. By attained dexterity in its application, he becomes a craftsman ...
>
> The layman stands before this artificial product of art music, and very rightly can grasp nothing of it but what appeals directly to the heart [and] this only meets him in the unconditioned ear-delight of Melody.[36]

Modern clinical research has established that a principal significance of melody is the communication of feeling and that we carry some of this information genetically into birth.[37] For the conductor who wishes to study in depth how melody expresses emotion, we recommend the remarkable book by Deryck Cooke, *The Language of Music* (Oxford: Clarendon, 1990).

On Harmony

We would not say that harmony is taught as mathematics, although Wagner used that word.

> Counterpoint ... is the Art's artificial playing-with-itself, the mathematics of Feeling ... Incapable of answering any *soul-need* ... The cashbook of a modern market-speculation.[38]

We regard harmony as taught rather like a foreign language, another symbolic language. As with all languages, the reading of it is addressed to the eye and not the ear.[39] This creates a basic handicap for the musician, as Wagner also noted.

---

[35] *Der vollkommene Capellmeister*, op. cit., II, iv.

[36] 'The Art-Work of the Future,' in *Wagner's Prose Works*, op. cit., I, 129.

[37] Much of this is summarized in 'The Musical Brain,' in *U. S. News & World Report*, June 11, 1990.

[38] *Wagner's Prose Works*, op. cit., I, 118.

[39] Hence none of our students can hear what we talk about in harmony classes. Ironically, many popular musicians who cannot even read music have functional, aural perception of harmony.

The eye knows but the surface of this sea; its depth the depth of Heart alone can fathom.[40]

[40] ibid., I, 112.

In what music school are we taught to *feel* harmony?

For the conductor, a central issue with harmony is the balance of the performing forces, which often have uneven numbers of players on the various chord tones. We assume all conductors are familiar with what is called the 'pyramid principle' of balance, by which stronger low tones and weaker high tones produce better hearing of the chord, not to mention a more pleasing homophonic sound. The physiological need for this is to overcome somewhat the brain's tendency to 'boost' the partials in the octave beginning with third-space C in the treble clef.

But the reader may be surprised to know how long this has been a secret of the conductor's art. The earliest reference we know is in a treatise on singing, *De modo bene cantandi*, of 1474, by Conrad von Zabern, who was associated with Heidelbeg University. After much objection to singing in the upper register, which he finds too loud, he offers this principle:

> Whoever wishes to sing well and clearly must employ his voice in three ways: resonantly and trumpet-like for low notes, moderately in the middle range and more delicately for the high notes—the more so the higher the chant ascends.

A particularly interesting discussion of this idea is found in the *Syntagma Musicum* (1619), by Michael Praetorius. In the third volume, which concentrates on performance practice, Praetorius discusses a very important variant of this principle, using it in the third dimension to produce cadence releases which are staggered with the lowest note sounding last. He really seems to intend this as a secret for educated conductors for in describing this he suddenly departs from the German language and switches into Latin.

Michael Praetorius, copper engraving

> As a piece is brought to a close, all the remaining voices should stop simultaneously at the sign of the conductor or choir master. The tenors should not prolong their tone, a fifth above the bass or lowest voice … after the bass has stopped. But if the bass continues to sound a little longer, for another two or four *tactus*, it lends charm and beauty to the music [*Cantilenae*], which no one can deny.

Erasmus applied this same principle with regard to speaking, observing that even 'donkeys take longer over the low note than over the high one.'[41]

With regard to wind bands, a particularly interesting discussion of this principle was published in 1845 by Wilhelm Wieprecht in a Berlin newspaper. He lists all the instruments of the military band in three categories (reading top to bottom): 'to be played lightly,' 'to be played stronger' and 'to be played very strong.' Wieprecht, in fact, coined the expression 'acoustic pyramid.'

[41] 'The Right Way of Speaking Latin and Greek,' [1528] in *The Collected Works of Erasmus* (Toronto: University of Toronto Press, 1992), XXVI, 422ff.

On Form

Franz Liszt, in a letter of 1883 to the Russian composer César Cui, made this observation regarding form in music.

> Doubtless *form* in art *is* necessary to the expression of ideas and sentiments; it must be adequate, supple, free, now energetic, now graceful, delicate; sometimes even subtle and complex, but always to the exclusion of the ancient remains of decrepit *formalism*.

Yet, this 'decrepit formalism' is what we are mostly taught of form in music schools. As in the case of rhythm and harmony, we are certainly not taught to *feel* form. But, 'to feel and see the whole work laid out before you as you begin,' was to Von Karajan the goal of the study of form.[42]

In addition, one cannot help but notice that earlier musicians and writers did find feeling associated with form. First, there are innumerable instances where an early writer associated specific emotions with a particular dance form or a specific type of popular music. Johannes de Grocheo, for example, in his treatise, *De Musica* (ca. 1300 AD) writes of the choral song, *ductia*,

> This influences the hearts of girls and young men and keeps them from vanity and is said to have force against that passion which is called love or Eros.

In early examples such as this, however, the line between form and style is not entirely clear. So what about the familar 'architectural' forms we study in school, the sonata form, the

Franz Liszt, by Wilhelm von Kaulbach, 1856

[42] *Conversations with Von Karajan,* op. cit., 97.

rondo, etc. Can feeling be associated with them? Here is what Johann Mattheson (1681–1764) experienced as a listener in the form of a single movement.

43 Mattheson, op. cit., II, xii, 34ff.

> If I hear the first part of a good overture, then I feel a special elevation of soul; the second expands the spirits with all joy; and if a serious ending follows, then everything is brought together to a normal restful conclusion.[43]

Roger North (1653–1734) also writes of feeling associated with form, including the earliest written rationale for the *ritornello* principle.

44 Quoted in John Wilson, *Roger North on Music* (London: Novello, 1959)., 69.

> It is certain that the melody [*air*] of music is improved by repetition, and is always better the second time than the first, and so on, till some novelty suppresseth it. For this reason it is that we have so many repeats and *ritornellos*.[44]

Roger North, by Peter Lely

This pleasure from recognition of the familiar that North speaks of, like the 'here I am back home again' feeling when one hears the beginning of a recapitulation, are feelings made possible by form. The conductor will not fail to account for this aspect of form so long as he is a listener too.

Part IV
On Conducting Technique

11 *On the Purpose of Rehearsal*

THE REHEARSAL IS WHEN MUSIC FIRST COMES TO LIFE. It is important to remember that the score and parts are not music, they are merely a notated, symbolic language. That is why other languages, such as German, do not confuse *'die Musik'* with the parts, which are called *'die Noten.'*

Therefore, if the rehearsal is when music comes to life, then there should be much in common with a performance. This is what one observes in a fine modern orchestra, the rehearsal has all the intensity and sincerity of a performance. Furthermore, most of the 'rehearsing' is done while the music is playing, not by the conductor talking over the music, but by the non-verbal communication of the elements of style and emotional meaning. This is entirely appropriate since much of music is too subtle to be effectively explained by words anyway. For the fine professional conductor the concern is not one of how to rehearse, but how to communicate.

In the school environment, since some conceptual teaching must also be done, many conductors have become accustomed to 'rehearsing' by talking. The school rehearsal thus becomes play—talk—play—talk, etc. The critical failure is if during the 'play' intervals the music does not become emotionally alive. Actually, this modern school custom of thinking of the rehearsal as a place for talk, and the concert a place for music, has its roots in nineteenth-century orchestral tradition—when orchestras had more time for talk. It is from this background that the important conductor, Felix Weingartner, could write,

> At the rehearsals the conductor is mostly nothing more than a workman, who schools the men under him so conscientiously and precisely that each of them knows his place and what he has to do there; he first becomes an artist when the moment comes for the concert.[1]

But this is wrong, in every respect. The rehearsal must be a place of music. We will return to this subject in the following chapter, but for now the question is another purpose—*what* do we rehearse?

[1] Felix Weingartner, *On Conducting* (New York: Kalmus), 56.

The question of what we rehearse is inseparable from the question of the responsibility owed the composer. This is a rather complex question, due to the fact that there are *three* versions of the score present during rehearsal. One version of the score is on the music stands, the printed score and parts, the version of the music written on paper by the composer. But another version of the score is that heard in the room, which may be different from the printed version because the players are contributing their own insights and experience. This version may be different from the score for other reasons in school rehearsals! Yet another version of the score is the one in the head of the conductor, which consists of what he believes the composer really had in mind when he wrote the notes he did. This version can be quite different from the first two.

The complexity of the question of the responsibility to the composer can be seen if we consider, for example, the definition of 'precision' with respect to the rehearsal. With regard to the printed version of the score, 'precision' has to do with the correction of errors or inconsistencies in the parts. But with regard to the second version of the score, the one heard, 'precision' has to do with the *execution* of the printed version. For the conductor, 'precision' means something still different—bringing the version heard in the room into correspondence with the version of the score in his head.

If there are three different versions of the score in the rehearsal room, which version do we conduct?

Does one conduct the version of the score on the music stand?

The first problem with conducting the version of the score on the music stand is that it is a past tense document, while the essential character of music is that it occurs in the present tense. The score is also past tense with regard to the composer, who may even be dead. The composer does not live by virtue of having left a score; he can only come to life through performance. It was in this context that the great pianist, Artur Schnabel (1882–1951), once said to a conductor during their rehearsal of a Beethoven concerto, 'You are there, and I am here. But where is Beethoven?'[2]

[2] Quoted in Nat Shapiro, *An Encyclopedia of Quotations About Music* (New York: Da Capo, 1977), 78.

If the composer is not present, the conductor, thinking of himself as the composer's representative, may error through the most sincere devotion toward the score. So much reverence does he give the printed score, that he feels compelled to highlight every detail, with the result that nuance becomes exaggeration. On this subject, Berlioz has written,

> The intentions of the poor composer are completely disfigured; and those of the conductor, however honest they may be, are like the caresses of the ass in the fable, who killed his master by fondling him.³

3 Hector Berlioz, 'On Conducting,' in *Treatise on Instrumentation* (New York: Kalmus, 1948), 419.

It is a particularly American viewpoint that one sometimes hears, when a critic cries, 'Let the music speak for itself,' which means, 'Just play what is on the page.' But Koussevitzky explained why this fails to bring the composer to life, if, indeed, it is even possible for any musician to just 'play what is on the page.'

> Nowadays we can often hear 'authorities' exclaim, in reviewing a performance: 'Let the music speak for itself!' The danger of this maxim lies in its paving the way for mediocrities who simply play a piece off accurately and then maintain that they 'let they music speak for itself.' Such a statement is not right, in any event, because a talented artist renders a work as he conceives it, according to his own temperament and insight, no matter how painstakingly he follows the score markings. And the deeper the interpreter's insight, the greater and more vital the performance.
>
> A perfect rendition of a work can have two different aspects which are equally faithful to the score. One part can be called mechanically perfect, the other organically perfect. The first gives the listener the beauty of mathematical balance, symmetry and clarity, the second the complete, vital, pulsing *elan vital* of the composition. The one wants to present a pretty facade, while in the other the musical creation—its basic idea—comes to life. The one may be compared to a completely symmetrical building, the other to a great Gothic cathedral, in parts asymmetrical and yet an organic unit. The one is always friendly and pleasant, but always retains something superficial, like a lively stage set. The other touches the listener, arouses him, fuses him with the reality of the basic idea, and allows him to experience the *elan vital* of the composition.⁴

4 Quoted in Carl Bamberger, *The Conductor's Art* (New York: McGraw-Hill, 1965), 144.

Serge Koussevitzky, photograph taken between 1920 and 1950, George Grantham Bain Collection, Library of Congress

Bruno Walter agreed that 'even an utterly *faithful* performance will reveal the peculiarities of the interpreter's personality.'⁵ In another place, he expands on this thought.

5 Bruno Walter, *Theme and Variations* (New York: Knopf, 1946), 47.

> Let us not underrate the importance of personality in musical execution! Its life gives life to a musical performance, its fire glows in it; surely a performance will be blunted by a dull interpreter, chilled by his coolness? Even though music, by virtue of its inborn warmth, may not entirely freeze to death under the breath of a frosty interpretation, there is such a thing as a virtually soulless performance, a virtually expressionless execution—as well as intentional, but misguided 'objectivity' in interpretation—particularly with regard to compositions of earlier periods. The plain truth is that a style of objectivity, a style of interpretation that is intentionally or unintentionally soulless, or even merely impersonal, must needs do an injustice to every piece of music, for there is none that has not sprung from some elevated state of the soul.[6]

[6] Bruno Walter, *Of Music and Music-Making* (New York: Norton, 1957), 78.

We would guess that it is probably impossible for any musician to play exactly what is on the page, for the simple reason that turning a dead score into live music precludes it.

But there is another question regarding the conductor's responsibility to the composer. What if we find a wrong note in the score? Is it our responsibility to play what is on the page, even if incorrect? Or is it the conductor's responsibility to make the composer sound better by correcting his mistakes? Before the modern Neue Ausgabe publication of the C minor Partita by Mozart almost every conductor faithfully performed the error in the final chord of the composition. Faithful to a fault!

Most conductors go further, as for example Solti, who, in his memoirs, makes it clear he did not hesitate to change tempo or dynamics in order to make the composer sound better.[7] But, how far is too far? Most conductors today would not follow the example of the great late nineteenth-century conductors, Mahler among them, who freely rescored earlier masterworks. This tradition no doubt began much earlier, when conductors simply used whatever instruments were at hand. Even Mozart did not seem to care whether a clarinet or a viola played a particular part in one of his symphonies, so long as someone played the part. In any case, things had become quite out of hand by the beginning of the nineteenth century. It was a practice which often drove Berlioz into a rage, causing him sometimes to stand up in the audience and scream at the conductor during a concert. Here is a typical example of one of his outbursts.

[7] Sir Georg Solti, *Memoirs* (New York: Knopf, 1997), 196.

We have the example of Kreutzer making numerous cuts in one of Beethoven's symphonies at the time of the last *concerts spirituels* at the Opera, after which we see Habeneck altering the orchestration of another (For the last twenty years the C minor Symphony has been performed at the Conservatoire without the double basses at the beginning of the scherzo. Habenek thinks they do not sound effective. Telling Beethoven how he should have written!). In London you hear *Don Giovanni*, *Figaro* and *The Barber of Seville* with additional parts for bass drum, trombones and ophicleide supplied by Costa. But if conductors are free to tamper with works of this kind at will and add or subtract as they please, what is to stop a violin or a horn, or any back-desk player, from doing the same? It will be the translator and the editor next, even the copyist, the engraver and the printer, who will have a fine precedent for doing the same (this is just what is happening).

Is this not the utter ruin and destruction of art? And ought not we, all of us who are in love with the glory of art and vigilant to protect the inalienable rights of the human spirit, ought we not, when we see them attacked, to rise up in our wrath and pursue and indict the malefactor, and cry aloud for all to hear, 'Your crime is contemptible—despair! Your stupidity is criminal—die! May you be scorned! May you be hissed and hooted! May you be accursed! Despair and die![8]

[8] Berlioz, *Memoirs*, ed., David Cairns (London: Gollancz, 1969), 92.

Does one conduct the version of the score heard live in the rehearsal hall?

On the rational side of our personality, with regard to language and mathematics for example, it is necessary that we agree with society's definitions in order to function. We can not each have our own answer to 'how much is two plus two?' But on the experiential side of our personality, as in the case of music or love for example, we can have individual values and beliefs. It is one of the virtues of music, as Mahler once explained.

But the chief thing is still the artistic conception, which no mere words can ever explain. Its truth shows a different face to each one of us—and a different one to each of us at different ages; just as Beethoven's symphonies are new and different at every hearing and never the same to one person as to another.[9]

[9] Quoted in Alma Mahler, *Gustav Mahler* (New York: Viking Press, 1969), 320.

It is possible in a large ensemble to have each individual take personal responsibility for his musical decisions. This would be the second form of the score in a pure sense, but then a conductor would be neither necessary nor wanted.

If a conductor is present it is understood that he will have the responsibility for achieving consensus. If he achieves this by measuring the performance against the first form of the score, the printed version, the entire process is reduced to little more than mathematics, for the results will either be right or wrong. This, in fact, is what the musically uninformed layman thinks the conductor does, and as in mathematics the musically uninformed layman can easily judge whether the music is 'right or wrong.' Plato, for example, wrote, in *Alcibiades I*, that the word, 'Musically,' is the very 'name for correctness in the art of music.'[10]

Erasmus (1469–1536), one who seemed to have little personal interest in music, also focused on accuracy. He refers to this in a discussion of the proverb, 'To strike the same wrong note.'

> Adopted from musicians, for whom it is a terrible thing to play a wrong note more than once on the same string. It can well be said of those who frequently go wrong in the same matter, or commit the same fault over and over again. The first lapse may be ascribed to chance or rashness, but to do it again argues stupidity or inexperience.[11]

In another place Erasmus says, 'music does not admit mediocrity.' This is found in his explanation of the Greek proverb, 'When you're offered turtle-meat, either eat or do not eat,' which means do not do anything half-way. He then adds the thought,

> Remember how many activities there are which are admirable if you throw yourself into them, and do harm if you are lukewarm; or which do not admit of mediocrity, like music and poetry.[12]

Lord Chesterfield, in his famous letters to his son, points to the purpose of the communication of emotions, but conditions this on the premise of accuracy in performance.

> The best compositions of Corelli, if ill executed and played out of tune, instead of touching, as they do when well performed, would only excite the indignation of the hearers, when murdered by an unskilled performer.[13]

[10] *Alcibiades I*, 108d.

[11] 'Adages,' in *The Collected Works of Erasmus* (Toronto: University of Toronto Press, 1992), XXXI, 393.

Desiderus Erasmus, engraving by Albrecht Dürer, 1526

[12] 'Adages,' in ibid., XXXII, 260.

[13] Earl of Chesterfield, letter to his son, July 9, 1750.

The musical conductor, on the other hand, understands that perfect precision, even if it could be achieved, is only the first step and not the goal of the rehearsal process. It is an indispensable part of the process, however, for, as Schumann wrote, it is precision which makes possible the next step, the unveiling of the *melos*.

> At rehearsal each musician must matter-of-factly work toward technical perfection in order to free the work of art from its mechanics.[14]

[14] Bamberger, op. cit., 62.

Walter makes this same point in his description of Mahler as a conductor.

> Without a sacred sense of order, leading almost to pedantry, the gifts of a genius were to him but an empty sound meaning nothing. When, however, he had succeeded, by his persistent demands upon singers and musicians, in achieving absolute distinctness and precision, the soul was permitted to spread its wings freely upon this secure foundation, and thus his performances produced the effect of spontaneous improvisation.[15]

[15] Bruno Walter, *Gustav Mahler* (New York: Greystone Press, 1941), 80.

Walter writes of this again in another place.

> Correctness is the indispensable condition and prerequisite for any musical interpretation that bears witness to the spirit and soul of a work. Exactness, cleanliness, orderliness, ie., rightness of notes and time, clarity of sound, and compliance with dynamic and tempo indications: these are the demands of correctness, and it is only from such a basis that meaningful music-making can evolve. Even the most fiery expression cannot do justice to a passionate composition if the spirit of order is lacking in its execution, if its passages are played untidily and its rhythm inexactly.[16]

[16] Bamberger, op. cit., 159.

And in yet another place he adds,

> Precision can never contain or effect spirituality; it can merely help to clear the way for spirituality to manifest itself. In all music-making, spirituality is the primary concern—that is the creed of every true musician.[17]

[17] Bruno Walter, *Of Music and Music-Making* (New York: Norton, 1957), 126.

Wagner refers to the spirit when he writes of a passage in the Ninth Symphony of Beethoven in which he had failed in both Dresden and in London to achieve what he thought the composer intended.

> To the dull-of-feeling it is hard to convey the difference between the plainly expressed intention of the master, as indicated in the score, and the expression given to this passage when strummed in such a banal fashion.

When he finally heard this passage performed well, in Paris, the result he recalled, 'seemed like a magic spell initiating me into the matchless mysteries of Spirit.'[18]

Which ever view point a conductor takes, either of measuring precision against a score, or treating precision as only an initial step, the question of discipline will be present. The fact that no musician appreciates being on the receiving-end of discipline prompted Oscar Levant (1906–1972) to observe,

> A conductor should reconcile himself to the realization that regardless of his approach or temperament the eventual result is the same—the orchestra will hate him.[19]

But another writer, Hubert Kupferberg, was perhaps more to the point when he quoted a member of the Philadelphia Orchestra:

> Show me an orchestra that likes its conductor and I'll show you a lousy orchestra.[20]

In Peter Paul Fuchs' survey of major conductors, he found most said only praise should be given in rehearsal, with criticism made in private.[21] There were exceptions, such as Bernstein, who observed that 'everybody learns from it.' Steinberg, observed 'I praise and criticize as the occasion demands ... I am not in favor of private consultations.' We might add that we noticed, during the year we spent studying with Eugene Ormandy, that he made all personal criticism only in his private office. There is powerful psychology at work in this. We saw men who, in the orchestra, were powerful and outspoken, but who, standing alone, trembled at knocking on Ormandy's door.

---

[18] William Ashton Ellis, *Wagner's Prose Works* (New York: Broude), IV, 301ff.

[19] *A Smattering of Ignorance* (1940).

[20] Quoting Goddard Lieberson, in *Those Fabulous Philadelphians* (1969).

[21] Peter Paul Fuchs, *The Psychology of Conducting* (New York: MCA, 1969), 135ff.

Perhaps the best model for all conductors on this subject was Bruno Walter. He wrote at length arguing against the treatment of people in a violent manner or through intimidation.[22] His view was that the conductor should be more like an educator.

[22] Bruno Walter, *Of Music and Music-Making* (New York: Norton, 1957), 119. 120. 122.

> The orchestral musician needs [a] warm climate for the full unfolding of his artistic abilities; under the chill of unfriendliness or mordant scorn, under the heat of impatience or anger emanating from the conductor's desk, they freeze or wither.

Finally, it is important to ask, how does the individual performer profit from rehearsal? Apart from the 'fun of playing music,' the various social enticements, etc., there is also an opportunity to learn. Leaving aside the important musical and stylistic learning opportunities, there is the extremely valuable, and almost unique in the school environment, opportunity to experience deep human emotions, or as Wagner used to say, to 'gaze into the inmost Essence' of oneself. But these insights will come from the music itself, and not from the words and explanations of the conductor. Thomas Ewens makes this point very well.

> It seems to me that this is a critical issue in art education and one which all parties—artists, art historians, art critics, aestheticians, *and* art educators—should get clear if efforts to reconstruct a viable program of art education are to succeed. Macmurray sees this very clearly. The proper artistic education of the young, he says, is 'a training in perception and expression, which in its full results would develop to the fullest measure of which the child is capable, his ability to be an artist; that is to say, to apprehend the world finely through his own sensibility, and to express it in spontaneous activity purely for the joy in doing so.'[23] Such a training in artistry is not to be based in the three academic disciplines Eisner invokes[24] but in the spontaneous emotional activities, attunements, discernments, appraisals, and imaginary experiments of the child. It is an education geared to making art as a fullness of life for its own sake. Its goal is not to train children's minds in the analysis and understanding of the works of others; its goal is to enable them to see and feel and judge for themselves and to be true to their own emotional experience. We might resume this point in homely terms: just as people, young and old, can enjoy sex and, as the Bible says, 'know' each other without benefit of clergy, so too can they enjoy and know art without benefit of art historians, art critics, and aestheticians.[25]

[23] John Macmurray, *Reason and Emotion* (London: Faber and Faber, 1972), 74ff.

[24] Elliot W. Eisner, *The Role of Discipline-Based Art Education in America's Schools* (Los Angeles: The Getty Center for Education, 1978).

[25] Thomas Ewens, 'In Art Education, More DBAE Equals Less Art,' *Design for Arts in Education*, March/April, 1988.

Dorothy Ling makes the same plea.

> The purpose of artistic experience is to keep open or reopen the doors of perception. It is only through these doors that the channels of creativity, communication, imagination, and affection can operate to connect us with our innermost selves and with reality. As the maximum intervention of all these channels is indispensable to education, it follows that artistic experience (not information) must be the axis of education ... Access to this experience must be immediate, free from all information, theories, and applied techniques; there is nothing to be taught, only experienced.[26]

[26] Dorothy Ling, *The Original Art of Music* (The Aspen Institute), 66–67.

It is because this deep emotional experience is so valuable to the player, that the conductor will have such difficulty getting anyone to really listen carefully to his verbal instructions. The players are there to make music. You can observe this yourself in anyone's rehearsal, from an elementary school to a professional orchestra—watch the faces, and eyes, of the musicians when the conductor begins to talk.

Does one conduct the version of the score in one's head?

Real precision comes only from the conductor's vision, having in his mind a clear concept of exactly how the music *should* sound. The mind is the source of *all* physical actions by the body, both voluntary and involuntary. If the conductor has a clear musical concept in his mind, he *will* be able to physically communicate it to the ensemble. As Peter Paul Fuchs says,

> Without trying to downgrade for one moment the necessity of beating clearly, my own experience has taught me that often the best results are obtained not so much by the beating pattern as by an unbendable inner conviction as to how the music should sound. This may be telepathy, but it works![27]

[27] Fuchs, op. cit., 57.

Bruno Walter shared this same viewpoint.

> Sufficient natural talent provided, the spirit cannot fail to develop the technique it needs. For this is indeed essentially a spiritual task since ... precision is only to a very limited extent of a mechanical nature—at bottom, its claims are musical, and the technique required to achieve it

must, therefore, arise and evolve from spiritual-musical impulses. By concentrating on precision, one arrives at technique; but by concentrating on technique one does not arrive at precision.[28]

Forming and conducting a vision of the music in one's head is really the theme of this entire book. Here we might only add that since this vision of the composer's intent becomes so personal with the conductor, he is left quite vulnerable. Anything he hears in rehearsal which does not perfectly correspond with this internal score can be not only a shock, but can cause a real sense of suffering on the part of the conductor. Solti used the analogy of a dream to explain this.

> A conductor's aim is to make the orchestra produce what he imagined during the weeks and months when he was studying the score. Toscanini once told his orchestra, 'I hate you all, because you destroy my dreams.' You have a dream and you try to realize it; if your dream is destroyed, you suffer. Rehearsals exist in order to try to realize dreams.[29]

There are many stories of the sensitivity of Toscanini in this regard. Von Karajan recalls an occasion when Toscanini was guest conducting the Vienna Philharmonic, became angry and stormed out only to find the doors had been locked at his orders. So, according to Von Karajan, Toscanini went into a corner and cried.[30] Toscanini himself once observed,

> Nikisch is good conductor—but make performance for public. And sometimes he do not look at score. When I conduct I am always prepared. I do not stand before public to show I am Toscanini—never! Always I try to do my best. And always conducting is great suffering for me. At home, with score, when I play piano, is great happiness. But with orchestra is great suffering—*sempre, sempre!*[31]

And on another occasion, in Salzburg in 1939, Toscanini observed, 'When Bruno Walter comes to something beautiful he melts. I suffer!'[32]

In this regard a final note about rehearsals is, in our view, important. Many conducting teachers focus getting the student to be able to hear variances between the second form of the score with the first, even planting wrong notes, etc., for this purpose. We feel this is largely a waste of time, for any

[28] Bamberger, op. cit., 169.

[29] Sir Georg Solti, *Memoirs* (New York: Knopf, 1997), 206.

[30] Richard Osborne, *Conversations with Von Karajan* (New York: Harper & Row, 1989), 69ff.

[31] B. H. Haggin, *Conversations with Toscanini* (Garden City: Doubleday, 1959), 62.

[32] ibid., 81.

conductor who knows the score will always hear these errors. We teach somewhat differently. We teach the student to concentrate on the third version of the score, not the first two. It is the third score version which is the compass for the rehearsal and performance and which the conductor must at all costs hang on to. In a sense the conductor must learn to ignore the score version in the hall, in its present tense moment. That is, in the case of poor playing, for example, he must remember *how* something was played, but not respond *to* how it is being played. If the conductor is only occupied with comparing score version two with score version one, in the case of an error, or poor playing, he will be likely to respond with a sentence beginning, 'You did not ... ,' or 'You are not ... '. No matter how this sentence concludes, it will be taken badly by the player. But, if the conductor is occupied in comparing score version two against score version three, in such an event he will be more likely to respond with a sentence beginning, 'We need ... ,' or 'Perhaps, if we could ... '. In drawing attention to version score three, instead of score version one, the player may disagree, but he will have no cause to be offended.

12   *The Technique of Musical Conducting*

ARE THERE SPECIAL TECHNIQUES which make a musically fine conductor? The distinguished conductor, Erich Leinsdorf, observed 'The qualifications for this elusive art and craft are a mystery to all but a very few experts.'[1] But if this is true, why is there a general feeling among musicians that the ability of a conductor can be almost immediately recognized? Richard Strauss quoted his father, an old horn player in the Munich opera, as declaring,

[1] Erich Leinsdorf, *The Composer's Advocate* (New Haven: Yale University Press, 1981), 167.

> When a new man faces the orchestra—from the way he walks up the steps to the rostrum and opens his score—before he even picks up the baton we know whether he is the master or we.[2]

[2] *Recollections and Reflections* (1922).

Georg Solti wrote that he could tell if a conductor has talent for conducting in five minutes.[3] Peter Paul Fuchs asked this question of a number of distinguished conductors.[4] Everyone agreed that it took about fifteen minutes and Leonard Bernstein said, 'one bar.'

[3] Sir Georg Solti, *Memoirs* (New York: Knopf, 1997), 207.

[4] Peter Paul Fuchs, *The Psychology of Conducting* (New York: MCA, 1969), 132.

But on what basis do musicians make this rapid decision? John Barbirolli believed they know 'immediately and instinctively.' Several said, if the conductor 'knows the music,' but only Josef Krips said if the conductor 'has a clear beat.' The answer to this question given by Bernstein is the correct one:

> The opinion is not formed in an intellectual way. He knows whether you have the capacity to convey your feelings and whether you have feelings to convey.

Bernstein goes right to the heart of the issue, for what the fine conductor does, above all else, is to *personify* the emotional meaning of the music to the orchestra. This was what was meant when Von Karajan quoted Klemperer as defining conducting as the 'power of suggestion.'[5] Because, as we have discussed earlier, the facial and body motions expressing emotions are universally understood, the experienced conductor can communicate sophisticated musical ideas, in an instant, to

[5] Richard Osborne, *Conversations with Von Karajan* (New York: Harper & Row, 1989), 105.

a large number of musicians, bring them to a consensus, and through them transmit the spiritual message to the audience. The great German conductor, Wilhelm Furtwängler (1886–1954), once made this very point.

> What one can teach an orchestra in rehearsals, even extended, highly concentrated, and very precise rehearsals, is little in comparison with what can be done right from the start and in a few moments, through the type of beat and the related instinctive (that is subconscious) method of communication ... It is on this that the instinctive appreciation which the public bestows on a conductor is based.[6]

[6] Quoted in Carl Bamberger, *The Conductor's Art* (New York: McGraw-Hill, 1965), 213.

The Berlin Philharmonic Orchestra and conductor Wilhelm Furtwängler in a work break in a concert hall of the AEG factory in Berlin. Bundesarchiv, Bild 183-L0607-504 [CC BY-SA]

Assuming musical competence, it is, then, primarily the ability to communicate feeling which characterizes the fine conductor. Consequently, one finds this common thread running through all eye-witness descriptions of famous earlier conductors. Berlioz, for example, was described as a conductor in a letter by Moscheles, the teacher of Mendelssohn, as follows:

Berlioz's conducting inspired the orchestra with fire and enthusiasm, he carried everything as it were by storm.[7]

[7] Weimar, November, 1852.

Berlioz himself expressed the definition of a fine conductor very clearly:

> The players must feel that the conductor feels, understands and is moved; then his emotion communicated itself to those whom he conducts. His inner fire warms them, his enthusiasm carries them away, he radiates musical energy. But if he is indifferent and cold, he paralyzes everything around him, like the icebergs floating in the polar sea, whose approach is announced by the sudden cooling of the atmosphere.[8]

[8] Hector Berlioz, 'On Conducting,' in *Treatise on Instrumentation* (New York: Kalmus, 1948), 410.

Felix Weingartner credited Wagner in particular for demonstrating to the conductors of the late nineteenth century the importance of the conductor's role in providing 'the spiritualizing internal factor that gives the performance its very soul.'[9] In another place, he describes the emotional intensity of Wagner as conductor.

[9] Felix Weingartner, *On Conducting* (New York: Kalmus), 5.

> Added to this desire for clarity in Wagner was the passionate temperament with which, aided by a keen understanding, he threw himself into his work; he brought to it also a faculty of immediate communication with the players and imposition of his will on them ... *There is no performance of genius possible without temperament.* This truth must be perpetually insisted on ... Temperament, however, can be given neither by education, nor conscientiousness, nor, by the way, by favor; it must be *inborn*, the free gift of nature ... But [performances of genius] are quite incomprehensible to those 'aesthetes' who consider them as problems of the understanding and would solve them, like a mathematical problem, by analysis.[10]

[10] ibid., 10ff.

Similar examples range from Bruno Walter's characterization of Mahler as a conductor with the 'emotional communication of a universal mind'[11] to Davenport's recollection of a dress rehearsal for *Die Meistersinger* which concluded with both Toscanini and the entire cast in tears.[12]

But the important question for this chapter is how does one learn, or develop, the ability to personify the range of emotions in a composition? The usual techniques of method acting or mime are completely out of the question because they teach only the *representation* of an emotion, whereas the conductor

[11] Bruno Walter, *Gustav Mahler* (New York: Da Capo, 1970), 8.

[12] Marcia Davenport, *Too Strong for Fantasy* (New York: Scribner's, 1967), 229.

must communicate the genuine thing. Probably one becomes better at personifying the music not by practicing gestures before the mirror, but by studying the score—contemplating and clarifying one's understanding of the emotional content of the composition. But with regard to score study, we must repeat a basic theme of this book: it is not the notes on paper we project, but what they represent. This is what Ferruccio Busoni (1866–1924) meant when he wrote,

> Notation, the writing out of compositions, is primarily an ingenious expedient for catching an inspiration, with the purpose of exploiting it later ... It is for the interpreter *to resolve the rigidity of the signs* into the fundamental emotion.[13]

[13] *Sketch of a New Aesthetic of Music* (1911).

Certainly, resorting to the use of words in rehearsal has very little influence on an orchestra's capacity to project emotions. As Leonard B. Meyer once observed,

> Verbalizations of emotions, particularly those evoked by music, are usually deceptive and misleading.[14]

[14] *Emotion and Meaning in Music* (1956).

In any case, as Solti pointed out, 'If a conductor is clear in his gestures he doesn't really need words.'[15] In another place, Solti adds,

[15] Sir Georg Solti, op. cit., 37.

> When you stand in front of the orchestra, you must never try to show off your aesthetic or philosophical ideas. You must address the musical problems as they arrive.[16]

[16] ibid., 115.

Sir George Solti, by Allan Warren, 1975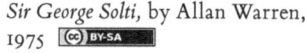

In this regard, Fuchs doubts the value of 'impressionistic' language, such as 'give me the glow of a sunset' and specifically disallows any sentence beginning 'Somehow this isn't …'.[17] The 'somehow,' he stipulates, must be expressed in technical terms. We agree that 'impressionistic' words seem to be rather ineffective (other than when used for humor), but we have found that emotional terms can be very effective. Amazing changes take place when one says to an ensemble something like, 'I don't hear any *pain*.'

Max Rudolf agreed that it is not words that are successful in rehearsal, and introduces a new word, *personality*:

[17] Peter Paul Fuchs, op. cit., 54.

> There are limits to the conductor's efforts to translate his intentions into technical language. The intrinsic meaning of music, the subtleness of a phrase, or the dramatic impact of an emotional outburst may not be felt by all the players unless the conductor possesses the suggestive power of revealing what is 'behind the notes.' How to do this cannot be taught. Each conductor must find his own way to project his feelings, by virtue of his personality.[18]

[18] Bamberger, op. cit., 289.

This word, 'personality,' is one often used by great conductors to describe this aspect of their craft. For example, William Steinberg said,

> I think mainly that every man develops his own method with which he expresses himself after his own nature and that the only factor that counts is the power of his personality.[19]

[19] ibid., 306.

And Hermann Scherchen:

> The secret of art is the secret of personality, whose infinitely various possibilities cannot be counted.[20]

[20] ibid., 224.

And Bruno Walter:

> His spiritual mediation, drawing inspiration from the work, is then needed to give an individual stamp to this actual, that is sounding, unity; the seal of personality must be set upon it.[21]

[21] ibid., 162.

What exactly are they talking about? They are clearly not talking about personality in its customary usage in show business. We think that a word which better represents what they are talking about is 'personification.' This is the real heart of the matter, the distinguishing characteristic of all great conductors. The conductor must personally project the style and emotional content of the score. The ability to do this is the primary conducting technique of the musical conductor. As Peter Paul Fuchs concluded,

> The conductor must be involved with the music that he conducts, otherwise his work will be nothing but undistinguished time beating.[22]

[22] Peter Paul Fuchs, op. cit., 56.

Lebrecht quotes a member of the Boston Symphony Orchestra as saying, 'We're desperate to have someone come and conduct us in the German literature, and be *inspired*.'[23] Bruno Walter used another form of this word.

[23] Norman Lebrecht, *The Maestro Myth* (New York: Citadel, 1993), 138.

> By inspiriting I mean the incessant impletion of music-making with expression, that is, with the vivid, ever-changing sentiment which the musical—or dramatic—consecution calls forth in the performer. Since all music originates in the soul and can never, therefore, be soulless or lacking in feeling, nothing but an unceasing inspiriting of interpretation can do justice to it.[24]

[24] Bruno Walter, *Of Music and Music-Making* (New York: Norton, 1957), 128.

To do this effectively, of course, the feelings of the conductor must be genuine. It therefore follows that the experience can be, for the conductor, very intense. Bruno Walter writes 'impulsive intensity,'[25] and in another place, of 'intense empathy.'[26] Peter Paul Fuchs notes that the state of concentration is so intense in conducting that a major work can seem like a lifetime.[27] Von Karajan observes of Mahler's Ninth Symphony, 'Coming to the end of this symphony is one of the hardest tasks in all conducting.'[28] And of the Berg *Three Orchestral Pieces*, he reflects,

[25] ibid., 113.
[26] ibid., 112.

[27] Peter Paul Fuchs, op. cit., 68.

[28] Richard Osborne, *Conversations with Von Karajan*, op. cit., 118.

> To conduct it is a devastating experience: it takes up all your mind and it will take you two or three days to recover from it.[29]

[29] ibid., 123.

Regarding the acquisition of this ability to personify to the orchestra the emotional content of the music, we have quoted above Bruno Walter's belief that 'Sufficient natural talent provided, the spirit cannot fail to develop the technique it needs.'[30] Walter is quite correct about this and it is made pos-

[30] Bamberger, op. cit., 169.

sible through the process by which our brain works the body as a machine. To make the body members function we need only a simple image in the mind. To walk out a door, for example, we simply form the image of walking out the door. We do not think 'pick up the left foot, put it down, pick up the right foot, put it down,' etc. The center fielder in baseball, in order to catch a flyball, thinks only 'catch the ball,' yet his mind performs an extraordinary array of calculations which include the influence of gravity, wind factors and speed of the ball. Yet, the brain does this so rapidly that he invariably begins to run at the instant the ball is hit to exactly the spot where the ball will fall. Even the most stupid center fielder in baseball will not run in the wrong direction at the crack of the bat.

This illustrates, we hope, how the mind works with respect to what Walter was trying to describe. All we actually need is an image in the mind, a *precise* image of style and emotion regarding how the next moment should sound, and the brain *will* produce the musically appropriate gesture. From the conductor's perspective, this image can be formed only by study and reflection. But since this is not a technique which has a rational basis, it may well be that the players are unaware that they have seen a specifically developed technique, as Eugen Jochum points out.

> A phenomenon becomes visible that most likely represents the particular core of conducting talent: a peculiar physical predisposition to receive a musical happening (with all of its accumulations, tensions, and resolutions, with all of its melodic, rhythmic, and other elements) and transmit it through conscious as well as involuntary gestures, so that the player responds with a physical perceptiveness, far below the threshold of rational understanding.[31]

Steinberg expresses this a bit more surreptitiously:

> The best possible solution is not to let the players find out the method, so that they are simply carried along and do not know what is happening.[32]

One avenue for the development of this ability to project feeling which is mentioned by several fine conductors, is the general spiritual development of the conductor himself. Bruno Walter writes,

---

[31] ibid., 263.

[32] Fuchs, op. cit., 133.

> In this respect, too, innate talent is of decisive importance—a talent for asserting one's own personality—and it needs to be developed by constant endeavor and by making the most of daily experiences.[33]

[33] Bruno Walter, *Theme and Variations* (New York: Knopf, 1946), 82.

When Bruno Walter used the expression 'daily experiences,' he was talking about pursuits of a spiritual and humanistic nature which offer the conductor the potential for growth. For, as Hermann Scherchen writes, this is at heart a spiritual profession.

> To acknowledge that the conductor's domain is largely spiritual is to realize the exceptional character of his art; one can then appreciate the great artistic and human attributes which must be possessed by the true conductor.[34]

[34] Bamberger, op. cit., 223.

William Steinberg adds that the development of such great character is not only necessary for the actual musical work, but to build the kind of character that will keep one safely on track aesthetically.

> He who besides integrity, possesses all implied spiritual traits and virtues of character which he polishes in the furnace of intuition and inspiration, and he who can muster enough modesty to hide himself from the eyes of a crowd craving to be entertained or provoked.[35]

[35] ibid., 308.

Anyone who ever had the opportunity to observe Bruno Walter, was fortunate to see an extraordinary example of a conductor who personified these great human and spiritual qualities. Peter Paul Fuchs describes a rehearsal he observed:

> I heard him speak to the performers, patiently pleading with them to do justice to the spiritual essence of the work, to try to feel everything that was in it ... No one remained untouched ... everyone ... felt purified by his presence.[36]

[36] Fuchs, op. cit., 142.

Not only does the conductor bear the responsibility of projecting this spiritual essence of the score, its *melos*, but he must do it in such a way as to draw the player into a common intuitive understanding of the work. One of the most extraordinary illustrations of a conductor's effort to bring his musicians into this common understanding is described by Wagner, in his essay on conducting. He recalls the first performance in Paris of Beethoven's Ninth Symphony, at a time when the work was still quite unknown generally. Even though the conductor, Habeneck, had available the best orchestra of Paris, he rehearsed the work for three years before performing it before the public! His long study with the orchestra was not due to the technical difficulties, but for the purpose,

> not to rest until the new Beethovenian *melos* had dawned on every member of his orchestra and been correctly reproduced by each.[37]

[37] William Ashton Ellis, *Wagner's Prose Works* (New York: Broude), IV, 301.

Robert Schumann also discussed this critical subject of the conductor's duty to draw in the feelings of the players.

> Is it not then as if the spirit of the composition is projected from the podium upon the orchestra? And, conversely, an uninspired conductor can, in spite of the most military of methods, achieve at best a mechanical brilliance. The orchestra should not be a mechanism which plays its tones like a clock, but the individual emotions of each participant should attach itself to the spirit of the composition. It is not the playing of forte and piano which renders the spirit of the composition but the conception and execution of it as a work of art.[38]

[38] ibid., 64.

This is the essential challenge of the rehearsal. In achieving this, the conductor faces some formidable obstacles which have their origin in the fact that the players have a fundamentally different perspective regarding their performance. First, while the conductor must communicate the non-rational, non-verbal, non-notational form of the music, he stands before a group of players whose basic training is entirely of a rational, notational and technical nature. This kind of teaching, so characteristic of the world of the studio teacher, is very limited, as Hermann Scherchen points out.

> Performers acquire a knowledge of the instrument they play, but never of the works they wish to perform. The technique of the instruments has become an end in itself. The player devotes the whole of his labor to this, but has practically no acquaintance with the technique of composition. And he knows even less of the creative force.[39]

[39] ibid., 223.

Bruno Walter's solution to this problem is simply to encourage every hint of emotional involvement by the players.

> If individual taste or personal emotional participation are ruthlessly suppressed, the result will be a sort of emotional impoverishment of the performance. The conductor should strive to encourage every sign of emotional participation in the orchestra.[40]

[40] Bruno Walter, *Of Music and Music-Making*, op. cit., 123.

As significant as this difference is between how the conductor and player come to the rehearsal prepared to think about the music, there is another, psychological, difference which Bruno Walter calls 'the profound difference.'[41] This difference lies in the fact that only the conductor has a score. Through his *melos*-searching study, the conductor arrives at the rehearsal hall filled with the spirit of the music, imagining an idealized form of the music and hearing in his ear a perfect performance. The individual player, however, can not be expected to arrive filled with the spirit of the music. Even if he were so dedicated as to study his part before rehearsal, that part, say a second trombone part, or even a first violin part, is too fragmented and incomplete to be able to fill him with the spirit of the music. The most the conductor can hope for, says Bruno Walter, is that the player will just arrive at the rehearsal with a sense of good-will.

[41] ibid., 111ff.

What happens when these two diametrically opposed psychological states of mind meet, with the first downbeat, has an enormous impact and influence on the entire rehearsal which follows. The conductor, filled with the emotions of the music at hand, looks out on a sea of faces which are neutral at best, but often tired and bored, and gives the downbeat. The first sound the conductor hears brings a jolting conflict with the idealized image of the music he hears in his mind. At this moment the psychological state of the player is unchanged, for he is unaware of anything having happened. But the conductor is demoralized, a state which Bruno Walter compares to a heavy weight pressing down on him. The conductor who does not anticipate this very natural human situation may well respond with negative feelings toward the players, perhaps even anger. This is also human nature, but the result is even less response from the players, followed by more negative feelings by the conductor, and so on.

This difference in the psychological states of mind at the beginning of the rehearsal is real and predictable. It is also obvious that it must be the conductor himself who overcomes this problem and fills those empty faces with the spirit of the music, thus turning the direction of the rehearsal from a negative atmosphere to a positive one. But how?

At this moment the rational side of his personality will only work against the conductor. The conductor who begins to talk, whether explaining the music, or demonstrating his knowledge of the music, only disconnects the players from their experiential involvement in the music and all that it entails. They are there to play music and when the conductor switches to a different mode, to the rational, they simply 'turn off.' What conductor has not experienced this?

It is only the experiential and feeling side of the personality which comes to the conductor's aid since this is more closely related to the central essence of music itself. Bruno Walter explains how the conductor does this.

> What must come to his rescue here, is an intense empathy with the mind of the players that will teach him to put life into the orchestra, raise its tension towards his own, fire the musicians and his own fire, and kindle their activity by his.
>
> Such empathy will help him make the orchestra into an instrument on which he can play with the freedom of a soloist. But what are the artistic means of realizing those highest orchestral achievements in which his conception, his own self, can find audible expression? I shall not trouble to try and explain the strongest and most effective means, for it is, at the same time, the most obscure: I mean by this the forcible, direct influence which the born conductor, by virtue of his inner musical intensity and the sheer power of his personality, exerts on his musicians. The forces that emanate from him create an atmosphere of spiritual communion which gives elemental spontaneity, completeness, and conclusiveness to the musical performance. Every truly sympathetic observer will have perceived in this collaboration of conductor and executants the workings of deep, instinctive forces of the soul, together with such as are elucidated by consciousness ... This instinctive faculty for immediately transmitting one's own musical impulses to the orchestra is the sign of true talent for conducting.[42]

[42] ibid., 174.

Finally, the ability to focus the rehearsal on the emotional content and meaning of the music stimulates the players to understand how their part contributes, and to make the necessary corrections to that end by themselves. This is a technique of rehearsal far superior to the conductor being the rational policeman whose duty is to constantly seek and 'correct.'

Furthermore, this technique leads to a much faster paced rehearsal, particularly if the conductor is rehearsing without a score. This is an essential point for we live in an age when time has an entirely different meaning and price. We will never again have the luxury of the endless rehearsals which characterized an earlier time, when time itself had little value in so far as the player was concerned. For today's conductor who worries over the limited rehearsal time available to him, let him imagine the following and dream of an earlier life:

Wagner once held twelve rehearsals just for the string basses for the recitative bars at the beginning of the fourth movement of the Beethoven Ninth Symphony.[43]

With world-class orchestras, Mengelberg took a month to prepare *Till Eulenspiegel*, Toscanini once insisted on twelve rehearsals for *La Mer* and the first *Rite of Spring* needed one hundred and twenty rehearsals! Barbirolli required fifty hours of rehearsal before doing Mahler's Ninth Symphony with Berlin, Abbado needed forty rehearsals for *Wozzeck* at La Scala and Erich Kleiber held thirty-four full orchestral rehearsals for the same opera.[44]

Von Karajan recalls sixty or seventy rehearsals for the Bach B Minor *Mass* or Beethoven *Missa Solemnis*.[45] He consumed sixty hours of rehearsal and made a recording of Mahler's Fifth Symphony with Berlin before playing it before the public.[46]

Once, at La Scala, Toscanini held sixty rehearsals for Bellini's *Norma* and then canceled the production.[47]

For his first concert as music director with the Los Angeles Philharmonic, Giulini asked for eighteen hours of rehearsal for Beethoven's Ninth, not for the purposes of technical work, but 'to make human contact.'[48]

Finally, in this regard, we might quote an interesting discussion of Mahler as a conductor, written by his young disciple, Arnold Schönberg.

> Certainly, many have extolled his demonic personality, his unheard-of sense of style, the precision of his performances as well as their tonal beauty and clarity. But, for example, among other things, I heard one of his 'colleagues' say that there is no special trick to bringing off good

[43] Richard Wagner, *My Life* (New York: Tudor, 1936), 401.

[44] Norman Lebrecht, op. cit., 161, 217, 233.

[45] Richard Osborne, *Conversations with Von Krajan*, op. cit., 48.

[46] ibid., 118.

[47] Marcia Davenport, op. cit., 128.

[48] Gerald Stein, 'Giulini: On Preparation, Rehearsal and Performance' in *The Instrumentalist* (October, 1980).

Willem Mengelberg, George Grantham Bain Collection, Library of Congress

Erich Kleiber, George Grantham Bain Collection, Library of Congress

performances when one has so many rehearsals. Certainly there is no trick to it, for the oftener one plays a thing through, the better it goes, and even the poorest conductors profit from this. But there is a trick to feeling the need for a tenth rehearsal during the ninth rehearsal because one still hears many things that can become better, *because one still knows something to say in the tenth rehearsal.* This is exactly the difference: a poor conductor often does not know what to do after the third rehearsal, he has nothing more to say, he is more easily satisfied, because he does not have the capacity for further discrimination, and because nothing in him imposes higher requirements. And this is the cause: the productive man conceives within himself a complete image of what he wishes to reproduce; the performance, like everything else that he bring forth, must not be less perfect than the image. Such re-creation is only slightly different from creation; virtually, only the approach is different.[49]

[49] *Style and Idea.*

13 On 'Standard Conducting Technique'

MOST BOOKS ON THE ART OF CONDUCTING, and most courses in conducting, concentrate a great deal on the so-called 'standard conducting technique,' in particular the 'patterns' which the conductor describes with his baton. Erich Leinsdorf suggests that this whole general concept of a conducting 'technique' had its origin in the European 'operatic routinier' conductor.

> The best of this breed are able, with little or no rehearsal, to hold a show together, steering it with imperturbable assurance past cliffs and narrows and through stormy passages into the safe harbor of the final curtain. These are the prototypes who pass for 'technicians of the baton,'[1] relying on the unequivocal clarity of their signals. At the opposite end of the scale is the conductor who at first sight seems awkward, whose every upbeat or start of a new tempo causes a minor nervous crisis—and who yet produces without fail performances of distinction.[2]

His final sentence seems to question whether this 'standard technique' has any real influence on the musical results. Peter Paul Fuchs, in a survey of major conductors, found nearly all professed to be unaware of their gestures and not particularly concerned.[3] And Steinberg observed,

> Both from my own experience and from the observations of others I learned that an orchestra simply does not care what kind of a diagram is beaten before their noses.[4]

These observations clearly raise the question whether there is any real musical function in the so-called 'standard conducting technique.'

[1] Wagner also wrote a humorous account of the 'virtuoso of the baton' of the opera house. See William Ashton Ellis, *Wagner's Prose Works* (New York: Broude), VII, 114. The musically uninformed layman often thinks that the essential job of the conductor is to 'keep the players together.'

[2] Erich Leinsdorf, *The Composer's Advocate* (New Haven: Yale University Press, 1981), 179.

[3] Peter Paul Fuchs, *The Psychology of Conducting* (New York: MCA, 1969), 134.

[4] Quoted in Carl Bamberger, *The Conductor's Art* (New York: McGraw-Hill, 1965), 305.

Does 'standard conducting technique' have a value?

Few important conductors have ever given much credit to this 'standard technique' which is taught in conducting books and courses. Furtwängler, for one, wrote,

> There is nowadays a conducting technique which is taught in books and is practiced everywhere—a standardized technique, as it were, which produces a standardized orchestral sound. It is the technique of routine whose aim is simply precision. Here something which should be a natural prerequisite to the proper leading of every orchestra is made into a final purpose, an end it itself.[5]

[5] ibid., 207

The traditional patterns, which show what Furtwängler called, the 'corners, the rhythmical intersections' of the music, are certainly elementary in and of themselves. Of the little skill required to do this, Hindemith once observed,

> Even the most refined technique of beating time requires scarcely more skill than a good percussion player needs for his job.[6]

[6] ibid., 237.

Likewise, the musical results also have little to do with the baton, as Leinsdorf points out.

> 'Technique' means *knowledgeable* technique, for it has little, if anything, to do with the stick.'[7]

[7] Erich Leinsdorf, op. cit., 179.

Most experienced conductors would probably agree that the chief value of the baton itself is simply clarity and precision.[8] This value can only be obtained, by the way, if the baton is pointed straight toward the orchestra, which results in a very concentrated visual point. A bent baton results in a swath of light rays and will not materially influence precision. This bent hand position is what one sees ninety-nine percent of the time because it results from the natural design of the hand [designed to swing in trees]. It nearly always follows that such conductors do not actually use the baton, but merely hold it as a kind of status symbol. By 'use it' we mean showing everything with the tip of the stick.

[8] See, for example, Bruno Walter, *Of Music and Music-Making* (New York: Norton, 1957), 88ff, and Peter Paul Fuchs, op. cit., 24.

Conductors who do not have the technique to actually use the baton often feel more at ease not using one at all. There have been famous conductors who have conducted without a baton. Fuchs reported that when Ormandy was asked why he returned to using a baton, after not using one for many years, that he answered that his physician assured him it would add five years to his life. Ormandy told me a different story. It is a tradition in Europe that, as a courtesy, the orchestra will put a baton on the conductor's stand. Ormandy told me that when guest conducting in Europe, he saw the baton lying there and in a 'spur of the moment' decision simply picked it up and used it, continuing to use one thereafter.

I, myself, conducted for a number of years without a baton, believing I could be more expressive. But it was attending a concert by Solti in Chicago that I became convinced that there were things I could not do without a baton.

In any case, most perceptive musicians conclude that it is not the baton, and its associated technique, that communicates with the orchestra, but the entire body of the conductor. Charles Gounod, for example, in a discussion of conducting, wrote,

> It is an error to think that the conductor can make himself entirely understood by means of the baton or the bow which he holds in his hand. His whole demeanor should instruct and animate those who obey him. His attitude, his physiognomy, his glance should prepare the musicians for that which is demanded of them; his expression should cause them to anticipate his intentions, and should enlighten the executants ... In short, the conductor is the ambassador of the master's thought; he is responsible for it to the artists and to the public, and *ought to be* the living expression, the faithful mirror, the incorruptible depositary of it.[9]

[9] Charles Gounod, *Memoires d'un Artiste* (Paris, 1896).

Georg Solti also emphasized the importance of the use of the rest of the body, and not just the baton, for communicating with the orchestra. In a discussion of studying Mahler's music with Bruno Walter, he observed,

> Walter had a strange, not very clear beat, but he was proof that the beat is not an essential part of a conductor. You are conducting with your eyes and with your soul.[10]

[10] Sir Georg Solti, *Memoirs* (New York: Knopf, 1997), 114.

In another place, he adds,

> If your imagination is clear, then you will communicate with the orchestra even if your beat and technique are not first-rate ...
>
> The inexplicable miracle of conducting is that the body, eyes and soul of a conductor transfer something intangible and unique to an orchestra.[11]

[11] ibid., 207.

Leopold Stokowski made a similar observation.

> Conducting is only to a small extent the beating of time—it is done far more through the eyes—still more it is done through a kind of inner communication between players and the conductor.[12]

[12] Quoted in Carl Bamberger, op. cit., 199.

The United States premiere of Mahler's Symphony No. 8 in E♭, with the Philadelphia Orchestra conducted by Leopold Stokowski.

It is this total body and eye communication which accounts for the success of some very famous earlier conductors who used very small and almost inconsequential baton patterns. Their conducting was done with the rest of the body. Sir Adrian Boult recalled hearing the legendary Nikisch conduct the Brahms C Minor Symphony in a performance which brought the audience to what he called 'white heat' and was the most thrilling performance he had ever heard. Yet, when it was over, he relates,

Arthur Nikisch, by Ernst Oppler

It occurred to me that Nikisch's hand had never been raised higher than the level of his face throughout the entire last movement. The long stick held by those tiny fingers almost buried beneath an enormous shirt-cuff had been really covering quite a small circle the whole time, though the range of expression had been so wide; and if the arm had ever been stretched to its full length, some catastrophe must have occurred, like an earthquake or the destruction of the building.[13]

Anyone who ever had the pleasure of hearing Fritz Reiner will recall the eruptions of sound he could obtain from the Chicago Symphony Orchestra with only the sudden outward movement of one finger. It is interesting, however, that Fuchs says a member of the Chicago Symphony Orchestra confided to him that it gave him 'physical agony' to hear rousing fortissimos while the conductor's (Reiner) beat never exceeded a radius of three inches.[14] If one recalls our earlier discussion of the genetic relationship of movement and music, such a confusion between eye and ear might indeed induce physical discomfort.

Another often mentioned with regard to very little physical activity while conducting, was Richard Strauss. Fuchs reports seeing Strauss conduct a great performance with the right hand only, and barely visable at that, and with the left hand permanently at his side.[15] Solti had a similar recollection.

> He moved with difficulty and could not see or hear well, but his small gestures and brilliant conducting technique communicated everything he wanted to the orchestra.[16]

Solti adds that Strauss criticized him for waving his arms so much. But Strauss' wife added that Strauss conducted that way as well, until warned not to by a doctor.[17]

We recall being present for the rehearsals on the occasion of the first return, after many years, of Stokowski to his former orchestra, the Philadelphia Orchestra. Stokowski, more than ninety years old, conducted only with his fingers, being too frail to use his arms, or even to stand. But these rehearsals were so charged with emotion due to the occasion, and the music, the Second Symphony of Mahler, that enormous emotional reactions erupted in the orchestra from hardly any movement at all. But these are exceptions, very rare exceptions, and should be considered as such.

[13] ibid., 216.

Fritz Reiner, George Grantham Bain Collection, Library of Congress

[14] Peter Paul Fuchs, op. cit., 67.

[15] ibid., 10.

[16] Sir Georg Solti, *Memoirs*, op. cit., 72.

[17] ibid., 80.

Most experienced conductors would no doubt agree that if there is a value to the traditional gestures and patterns, that value lies in direct proportion to the music itself. In other words, the patterns do not reflect any 'standard' science, but vary in size and character to reflect the stylistic and emotional meaning of the music. As Gounod expressed it above, the conducting gestures '*ought to be* the living expression, the faithful mirror, the incorruptible depositary of [the music].' This is what Arnold Schönberg saw in Mahler's gestures as a conductor.

> Never a movement which was not exactly consistent with its cause! It was just as large as it had to be; it was executed with temperament, with life, energetically, powerfully, for temperament is the executive of conviction, and it will never be inactive ... To emulate him means always to be as one's own feelings dictate.[18]

[18] *Style and Idea.*

Felix Weingartner also stressed the importance of the intimate relationship between the music itself and the gestures.

> Some conductors are reproached with making too many gestures ... A pose of assumed quiet is however just as repellent. In our music there are, thank God, moments when the conductor must let himself go if he has any blood in his veins. An excess of movement is therefore always better than its opposite, since—at any rate as a rule,—it indicates temperament, without which there is no art ... The expression of each passage will generate an appropriately great or small motion of the baton.[19]

[19] Felix Weingartner, op. cit., 44.

Peter Paul Fuchs wrote of this same principle, that the gesture must reflect the music and not a 'standard technique.'

> If the conductor's gestures are to inspire the musicians with the proper expression, then the expression should in some way be found in the gestures themselves.[20]

[20] Peter Paul Fuchs, op. cit., 63.

He also quotes Giorgio Polacco, 'one of the best known opera conductors,' in a comment which is relative to the brain–body relationship which we have discussed in the previous chapter.

> To teach conducting is nonsense. If a man has musical talent, has mastered the score and knows exactly what he wants from the performers, his hand will follow his intentions without difficulty.[21]

[21] ibid., 9.

Before continuing, we must mention here that some distinguished conductors follow the practice of fully accommodating gesture to emotion during rehearsal, but are deliberately more restrained in concert. Toscanini was of this school. Accounts of him in rehearsal depict an entirely different conductor than that seen by the public. One describes him as 'uninhibitedly vigorous,' even stamping his feet.[22] Another reports him cueing the strings 'like lashes of a whip (in a Mozart symphony!).'[23]

[22] B. H. Haggin, *Conversations with Toscanini* (Garden City: Doubleday, 1959), 64.

[23] Marcia Davenport, *Too Strong for Fantasy* (New York: Scribner's, 1967), 193.

Can conducting gestures be planned or practiced?

Oscar Levant (1906–1972) once uttered the witty description of Leonard Bernstein, 'He uses music as an accompaniment to his conducting.'[24] George Szell (1897–1970) once observed,

[24] *The Memoirs of an Amnesiac* (1965).

> Conductors must give unmistakable and suggestive signals to the orchestra—not choreography to the audience.[25]

[25] Quoted in *Newsweek* (January 28, 1963).

Comments such as these suggest that some conductors think about gestures as something independent and apart from the music itself, that they think of 'choreography.' I regard such comments as demeaning to the profession, for no conductor worthy of the name would find his choreography more interesting than his music. Bernstein, in particular, has been unfairly criticized in my opinion. I never saw a gesture of his that was not expressive of the music. I recall one occasion in Vienna, when he was conducting the Beethoven *Missa Solemnis*. At one climax, Bernstein (who was a very short man) leaped into the air well above the podium. In the moment, I regarded it as perfectly expressive.

On the other hand, there is a curious school of conducting in the United States at the moment which is based on a negative psychology which theorizes that by conducting smaller patterns you force the players to watch these patterns more closely. This is undoubtedly true, but at a dear price—for it teaches the players to use their eyes in rehearsal instead of their ears. Furthermore, any such philosophy by which the conductor concentrates on *technique itself*, is nothing more than mannerism. We wonder if any conductor can think about technique while conducting and still be deeply involved in the music itself.

Sometimes one hears a statement similar to one once made by Josef Krips, who is said to have observed, 'a conductor who has learned not to interfere with the playing of the orchestra is already a pretty good conductor.'[26] Taken at face value, this is also a kind of mannerism of the worse kind. But we regard all such statements as facetious.

[26] Peter Paul Fuchs, op. cit., 14.

Rehearsal planning

The conductor who works in the educational environment might be surprised to learn of the precise planning of rehearsals far into the future by professional conductors. When at Covent Garden, Solti kept a detailed rehearsal calendar for two years ahead.[27] When we were in Philadelphia, in 1967–1968, each member of the orchestra was given a published pocket calendar for the *following* year with not only the exact times of rehearsal, but the repertoire to be rehearsed each day.

[27] Sir Georg Solti, op. cit., 131.

There is some value to this beyond the obvious practical considerations. We have often encouraged students to experiment with a plan such as the following. Suppose for the next concert you have ten two-hour rehearsals and you will program Schwantner's *And the Mountains Rising Nowhere*, Maslanka's *A Child's Garden of Dreams*, the Persichetti *Symphony* and Husa's *Music for Prague 1968*. The question is how many of these twenty hours to give each work. So, at first you might put on paper,

Schwantner	5
Maslanka	5
Persichetti	5
Husa	5

But, you realize the Maslanka is a much longer composition than the other three, so you alter the hours to read,

Schwantner	4
Maslanka	8
Persichetti	4
Husa	4

Now it is apparent that you can't completely rehearse either the Persichetti or the Husa in four hours. So now you decide,

Schwantner	4
Maslanka	6
Persichetti	5
Husa	5

We still regard the Husa as questionable, so Persichetti must yield to Husa. Thus we arrive at,

Schwantner	4
Maslanka	6
Persichetti	4
Husa	6

Now we realize, before the first rehearsal, that we are going to have to work rapidly when rehearsing Persichetti. We will limit where we stop to talk and we will allow the process of playing the work itself to permit the more obvious problems to 'solve themselves.'

Next we encourage the student to actually block out the twenty hours, say in half-hour segments. So we will plan for the first day to rehearse the Persichetti first movement the first half-hour, followed by Maslanka, etc. With a little experience, one can actually post the schedule several weeks in advance and feel perfectly comfortable in having done so.

There is, first, the obvious advantage in the choice-making in the above illustration, and in realizing, and deciding, in advance where time must be given and where not. But in having gone through this process one finds an even more compelling advantage. Somehow a kind of internal rehearsal clock gets implanted in the brain and one will feel vividly on any given day whether a particular composition is ahead of schedule or behind. And if one composition is taking longer than expected, the chart permits an invaluable means of determining where adjustments must be made.

There will never be enough rehearsal time! Even in former days when conductors could demand more rehearsals than is possible today, they never felt they had what they needed. The explanation for this is very simple: the conductor has an idealized concept, the perfect performance, while he must in fact come to terms with the sure fallibility of human nature. We might as well state it in the form of a rule: There will never be enough rehearsal time to create a perfect performance. Therefore every conductor must learn where to compromise, making sure the available time will be well invested. The more detailed thinking the conductor can do before rehearsal, the more economically he can use his time, even in the first rehearsal.

In this regard we must raise the question of the philosophy of 'reading through' a composition at the beginning of the first rehearsal. Many fine conductors, including Solti,[28] believe strongly in this practice. The primary reason for taking the time to do this is usually given as 'to give the player's an idea of the piece,' or something of that nature. This, in our opinion, is a mistake. What really happens is that the players have implanted in their ears the very worst image of the composition, with poor balances and a host of technical problems. Further, the question might be raised whether the players, being absorbed in sight-reading, really hear much of anything the first time through.

There is a great price paid for this practice. Each composition will have a final number of minutes of rehearsal, whatever that amount of time turns out to be. The result is that the time taken at the beginning to 'read,' becomes time taken from the total. Thus it turns out that time is really lost from the other end, time that could have been used for final polish. Therefore these minutes devoted to 'reading' are the most expensive minutes of all and will always, in our view, detract from the final result.

We encourage, instead, the practice of beginning the very first rehearsal with all the intensity and musicality of a performance. Even if we end up only playing a minute or two before stopping, that intensity and musicality will draw in the player, will reveal immediately to him how his part relates to what he hears and makes it possible for him to make changes and corrections on his own.

[28] ibid., 74, 181.

Part V
On Performance And The Public

14 Regarding Performance

ALTHOUGH ACCOUNTS OF CONTEMPLATIVE LISTENERS are as old as Western European literature, it is only with the Renaissance that one begins to read of the kind of thoughtful advance planning associated with modern concerts. Baldassare Castiglione (1478–1529), a diplomat for the duke of Urbino and popes Leo X and Clement VII, was the author of one of the most famous books of the Renaissance, *The Courtier* (*Il Cortigiano*). This famous book of etiquette recommends an aesthetic environment for art music: a relaxed atmosphere, when no one has pressing business at hand, when the listeners are in the proper mood, and when ladies are present. The gentleman only sponsors private performances, not before large audiences or the common people.

Baldassare Castiglione, by Raphael, 1514–15

[1] *The Courtier*, trans., George Bull (New York: Penguin Books, 1967), II, 120ff

> Then as to the occasions when these various kinds of music should be performed, I would instance when a man finds himself in the company of dear and familiar friends, and there is no pressing business on hand. But above all, the time is appropriate when there are ladies present; for the sight of them softens the hearts of those who are listening, makes them more susceptible to the sweetness of the music, and also quickens the spirit of the musicians themselves. As I have already said, one should avoid playing in the presence of a large number, especially of the common people.[1]

A particularly interesting document is associated with the famous Baïf Academy in Paris, chartered under Charles IX in 1570. The statutes regarding the performances by its member-musicians deal with rehearsal requirements as well as personal issues such as restrictions against quarrels and fighting amongst members—within one hundred feet of the concert site! Some of the most interesting language in this document is addressed to the audience members of these private concerts. When performances are underway, the listeners must not speak, whisper, nor make any noise. No one can enter during a song, but must await its conclusion. Interestingly enough, the listeners were not to approach the musicians in the private place where they prepared before the performances.

All this brings us to the point that the modern conductor must take some responsibility over the environment in which the concert takes place. A concert is not an entertainment event but something much more spiritual in character and everything surrounding the concert affects this quality: the setting of the stage, the hall, the lighting, what the players wear, etc. Of particular importance is how the conductor begins each composition, how he frames and establishes the character of the music even before the first tone is sounded.

Solti speaks of the discomfort of the audience which has to listen to someone talking before a performance. 'People go to hear music, not to listen to speeches,'[2] he reminds his readers. This is actually a very important psychological, and even physiological, issue. We have seen many concerts where the conductor, erroneously believing he was making music more palatable to the audience, introduced each work with lengthy comments. Physiologically this only makes it difficult for the listener to shift gears to listen to music and we guarantee that any musical fragments pointed out beforehand, such as 'later the composer presents this upside down,' will never be heard by the listener—nor should they. We want the listener to be caught up in the emotional meaning of the music, not in rational concepts which have nothing to do with the purpose of listening to music, as we have repeatedly stressed in this book.

Even worse is the conductor who comes out at the beginning of a concert and wanders around the stage, whispering little things to players who giggle. This kind of 'inside humor' is very offensive to the audience.

Within the general context of the environment, there are important acoustic realities which the conductor may or may not have much control over. One only begins to find discussion of this problem during the Baroque. Roger North suggests that the listener needs to be a certain distance from the music, although unfortunately he does not elaborate on this idea. This occurs to him as he is objecting to the difficulty the listener has in hearing fast, multi-part instrumental works such as fugues, or fugal allegros.

[2] Georg Solti, *Memoirs* (New York: Knopf, 1997), 101.

Perhaps an ear placed in the middle of the performers may distinguish somewhat, but at a decent position, the sum is a musical din, and no better; and music, like pictures, ought to have a just distance, or else the parts it consists of, which in all entertainments ought to be perceptible, will blend as in a mist.[3]

Francis Bacon observes that sounds are better if one's mind is concentrated on only one sense: hearing. Therefore he suggests that music sounds better at night than during the day.[4] It is for this reason why we wear black clothes for classical concerts; colors would distract the listener by introducing a stimulus for another sense, the eye.

Charles Gounod raised the question of tempo, relative to the hall. He believed that tempi should go slower in a large hall than a smaller one.[5] William Finn, the choral conductor, also emphasizes this point, as well as the question of whether various concert halls are themselves sensitive to specific keys.[6] We once conducted in a sixteenth-century hall in Austria which resonated vibrantly to each E♭ major chord as it sounded.

The above issues are all relative to the perspective of the listener, which is also an interesting problem with respect to recordings. Eugene Ormandy once told me that for recordings one should always perform slow movements at a faster tempo than one would use in a live performance, the argument being that the listener at home would be distracted and would not have the attention span necessary for contemplative listening to a slow movement. Von Karajan once mentioned that the recording engineers tried to get him to use faster tempi in general for recordings. He called the idea nonsense and refused.[7] Haggin, during his conversations with Toscanini, found that the maestro, while pleased with his perception of tempo in concert, was often displeased with his tempi when hearing his own recordings.[8]

Of course, few composers give thought to acoustics or the environment of the performance. Conductors are left to struggle with a number of additional problems which affect the performance, such as the nature and size of group, hall, acoustics and the size of audience. An early exception was Anton Reicha, who included an extraordinary handwritten note in the score of his Symphony for band (1815),[9] in which he discusses the nature of the performance site he had in mind,

---

[3] Quoted in John Wilson, *Roger North on Music* (London: Novello, 1959), 189.

[4] 'Natural History,' Section 230ff, in James Spedding, ed., *The Works of Francis Bacon* (Cambridge: Cambridge University Press, 1869). In Bacon's utopian study, *The New Atlantis*, he presents an extraordinary proposal for an acoustic studio, a 'sound-house.'

[5] Charles Gounod, *Memoires d'un Artiste* (Paris, 1896).

[6] William J. Finn, *The Conductor Raises his Baton* (London: Dobson, 1946), 75, 62, 69, 71. He also discusses the influence on acoustics by such things as floral displays.

[7] Richard Osborne, *Conversations with Von Karajan* (New York: Harper & Row, 1989), 128.

[8] B. H. Haggin, *Conversations with Toscanini* (Garden City: Doubleday, 1959), 18.

[9] 'Musique pour célébrer la memoire das grands hommes et des grands événements.'

the space between players, exact adherence to the instrumentation—together with his plea for a good conductor who will study the score!

Peter Paul Fuchs has written at some length about the psychological frame of mind of the conductor immediately before a concert.[10] He acknowledges that the conductor will always have some apprehension, since he knows that no performance is ever fully rehearsed. On the other hand, we, and we would suppose most conductors as well, have found that there is great compensation in the fact that for once one truly has one hundred percent attention and concentration from the ensemble, a state which can sometimes produce miracles. For the period before the concert Fuchs cautions the conductor against such things as drinking, or having arguments which might detract from his concentration. This is a time to gather his thoughts together, to prepare himself for the 'holy office.' We might add that the same is necessary before ordinary rehearsals. A school conductor should make every effort to keep the hour before rehearsal free.

In the final seconds before the first down-beat, Fuchs stresses that the conductor must have no thought of the audience, or how he might look. He must appear as if saying to the orchestra, 'this is our great moment: now we shall make beautiful music together.' The highest priority is to 'concentrate completely on the intended sound of the first measures of music he is about to conduct.'

Leonard Bernstein, writing of these final moments before the concert, found a magical moment, a moment when the audience is ready, the players are focused and the conductor has brought his mental and spiritual forces to a point of concentration.

[10] Peter Paul Fuchs, *The Psychology of Conducting* (New York: MCA, 1969), 71ff.

> How can I describe to you the magic of the moment of beginning a piece of music? There is only one possible fraction of a second that feels exactly right for starting. There is a wait while the orchestra readies itself and collects its powers; while the conductor concentrates his whole will and force toward the work in hand; while the audience quiets down, and the last cough has died away. There is no slight rustle of a program book; the instruments are poised and—bang! That's it. One second later, it is too late, and the magic has vanished.[11]

[11] Quoted in Carl Bamberger, *The Conductor's Art* (New York: McGraw-Hill, 1965), 271.

Also at this final moment, the young conductor, in particular, may find a natural enemy in stage-fright, for it has the capacity to rob him of the ability to concentrate fully on the music. Nothing comes to the conductor's aid so much as knowing the score thoroughly. Somehow it never helps with these kinds of problems to be told that every artist experiences them, but it is surprising to imagine Toscanini having this problem!

> I am always so nervous when I have to step before the orchestra—even after all these years—it is as though the first time I conduct![12]

[12] ibid., 310.

It helped me in my younger days to remember that what we call stage-fright is actually a hormone which is released by the brain into the body to enable the body to do its best work in a time of stress. Therefore it is a good sign; we should be alarmed if we *don't* have this feeling.

Now the music begins and from this moment on the conductor functions in a state of concentration which very few other professions ever demand. He must not only see in advance both the whole and the details of an experiential work of art, see those things not notated on paper and be responsive to all these things and communicate them to the audience. But, even more than this, the conductor must mediate whatever comes as a result of the work being *live*. It might be more accurate to say, *alive*, for even the passage of a few hours of time causes each player, as well as the conductor himself, to be in fact different people, people more mature, with a different experiential perspective. Thus live music is truly *alive*, existing only at that precise moment in that precise way and never again in that way.

The conductor may *feel* at this moment that some things should be played differently than in rehearsal for very good musical reasons, which have their foundation in the fact that this is a truly *live* moment, unique in all of its circumstances which in particular include the acoustics and the audience. Significant changes will be rare, if one has done his duty in score study and reflection. We should confide one of these rare occasions, in which we suddenly understood the composer's intent for a particular passage while walking to the concert, requiring, as a matter of loyalty to the composer, to perform it differently 'on the spot' without the opportunity to warn the ensemble. We were guest conducting the United States Army Field Band, in the performance of an Offenbach overture. Near the end is a passage where a measure is repeated a number of times, which we first took to mean an implied *crescendo*. Walking to the concert site, it suddenly seemed embarrassingly conspicuous that what the composer really expected here was an accelerando. With a fine ensemble at hand, it was, of course, no problem accomplishing this during the concert.

Because the performance will *never* resemble the last rehearsal, some conductors find they listen entirely differently to the ensemble during a concert. Sometimes, as in the case of Josef Krips, this takes on the character of being almost detached from the performance in some respects.

> In concert, provided that a piece has been well rehearsed, I conduct it without really listening to the playing. It is my feeling that if I listen closely and control every note that is being played, I am *behind* the orchestra. In reality, a conductor during the performance of a symphonic piece *cannot* listen! He *experiences* the music.[13]

[13] Fuchs, op. cit., 135.

Another important aspect of the music being live, is that it exists in time, in present tense, with each fragment of its existence forming delicate psychological relationships related to time itself. As Fuch points out,

> The slightest slip of concentration on [the conductor's] part can ruin a performance, not necessarily in the sense of bringing it to a dead stop, but by disturbing the delicate balance which is the essence of any artistically viable interpretation. The parts of a symphonic performance fit together like the pieces of a jigsaw puzzle: you cannot change an element without causing a dozen others to be displaced as a consequence.[14]

[14] ibid., 70.

When we were a student at the Akademie für Musik in Vienna, Hans Swarowsky used to emphasize the belief widely held in Vienna at that time that in the Classical repertoire there were specific tempo relationships between movements. In consequence, if one began the first movement slightly too slow, then all the following movements would have to be slower, and perhaps the following piece, and the intermission longer, etc., et. al. It represents a very heavy burden for that first downbeat!

The conductor's goals

An anonymous fourteenth-century English poem, 'The Pearl,' contains a passage which describes the goals of a 'full and clear performance' as including music of noble character and being in tune.[15] Those are still pretty good goals to aim for. Certainly, a fine conductor does have performance goals with regard to technical elements such as intonation. With regard to these kind of technical achievements, the standard should be so high that the conductor will never feel he has succeeded. It was in this context that the famous Baroque singing teacher, Tosi, offered this timeless advice:

> Whoever does not aspire to the first rank, begins already to give up the second, and little by little will be content with the lowest.[16]

Schumann made a similar observation.

> He who sets limits to himself, will always be expected to remain within them.[17]

Peter Paul Fuchs asks, 'What are the specific elements in an orchestra performance that make one feel it is great?'[18] He defines, by the way, a *great* performance as one in which the experience of the listener is 'overwhelmed amazement,' as compared to a *good* performance in which one feels 'grateful satisfaction.' Fuchs points to such elements as tonal beauty and clarity, but we believe on this subject he has failed to make clear the most important point. In the end it is not the performance by the orchestra which is important, but the music which it communicates. The important Renaissance philosopher, Pietro Aretino (1492–1556), went right to the heart of the matter when he stated that neither the gift nor the skill is of any importance without heart.[19]

The conductor's one great contribution to the concert lies in his role, and duty, to achieve the communication of the emotional meaning of the music, its *melos*, to the listener. Only the conductor and the performers can bring the music of the composer to life. This clear fact brought even the egotistical Wagner to his knees.

[15] Anonymous, 'The Pearl,' trans., Mary Hillmann (College of Saint Elizabeth Press, 1959), 877ff.

[16] P. F. Tosi, *Observations on the Florid Song* (London: Wilcox, 1743), VI, xxiv.

[17] *Diary*.

[18] Peter Paul Fuchs, op. cit., 120ff.

[19] Letter to Massiminiano Stampa, in Thomas Chubb, *The Letters of Pietro Aretino* (New Haven: Shoe String Press [Archon Books], 1967), 39.

> My belief is that the *performer* is the real, true artist. All that we create as poets and composers expresses a *wish* but not an *ability*: only the performance itself reveals that ability or *art*.[20]

[20] Letter to Franz Liszt, July 20, 1850.

But there is more to the conductor's preparation to perform this role than score study and highly disciplined rehearsal techniques.

> The value of a conductor's artistic achievements is to a high degree dependent upon his human qualities and capacities; the seriousness of his moral convictions, the richness of his emotional life, the breadth of his mental horizon, in short, his personality has a decisive effect on his achievements; if his personality is unable to fulfill the spiritual demands of the works he performs, his interpretations will remain unsatisfactory although their musical execution may be exemplary.[21]

[21] Bruno Walter, *Of Music and Music-Making* (New York: Norton, 1957), 106.

Why do great conductors place such emphasis on the development of spiritual and humanistic qualities?[22] They would answer, I'm sure, that these qualities are necessary if the conductor is to be able to see behind the notes on paper and perceive and understand the real experiential message of the great composer. All of which is prerequisite to the paramount goal of the conductor, the communication of the *melos*, as Weingartner points out.

[22] Can a composer who is a superficial person compose music which rises above a superficial level? I think not.

> How feeble is the applause one usually hears after an indifferently played classical symphony, in comparison with the uncontrollable enthusiasm aroused by an artistic interpretation of the same work! Then the masterpiece appears in its true form; to be able to make this true form visible, however, is the sacred task of the conductor, and to have fulfilled it is his only honorable—nay, his *only possible*—glory.[23]

[23] Felix Weingartner, *On Conducting* (New York: Kalmus), 19.

Certainly we must reject without discussion any such notions as those advanced by Gunther Schuller, who, among the many bitter comments in his book on conducting, makes the extraordinary claim, indeed he calls it a *fact*, 'that in the concert hall most listeners are most intent on *watching* a conductor than just *hearing* the music.'[24] Anyway, it's not a bad idea for the audience to watch the conductor. Anyone who is familiar with the ancient, and truly genetic, association between movement and music, would understand that one important

[24] Gunther Schuller, *The Compleat Conductor* (New York: Oxford University Press, 1997), 539.

aspect of the fine conductor is that he is the *visible* form of the emotional character of the music, much more so than the motion of the violin bows, for example.

In a further, undocumented bit of nonsense, Schuller states,

> And it is well known that the average listener hears mostly, or only, that which he sees.

This would certainly come as very surprising news to the recording industry, which sells huge quantities of recordings to persons who only listen to them and see nothing!

We also believe Wagner was mistaken when he stated that the audience was incapable of distinguishing between a poor performance and a poor composition.[25]

[25] William Ashton Ellis, *Wagner's Prose Works* (New York: Broude), IV, 291.

A word should also be said about about bowing because it may also be part of the environment of the performance in which the emotions of the audience are involved. We might take a lesson from our brothers of the stage. The fine actor who plays Hamlet will still be Hamlet for two or three curtain calls; only for the third or fourth curtain call does he become Richard Burton, or whomever. The purpose of this is to allow the audience to gradually come down from the high of their emotional involvement. The worst opposite example of this is the cinema which immediately turns on the lights at the end of a sad movie in their attempt to refill the hall with new bodies. Everyone is sitting there embarrassed, crying when the lights suddenly come on. In the case of the conductor, perhaps it is not appropriate after the last sounds of a work like *Apotheosis of this Earth*, to suddenly spring around and give the audience a great smile when you bow. Perhaps we too should remain in character; to do otherwise is to give the audience the impression that the deep emotions you were previously communicating were only a pretense.

Beyond this, the best looking bow is one that is *low* and *slow*. This is important. Most of us are by nature modest and we will feel the tendency to make a modest bow, such as a slight nodding of the head. Unfortunately, the audience takes this for exactly the reverse; to them it appears as aloofness! Some conductors express their modesty by giving a series of rapid, short bows. These do not look modest, rather only perfunctory and again not appreciated by the viewers. We might add that in Europe there is a tradition regarding how to bow and it is taught to music students.

We must also remember there is a social expectation involved here. Just as we expect applause, no matter what, the audience expects a sincere gesture in return. You are also thanking the audience as the representative of your ensemble when you bow. That alone should be sufficient argument for sincerity.

The audience

> Music remains meaningless noise unless it touches a receiving mind.[26]
> [Paul Hindemith]

[26] Paul Hindemith, *A Composer's World* (Garden City: Doubleday, 1961), 18.

> There is no such thing as music divorced from the listener. Music as such is unfulfilled until it has penetrated our ears.[27]
> [Yehudi Menuhin]

[27] *Theme and Variations* (1972).

They are, of course, correct. Music has little purpose without a listener, and the same is true for sound itself. The correct answer for the old riddle, 'If a tree falls in a forest where there is no one present to hear it, does it make a sound?,' is no. Sounds, like colors, in fact do not exist except in our minds.

History is rich in illustrations, and has long recognized, the role of the listener in music. Many tomb paintings of ancient Egypt show people listening to the musicians and the active role of the listener is equally vivid in the oldest of Western European literature, that of Homer. Homer makes clear, in this case, that the audience is listening in silence, and indeed one is moved to tears and therefore requests the change to music of a lighter character.

> For them the famous minstrel was singing, and they sat in silence listening; and he sang of the return of the Achaeans—the woeful return from Troy which Pallas Athene laid upon them. And from her upper chamber the daughter of Icarius, wise Penelope, heard his wondrous song, and she went down the high stairway from her chamber ... She stood by the doorpost of the well-built hall, holding before her face her shining veil ... Then she burst into tears, and spoke to the divine minstrel:

'Phemius, many other things thou knowest to charm mortals, deeds of men and gods which minstrels make famous. Sing them one of these, as thou sittest here, and let them drink their wine in silence. But cease from this woeful song which ever harrows the heart in my breast, for upon me above all women has come a sorrow not to be forgotten.'[28]

[28] A. T. Murray, trans., *The Odyssey* (London: Heinemann, 1960), I, 325ff.

There is a very interesting passage in Ecclesiasticus, one of the books left out by the redactor of the Old Testament, which reminds us of Aristotle's complaint that the musical entertainers at banquets prevented good conversation. Here, however, it is the reverse: don't talk while the music is being performed, for the music is the highpoint of a good banquet.

> Pour not out words where there is a musician, and show not forth wisdom out of time.
> A concert of music in a banquet of wine is as a signet of carbuncle set in gold.[29]

[29] Ecclesiasticus 32:1ff.

As music became more emotionally complicated during the late Middle Ages, in contrast to the cold, mathematical contrapuntal church music, descriptions of the listener become common. A frequent comment is that the power of music makes one forget everything, even one's self. Even in Dante's *Purgatorio*, we read,

> He thereupon began to sing, so sweetly
> That I hear the sweetness of it still inside me.
> My master and I, and all those people
> Standing there with him, seemed so delighted
> That nothing else appeared to touch our minds.
> We were all transfixed there, listening …
>   …
> From his mouth, and in such tender tones,
> That it made me lose awareness of myself.[30]

Statue of Dante Alighieri outside the Uffizi Gallery, Florence

[30] *Purgatorio*, II and VIII.

The Minnesinger classic, *Tristan*, by Gottfried von Strassburg, also mentions this. When Tristan played and sang,

> Many a man sitting or standing there forgot his very name. Hearts and ears began to play the fool and desert their rightful paths.[31]

[31] Gottfried von Strassburg, *Tristan*, trans., Arthus Hatto (Harmondsworth: Penguin Books, 1960), 89ff.

And again, Tristan was singing so 'enchantingly' and 'most marvelous' that the listeners, 'were rooted to the spot as long as he harped and sang.'[32] Others come to the shore to listen, Tristan plays, and 'he moved them all to pity.'[33]

In a performance of a song, in Boccaccio's *The Decameron*, in the seventh story of the tenth day, we find the listeners enchanted, still and attentive.

32 ibid., 141.

33 ibid., 143.

> These words Minuccio forthwith set to a soft and plaintive melody, such as the matter thereof required ... King Pedro being still at table, he was bidden by him to sing somewhat to his viol. Thereupon he fell to singing the aforesaid song so sweetly that all who were in the royal hall appeared enchanted, so still and attentive were they all to listen.[34]

34 *Decameron*, John Payne, trans., (Berkeley: University of California Press, 1982), II, 739.

Finally, at the end of his *The Decameron* Boccaccio correctly observes that the receptive listener is part of the chain of aesthetics.

Giovanni Boccaccio, by Raffaello Sanzio Morghen after Vincenzo Gozzini, 1822

> Again, such as they are, these stories, like everything else, can work both harm and profit, according to the disposition of the listener.[35]

35 ibid., II, 796.

By way of contrast, in one of his stories Boccaccio presents a musician who cannot find the necessary inspiration, resulting in listeners who are clearly not caught up in the experience.

> At the same time they lent their ears to Ameto's song; but it seemed to him as if the gods had not given him heed—for [the listeners] hindered him with pleasant quips, jeering now and then.[36]

36 *L'Ameto*, trans., Judith Serafini-Sauli (New York: Garland, 1985), 42.

Nowhere in Medieval literature do we find a composer so fervently interested in the reaction of the listener as we do in Machaut's 'Remede de Fortune.'

> How do you like it? What do you say? ... What do you think of my song? ... What do you say? ... Won't you tell me if I sing well or poorly?[37]

37 Guillaume de Machaut, 'Remede de Fortune,' trans., James Wimsatt and William Kibler (Athens: The University of Georgia Press, 1988), 280.

In speaking of how the eye takes in an entire painting at once, Leonardo provides an analogy with music whereby he reveals a striking awareness of the experience of the contemplative listener.

And from painting which serves the eye, the noblest sense, arises harmony of proportions; just as many different voices joined together and singing simultaneously produce a harmonious proportion which gives such satisfaction to the sense of hearing that the listeners remain spellbound with admiration as if half alive.[38]

An account of Cavalieri's lost *La Disperazione di Fileno* mentions that the singing of Archilei 'moved the audience to tears.'[39]

The poetry of Sannazaro (1456–1530) often suggests the contemplative listener, a prime requisite for Art Music. Even a poor singer, such as Ergasto in *Arcadia*, could move his listeners,

> though with his weak voice and his wretched tones he many times moved us to sighing.[40]

One listener, after experiencing 'a most intense pleasure,' was moved to tears.[41] In another place, even though hearing a song in a language not familiar, the music was heard 'by each man with the closest attention.' One, while the singing lasted, was 'profoundly absorbed, in a motionless and prolonged meditation.'[42]

In the *Don Quijote*, Cervantes (1547–1616), when Don Quijote and Sancho hear a well-trained singer, 'It filled them with wonder,' and they are described as 'listening carefully' as they heard a second song.[43] In another passage, Dorotea 'listened carefully' to a 'delicate, loving song.'[44] In one of his shorter novels, *The Illustrious Kitchen Maid*, Cervantes describes a singer who,

> sang in tone so melodious and captivating that it filled them with wonder and they could not choose but listen until the end.[45]

The listener is also often emphasized in the pastoral romances. In the first book of *Diana*, by Jorge de Montemayor (d. 1561), Sylvanus takes his bagpipe, plays on it a while and then sings 'with great sorrow and grief.' The listener, Syrenus,

> was not idle when Sylvanus was singing these verses, for with his sighs he answered the last accents of his words, and with his tears did solemnize that which he conceived [in the verses].[46]

---

[38] Quoted in Jean Paul Richter, ed., *The Literary Works of Leonardo da Vinci* (London: Phaidon, 1970), I, 59.

[39] Nino Pirrotta, in *Music and Culture in Italy from the Middle Ages to the Baroque* (Cambridge: Harvard University Press, 1984), 225.

[40] Ralph Nash, trans., *Jacopo Sannazaro, Arcadia & Piscatorial Eclogues* (Detroit: Wayne State University Press, 1966), 35.

[41] ibid., 117.

[42] ibid., 118ff.

[43] Miguel de Cervantes, *Don Quijote*, trans., Burton Raffel (New York: Norton, 1995), I, xxvii.

[44] ibid., I, xliii.

[45] *The Illustrious Kitchen Maid*, trans., Harriet de Onís, in *Six Exemplary Novels* (Great Neck: Barron's Educational Series, 1961), 268.

[46] Jorge de Montemayor, *Diana*, trans., Bartholomew Yong (1598), in Judith Kennedy, ed., *George of Montemayor's Diana and Gil Polo's Enamoured Diana* (Oxford: Clarendon Press, 1968), 15ff.

Another listener hears a singer's voice and 'awaked as it were out of a slumber, he gave attentive ear to the verses that she sang.'[47] Yet another singer, Arsileus, sang 'with so marvelous sweet grace and delectable voice, that he held all his listeners in a great suspense.'[48] Even Orpheus makes an appearance in this pastoral tale. First he sings while playing a harp and the listeners were so ravished they forgot everything.[49] Then he begins another song, 'such heavenly music that he suspended their amazed senses.'

During the Baroque, the German visitor, J. F. A. von Uffenbach, recorded his impressions of an oratorio performance given at one of the private male academies held in prince Ruspoli's palace in 1715.

> They performed a magnificent concert, or so-called oratorio, which so enraptured me that I was convinced that I had never heard anything of the kind so perfectly done before in my life ... Everyone listened so attentively to the excellent singers that not even a fly stirred ... Then the second half of the work was given, and that altogether the performance lasted some four hours.[50]

The careful observer of Baroque performance practice in Germany, Johann Mattheson, makes a wonderful observation on the listener.

> Whoever pays attention can see in the features of an attentive listener what he perceives in his heart.[51]

These examples will perhaps suffice in place of innumerable others. Ricardo Muti spoke of music as 'communion' between performer and public and any intrusion is sacrilegious.[52] This is why it is strictly forbidden for people to walk in or out of the auditorium while classical music is playing. Regarding the 'communion' between performer and listener, we once had a fine young Korean flutist who added the following thought as an endnote to a paper on performance practice.

> As a performer myself, I always try to listen to what the listeners want to hear in my playing. First I have to open ears in my mind to the listeners and let them know I'm ready for hearing them by smiling. While performing, if you can hear what they want to hear and follow their

[47] ibid., 54.

[48] ibid., 120ff.

[49] ibid., 143ff.

[50] Quoted in Malcolm Boyd, 'Rome: the Power of Patronage,' in *The Late Baroque Era* (Englewood Cliffs: Prentice Hall, 1994), 59.

[51] Johann Mattheson, *Der vollkommene Capellmeister* (1739), trans., Ernest Harris (Ann Arbor: UMI Research Press, 1981), I, 333, 52ff.

[52] Quoted in Norman Lebrecht, *The Maestro Myth* (New York: Citadel, 1993), 223.

will, then the performance will be an entirely different experience for you. That is how I enjoy my performances and my audiences' fabulous musical ideas![53]

Another form of audience participation is, of course, applause. Earlier composers were not at all offended by applause before the end of the composition, or even during a movement. Mozart, in fact, rewrote his 'Paris' Symphony in order to stimulate such applause. In a letter to his father, he explains,

> In the middle of the first Allegro was a passage which I knew could not fail to please. All in the audience were charmed by it, and there was great applause, but as I knew when I wrote it what an effect it would make, I brought it round an extra time at the end of the movement, with the same result, and so got my applause da capo.[54]

There a number of eyewitness accounts of such applause during a performance throughout the eighteenth and nineteenth centuries, frequently resulting in the repetition of arias or individual movements. But one must remember that not only were there no recordings, which allowed one to hear a favorite work again, but, since all music was live one did not hear music as frequently as one does today.

It was Wagner who brought these traditions to an end, instituting the tradition of applauding only at the end of a composition. Once, during a series of performances of *Parsifal*, he personally requested that the audience not applaud during the course of the performance. They did not, and so the following night Wagner appeared again explaining that it was OK to applaud at the end of each act.

It is the *listener*, not the score and not the performance, where the only meaningful concept of aesthetics in music can exist. This conforms exactly with the principles of aesthetics by Aristotle, who created this field of philosophy in his book on drama, *The Poetics*. After discussing all the elements (including music) which are necessary to a fine drama, he comes to the conclusion of his book but realizes that the end of all this is the impact on the observer. His subsequent discussion of the nature of the impact in different kinds of theater on the observer was the birth of aesthetics.

[53] Stacy Rim was her name.

[54] Quoted in Donald Tovey, *Essays in Musical Analysis* (London: Oxford University Press, 1959), VI, 22.

In music, we believe the question of aesthetics, the impact on, and the meaning for, the listener, is inseparable from the function and conditions of the performance of the music. We find four general classifications which characterize the nature of aesthetics in music.

I. Art Music

Art Music we believe is defined by four conditions, *all* of which *must always be present*. These are:

1. *Art music is inspired.* Art music is music in which it seems evident that the composer has made an honest attempt to communicate genuine feelings. Feelings, which may range from lofty and noble to superficial and vulgar, must be presumed to be generally recognizable in music, as they are in any other art form, including painting, sculpture, dance, and architecture. In Art Music, lofty and noble feelings are paramount. Due to the common genetically understood nature of emotions, it must also be understood that in music emotions or feelings can not be 'faked.' They will always be recognized as such by the contemplative listener.
2. *Art Music has no purpose other than the communication of its own aesthetic content.* Art Music is free of any purpose or function, save the spiritual communication of pure beauty.
3. *Art Music is that which enjoys a performance faithful to the intent of the composer.*
4. *Art Music must have a listener capable of contemplation.*

If any of these conditions are missing, the performance must result in a lesser aesthetic experience. For example, the Ninth Symphony of Beethoven played in a stadium, during the half-time of a professional football game, would fail for the lack of the presence of Condition Number Four. The same Symphony heard in a concert hall, but in a poor performance, not faithful to the intent of the composer, would fail for the lack of the presence of Condition Number Three.

II. Educational Music

Educational Music may or may not have the same conditions as Art Music, excepting Condition Number Two; it may or may not occur within an educational institution. Educational Music is didactic music, music which has the specific and *additional* aim to educate. In the strictest sense, if the *primary purpose* of Music is to educate, it cannot be Art Music—for Art Music has no secondary purpose.

III. Functional Music

Functional Music is music put at the service of something else. We include here, for example, all kinds of religious music, music for weddings, music for the military, and occupational music. Functional Music may share the same conditions as Art Music, excepting Condition Number Two.

One may ask, How can a Mozart Mass be called Functional Music, and not Art Music? If the observer were not contemplatively listening to the music, but were rather contemplating religious thoughts, then the Mozart Mass becomes merely a very high level of Functional Music. If, on the other hand, the observer is a contemplative listener of music, forgetting about religion, then the Mozart Mass is Art Music, but has failed in its purpose as church music.

IV. Entertainment Music

Entertainment Music is music with no object other than to please. It will always be missing Condition Four, the contemplative listener. For this reason, Entertainment Music may be inspired music, but the composer is unlikely to be inspired by lofty and noble emotions, knowing there will be no contemplative listener.

It is for these reasons that Entertainment Music can never be Art Music. But, one might protest, when a tired businessman goes to the opera at the end of his work day, is this not for him Art Music which is also a very high level form of Entertainment Music? Franz Josef of Austria once posed this very question. When Mahler was music director of the State Opera in Vienna, he once became frustrated because of the disruption of those arriving late. Therefore he began a policy of having all late arrivals placed in a separate room until the first intermission. When informed of this, the emperor was puzzled and observed, 'But after all, the theater is meant to be a pleasure.'[55]

[55] Quoted by Alma Mahler, Gustav Mahler (New York: Viking, 1969), 136ff.

The answer is no, Entertainment Music and Art Music can never be the same thing because of Condition Number Two: Art Music has no purpose other than the communication of its own aesthetic content. It is inconsistent with the nature of great art to have any extrinsic purpose, especially the purpose to amuse.

It is this fundamental characteristic of art music that it be without purpose, other than to express feeling, that Wagner addressed when he wrote,

> The highest principle of aesthetics, through it perceived, according to which being without purpose alone is beautiful, because, having a purpose in itself, in revealing its nature as lifted high above all vulgar ends it reveals at like time that to reach whose sight and knowledge alone makes ends of life worth following; whereas everything that serves an end is hideous, because neither its fashioner nor its onlooker can have aught before him save a disquieting conglomerate of fragmentary material, which is first to gain its meaning and elucidation from its employment for some vulgar need.[56]

[56] *Wagner's Prose Works*, op. cit., IV, 107ff. Later he observes that the State can never be part of high art because the State is only interested in purposeful ends.

The question of *how* music communicates from composer to performer to the audience was explained best by Socrates, using the brilliant analogy of the magnet.

> SOCRATES. The gift which you possess of speaking excellently about Homer is not an art, but, an inspiration; there is a divinity moving you, like that contained in the stone which Euripides calls a magnet, but which is commonly known as the stone of Heraclea. This stone not only attracts iron rings, but also imparts to them a similar power of attracting other rings; and sometimes you may see a number of pieces of iron and rings suspended from one another so as to form quite a long chain: and all of them derive their power of suspension from the original stone. In like manner the Muse first of all inspires men herself; and from these inspired persons a chain of other persons is suspended, who take the inspiration.
>
> ...
>
> Do you know that the spectator is the last of the rings which, as I am saying, receive the power of the original magnet from one another? Yourself, and the actor, are intermediate links, and the poet himself is the first of them.[57]

[57] *Ion*, 533d, 535e.

The aesthetic goal of this communication with the observer of drama was, for Aristotle, something he called 'catharsis.' It is probably the single most quoted sentence by Aristotle.

> A tragedy is the imitation of an action that is serious and also, as having magnitude, complete in itself; in language with pleasurable accessories, each kind brought in separately in the parts of the work; in a dramatic, not in a narrative form; with incidents arousing pity and fear, wherewith to accomplish its catharsis of such emotions.[58]

[58] *Poetics*, 1449b.24.

With regard to aesthetics, it is of course the famous heart of this definition, 'arousing pity and fear, wherewith to accomplish its catharsis of such emotions,' which interests us most and which is most directly applicable to the performance of music.

By 'pity,' he means empathy. He makes this clear when he defines this word in his book on rhetoric.

> Pity may be defined as a feeling of pain caused by the sight of some evil, destructive or painful, which befalls one who does not deserve it, and which we might expect to befall ourselves or some friend of ours, and moreover to befall us soon.

'Fear' goes beyond empathy with the action on the stage and becomes *personal*—what we see happening to the character on the stage might happen to us as well, if we make the same mistake. The play (or musical performance) which produces these effects reaches us in a deeper level than those arts we call entertainment. Entertainment we enjoy fully, but it never gets inside us, never reaches us at this deeper level. It is in the aesthetic work, when we experience 'pity and fear' that catharsis follows.

We sometimes explain this concept of catharsis to our students in an analogy with the cinema. We have all had the experience of going to the cinema with a group of friends and seeing a film in which, while it is running, we are totally involved—we laugh, we cry, etc. But, when it is over, it is over. We leave the theater talking about other subjects, friends, events in our lives, etc.

On the other hand, we have all had the experience of going to the cinema with a group of friends and seeing a film, but when it is over we leave the theater and no one talks! The impact of the film can stay with us for days or more.

The first is an entertainment experience. The second is an aesthetic experience—we have been reached on a deeper level.

A similar analogy could be made with musical performances. Some performances we applaud the accomplishments of the performers and go about our business, in other cases we are reached on a deeper level and something of the emotional experience stays with us. This is the fundamental distinction between the aesthetic and the entertainment in music. This is surely what Georg Solti had in mind, when he concluded,

> What you really remember is not the performance itself, but whether a performance touched you.[59]

[59] Georg Solti, op. cit., 211.

An extraordinary example of catharsis experienced by an entire audience may be found in a recollection by Marcia Davenport of a performance of the Verdi *Requiem* conducted by Toscanini, after which the entire audience silently got up and left without any applause.[60]

[60] Marcia Davenport, *Too Strong for Fantasy* (New York: Scribner's, 1967), 227ff.

All conductors have had experiences when the entire audience was transfixed by the music. These moments are our greatest reward. Similarly, all experienced conductors can 'feel' the level of attention by the audience even though the audience is behind the conductor's back. Sometimes, unfortunately, the audience's concentration suffers from circumstances and distractions over which the conductor has no control. One conductor, and one with a great deal of experience, who gave great weight during his concerts to the level of interest he perceived on the part of the audience behind him, was Sousa. If during the performance of some major work he concluded the audience was not interested he would simply stop and go on to a different composition. He did not wait for a conspicuous cadence, he made no explanation, he made no announcement of the new work, he just stopped and began a new composition.

15 On Programming

THE MOST COMMONLY HEARD ANSWER, when a conductor is questioned about the absence of quality music in his repertoire, is 'my audience will not let me play that kind of music.' This is a completely unfounded allegation, one which attempts to conceal the taste of the conductor and has nothing to do with the taste of the audience. So, before further discussion, we must set this superstition aside once and for all. The fact is that the audience, as a collective body, does not come to a concert *expecting* any particular music. They *do* come to a concert expecting a *concert*, a word which certainly carries its own connotations. We believe it is correct to say that all an audience really expects, or hopes for, in a concert is that it be good. One can find this expectation implied in a representative of the oldest literature of Western Europe, a fable by Aesop (620–560 BC) called, 'The Lyre Player.'

Statue of Aesop, Art Collection of Villa Albani, Rome, first to fifth century AD

> A lyre player of very little talent practiced constantly in a room with plastered walls, and from the echo he began to think that his playing sounded very well. So, in his vanity, he decided that he should go on the stage, but when he made his appearance and played very badly, he was run off with stones.[1]

[1] Nr. 121, in *Aesop*, trans., Lloyd W. Daly (New York: Yoseloff, 1961). We might remind the reader that in the age before recordings, musicians used echos as a means of hearing their practice.

What is good music?

Because in English all music is included under one word, 'Music,' some musicians make the mistaken conclusion that all music is therefore somehow equal. A wide variety of music is available to us which uses the same notational language, but to say this makes all music equal in significance is just as absurd as saying Shakespeare and comic books are equal in significance because they both use letters of the alphabet or words of the same language. The reason great literature and great musical literature are more significant than less significant works has to do not with the language (although, of course, Shakespeare and Mozart *did* use beautiful language), but with the importance of what it is that that language communicates.

Bruno Walter, by the way, was also agitated over the fact that we only have one word to cover everything.

> And how can it happen that music may descend from its lofty place, stooping to banality and vulgarity; how can one call by the same name of music what spills out from dance-halls and bars, or assaults us, with yowls and screeches, in the grotesquely distorted melodies, harmonies, and rhythms of jazz and allied forms of dance-music? ...
> The character of music, as that of every other art, can be superlatively ennobled by chosen individuals, or debased beyond recognition by the inept, inferior or perverse.[2]

[2] Bruno Walter, *Of Music and Music-Making* (New York: Norton, 1957), 18.

But what is good music? It is not a question that can be answered with complete consensus, like a question in mathematics, but there are some characteristics which most musicians would probably agree to be essential. Some of these characteristics have been recognized over a great period of time.

Athenaeus (fourth century AD) recognized two kinds of music. He first recalls a performance he heard which was a perfect example of the kind of music, or performance, which affords 'delight':

> He entered, and after drinking he took up his lyre and delighted us to such an extent that all were amazed at his playing, fluency being combined with correct technique, as well as at the tunefulness of his voice.

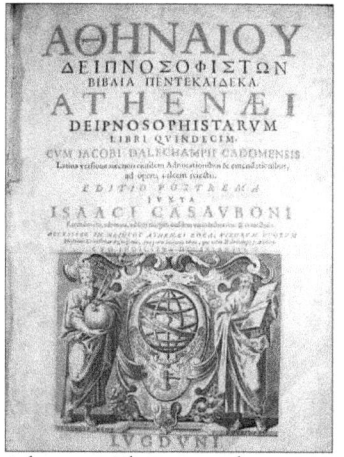

Athenaeus, *The Deipnosophists*, edited by Isaac Casaubon, 1657

But Athenaeus describes another kind of music in quite different language. In one place he concludes, 'It is plain to me also that music should be the subject of philosophic reflection.'[3] In another place he quotes a remark by Eupolis, 'Music is a matter deep and intricate,' adding his own observation that music is always supplying something new for those who can perceive.[4] This, in a word, was aesthetic music.

Erasmus (1469–1536) found, as a hallmark of a good work of art, that one's appreciation grows with repeated exposure. He discusses this relative to a proverb, 'Beauty bears repeating.'

> In general, there is such a power in excellent things that the more often and the more closely they are examined the more they please ... On the other hand, things which are falsely colored or commonplace sometimes have a charm to begin with, through sheer novelty, but soon grow ugly on repetition.[5]

[3] Athenaeus, *The Deipnosophists*, Charles Burton Gulick, (Cambridge: Harvard University Press, 1951)., XIV, 632.

[4] ibid., XIV, 623.

[5] 'Adages,' in *The Collected Works of Erasmus* (Toronto: University of Toronto Press, 1992), XXXI, 191.

This, by the way, explains why it is impossible to improve a bad composition by a good performance. The more rehearsal you devote to a poor composition the more you clarify and bring into focus the aspects of the composition which makes it poor in the first place.

The most important characteristic of good music is that it is *inspired* music, music written without purpose other than the composer's honest desire to communicate his feelings. This might be contrasted with what we call *constructed* music, such as the music being turned out in great abundance by educational publishers today. This music is designed for a certain portion of the educational market, designed for mass sales, and is carefully written to meet the technical needs of that market. But it is certainly not inspired music. It is exactly the kind of music Mendelssohn had in mind when he wrote,

> Music composed with a purpose will never reach the heart, because it does not come from the heart.[6]

[6] Letter to his family, September 2, 1831.

This kind of music has been around for a long time and many earlier musicians made the same complaint. Liszt can serve as a representative of numerous others.

> A work which offers only clever manipulation of its materials will always lay claim to the interest of the immediately concerned—of the artist, student, and connoisseur—but, despite this, it will be unable to cross the threshold of the artistic kingdom. Without carrying in itself the divine spark, without being a living poem, it will be ignored by society as though it did not exist at all, and no people will ever accept it as a leaf in the breviary of the cult of the beautiful.[7]

[7] Letter to August Kiel, September 8, 1855.

The deep significance of the distinction between 'inspired' and 'constructed' music first became clear to me years ago on an occasion when I was invited to rehearse four high school bands in music they were working on. I requested copies of the scores in advance in order to study them and received eight or so of these 'constructed' band pieces. As I studied them I wondered how I would ever fill an hour and a half of each band rehearsal with the joy of music using these particular scores. At the concert each band played two works with its own conductor, followed by an honor band consisting of members of each band, with whom I conducted only a short original band composition by Wagner, the *Huldigungsmarsch*. During the concert the audience of parents greeted each of these eight constructed, educational pieces with polite parental applause. After our performance of the Wagner the audience erupted with applause so enthusiastic, and so different in nature, that I was startled, and at a loss to understand why this feeble performance by the under-rehearsed 'honor band' had communicated so powerfully. It occurred to me that it was simply an expression of ordinary listeners upon finally hearing an inspired composition.

The paradox of programming *for* the public

When we mention the public we come face to face with a paradox unique to music among the arts. To begin, we might ask: Is the general audience *capable* of recognizing 'good' music? The answer is yes, as the above example of the parents listening to Wagner proves, and the reason lies in the fundamental issues of universality discussed earlier in this book. It is because of the universality of both music and emotions in the 'uneducated' public that Debussy could say, 'true fame comes solely from the masses and not from a more or less gilded and exclusive public.'[8]

The specific ability of the general audience to recognize good music has also been long recognized. There is, for example, a lengthy and interesting discussion of the aesthetics of performance by the emperor Julian (fourth century). His principal contention is that while some members of the audience, who have superficial taste, will respond to the outward appearance of the performance, one can be assured that the majority of the audience, even if uneducated, will respond to the genuine musical values in the performance. He also suggests that there were already by this time recognized aesthetic principles of music itself which were commonly understood by good musicians. He also defines the artistic performance as one which is genuine and inspired.[9]

On the other hand, the literature of Western Europe is filled with a great number of examples of important philosophers, poets and playwrights who have exhibited the greatest disdain for the taste of the general public. We will let one, Francesco Guicciardini (1483–1540), speak for them all.

[8] Quoted in Nat Shapiro, *An Encyclopedia of Quotations About Music* (New York: Da Capo, 1977), 107.

[9] *The Works of the Emperor Julian*, trans., Wilmer Wright (London: Heinemann, 1913), I, 299.

To speak of the people is really to speak of a mad animal gorged with a thousand and one errors and confusions, devoid of taste, of pleasure, of stability.[10]

Philosophers, in particular, made a point of excluding the public when discussing higher learning or the arts.[11] Aristotle, for example, concluded,

> It may be argued that the less vulgar is the higher and the less vulgar is always that which addresses the better public, an art addressing any and every one is of a very vulgar order.[12]

He is using the word, vulgar, of course in the sense of *vulgus*, meaning the common people, but he seems to suggest that great art cannot be understood by the masses.

Roger Bacon (b. ca. 1214) was even more outspoken in his disrespect for the masses, the 'unenlightened throng,' the 'ignorant multitude,' whom he says can never rise to the perfection of wisdom. For this reason, he maintains, the wise have always been an elite segment of society, separated from the masses. He found this true in religion ('as with Moses so with Christ the common throng does not ascend the mountain') and he cites a book by A. Gellius in which the author maintained that the great Greek philosophers had discussions among themselves at night, so as to 'avoid the multitude.'

> In this book he says that it is foolish to feed an ass lettuces when thistles suffice him. He is speaking of the multitude for whom rude, cheap, imperfect food of science is sufficient. Nor ought we to cast pearls before swine.

Similarly, Erasmus observed,

> The worst always pleases the most people, since the majority of men, as I said before, are prone to folly.[13]

This general distrust of the public can also be found in the views of some important composers. Wagner wrote,

> I assert that it is impossible for anything to be truly good if it is reckoned in advance for presentation to the public.[14]

---

[10] Francesco Guicciardini, *Maxims and Reflections*, trans., Mario Domandi (New York: Harper Torchbooks, 1965), C, 140.

[11] Cicero was a brave exception who did not object in principle to the idea that the orator, or artist, might aspire to be successful with his audience.
> Ambition is a universal factor in life, and the nobler a man is, the more susceptible is he to the sweets of fame. We should not disclaim this human weakness, which indeed is patent to all; we should rather admit it unabashed. Why, upon the very books in which they bid us scorn ambition philosophers inscribe their names! [Cicero, *Pro Archia Poeta*, x, 26]

[12] 'Poetics,' 1461b.27.

[13] 'Praise of Folly,' [1503] in *The Collected Works of Erasmus*, op. cit., XXVII, 116.

[14] William Ashton Ellis, *Wagner's Prose Works* (New York: Broude), III, 96.

And Schönberg agreed,

> If it is art, it is not for all; and if it is for all, it is not art.[15]

[15] Quoted in Nat Shapiro, op. cit., 237.

Antal Dorati believed that neither composer nor conductor should ever pander to the public taste of the moment.

> Art is not a civil service ... the composer does have a duty, but it is very high. It is a sacred duty. It is toward his art. The composer should not think about what pleases people. Art is creative expression.[16]

[16] Richard Carter, 'An Interview with Antal Dorati,' *The Instrumentalist* (December, 1980).

Peter Paul Fuchs is another who had serious doubts about the general audience, although his doubts are somewhat more qualified.[17] He seems surprised, after having *discussed* music with individual members of the audience and having found virtually no actual knowledge of music, to find that as a group they seemed to respond accurately to music. He cannot explain this. He also makes this odd judgment:

[17] Peter Paul Fuchs, *The Psychology of Conducting* (New York: MCA, 1969), 112ff.

> It seems to me that there is no harm in admitting it—only a comparatively small amount of the music offered in a symphony concert reaches the hearts and minds of the audience; the rest is heard but not listened to.

The tenor of his remarks seem to suggest that he presumes musical *knowledge* is required. But this is wrong, the audience needs no technical understanding in order to comprehend the important aspect of music, its *melos*. In reading his entire discussion, we could not escape the impression that he had a chip on his shoulder, perhaps reflecting his belief that *his* performances were not appreciated as much as he felt they deserved to be.

The reader can see in the above that there are two clearly distinct bodies of opinion with regard to the general public. As we have noted, this problem takes on special significance in the field of music. There is an apparent paradox here, which might be stated as follows:

> It is widely documented that music is genetically and universally understood by all men. Yet hardly any serious musician considers the highest form of his art to be that which most pleases the masses.

The solution to this paradox is found in making a distinction between the concept of the audience finding *pleasure* in the universality of music with the concept of the artist setting out *to please* the audience. The aesthetic danger is in progressing from the one to the other, as might be illustrated in the following chronology:

1. The artist performs and the audience finds pleasure in his performance.
2. The artist observes he has pleased the audience.
3. The artist now tries to please the audience.
4. His art has become entertainment.

This is personified in a recollection by William Finn, a distinguished choral conductor, of a celebrated baritone, John Charles Thomas, who,

> after [the conclusion of] Verdi's *Aida*, stood before a crowded house ... and sang 'Home on the Range,' to applause and cheers.[18]

[18] William J. Finn, *The Conductor Raises his Baton* (London: Dobson, 1946), 6.

The aesthetic problem here is a fine, but distinct, line between universality and popularity. This distinction was addressed by the Spanish writer, Baltasar Gracián (1601–1658). When a genuine art work communicates broadly, Gracián suggests, the artist should be pleased, even if he doesn't know why.

> Do not be alone in your condemnation of something which pleases a great many people. There is something good in it because it satisfies so many, and even though there is no explanation as to why it should be so, it is a source of enjoyment.[19]

However, it is quite a different matter to *aim* a work at the broad public.

Baltasar Gracián, anonymous, seventeenth century

[19] Baltasar Gracián, *The Oracle*, trans., L. B. Walton (London: Dent, 1953), Nr. 270.

[20] ibid., Nr. 28.

> Ah, how profoundly wise the man who was unhappy because his achievements pleased the many! A glut of popular applause does not satisfy sensible men ... Take no delight in the marvels of the multitude, which are no more than baubles, for general folly admires where exceptional discernment is undeceived.[20]

The aesthetic dangers implicit in the artist setting out to please the public have been commented on from the most ancient times. Plato discussed this in a lengthy discussion of the popular contests and festivals of music and dance in ancient Greece. In addition to discussing the subject of art which is addressed to the masses, he also makes interesting comments on the qualification of the judges, recommendations which are still worthy of note today: the judge must be highly qualified, he must have the courage not to be influenced by the audience, he must be honest and maintain the highest standards of performance.

Herm representing Plato, Roman copy after a Greek original from the last quarter of the fourth century, Vatican Museums, Photographer Marie-Lan Nguyen (2006)

> Thus far I too should agree with the many, that the excellence of music is to be measured by pleasure. But the pleasure must not be that of chance persons; the fairest music is that which delights the best and best educated, and especially that which delights the one man who is preeminent in virtue and education. And therefore the judges must be men of character, for they will require wisdom and have still greater need of courage; the true judge must not draw his inspiration from the theatre, nor ought he to be unnerved by the clamor of the many and his own incapacity; nor again, knowing the truth, ought he through cowardice and unmanliness carelessly to deliver a lying judgment, with the very same lips which have just appealed to the gods before he judged. He is sitting not as the disciple of the theatre, but, in his proper place, as their instructor, and he ought to be the enemy of all pandering to the pleasure of the spectators. The ancient and common custom of Hellas was the reverse of that which now prevails in Italy and Sicily, where the judgment is left to the body of spectators, who determine the victor by show of hands. But this custom has been the destruction of the poets themselves; for they are now in the habit of composing with a view to please the bad taste of their judges, and the result is that the spectators instruct themselves;—and also it has been the ruin of the theater; they ought to be receiving a higher pleasure, but now by their own act the opposite result follows.[21]

[21] *Laws*, 657d.

Petrarch also addressed the question of the obligation of the artist to the public, and concluded that for an artist to have the goal of pleasing the audience was wrong.

> It's idiocy to regulate our lives not according to intelligent reason but to suit popular fads … To follow the fashions of the vulgar mob, whose manners we laugh at and whose lives and opinions we despise, is to be more idiotic than the mob.[22]
>
> …
>
> Experience, the great teacher, is on my side, though the silly, unteachable mob is against me.[23]

[22] Letter to his brother, Gherardo, in Morris Bishop, trans., *Letters from Petrarch* (Bloomington: Indiana University Press, 1966), 92.

[23] Letter to Laelius, in ibid., 159.

Probably Petrarch felt this was an impossible goal to begin with, for he wondered, 'How can I please all? I have always striven to please only the few.'[24]

In another place, he returns again to his belief that, above all, one must not have the audience foremost in mind.

> No way is more prone to error or leads more directly to the brink of disaster, than the steps of the multitude. Almost everything which the crowd praises deserves to be condemned.[25]

Similar viewpoints are expressed throughout Western European history. To cite a later example, Wagner wrote in his essay on 'Public and Popularity' that good art must have no purpose, in the same way that that which is morally good is also without qualifying interests. The bad in art is that which 'aims to please.'[26]

For the ancient philosophers, this distinction between art and entertainment was based on a concern for the subsequent impact on society. Plato quotes Socrates' belief that amusement in any form, aside from the immediate pleasure, had a potential for harming the soul.

> SOCRATES. I would have you consider ... whether there are not other similar activities which have to do with the soul—some of them activities of art, making a provision for the soul's highest interest; others despising the interest, and as in the parallel case considering only the pleasure, of the soul, and how this may be acquired, but not considering what pleasures are good or bad, and having no other aim but to afford gratification, whether good or bad. In my opinion, Callicles, there are such activities, and this is the sort of thing which I term flattery, whether concerned with the body or the soul or anything else on which it is employed with a view to pleasure and without any consideration of good and evil.[27]

Plato believed that music had experienced a loss of discipline over the centuries in Greece. He saw an evolution from the noble old purposes to one of merely trying to please the crowd, resulting, he says, in licentiousness. It was his concern for this which results in his frequent plea for the importance of moral values in music.

[24] Letter to 'Socrates,' in ibid., 18.

[25] 'Remedies for Fortune Fair and Foul,' trans., Conrad Rawski (Bloomington: Indiana University Press, 1991), I, xi, 32.

[26] *Wagner's Prose Works*, op. cit., VI, 66ff.

[27] *Gorgias*, 501b. In *Laws*, 667e, he contends that the only positive entertainment is that which is amusing and provides neither harm nor good.

AN ATHENIAN STRANGER. Let us speak of the laws about music,—that is to say, such music as then existed,—in order that we may trace the growth of the excess of freedom from the beginning. Now music was early divided among us into certain kinds and manners. One sort consisted of prayers to the Gods, which were called hymns; and there was another and opposite sort called lamentations, and another termed paeans, and another, celebrating (I believe) the birth of Dionysus, called 'dithyrambs.' And they used the actual word 'laws' for another kind of song; and to this they added the term 'citharoedic.' All these and others were duly distinguished, nor were the performers allowed to confuse one style of music with another. And the authority which determined and give judgment, and punished the disobedient, was not expressed in a hiss, nor in the most unmusical shouts of the multitude, as in our days, nor in applause and clapping of hands. But the directors of public instruction insisted that the spectators should listen in silence to the end; and boys and their tutors, and the multitude in general, were kept quiet by a hint from a stick. Such was the good order which the multitude were willing to observe; they would never have dared to give judgment by noisy cries. And then, as time went on, the poets themselves introduced the reign of vulgar and lawless innovation. They were men of genius, but they had no perception of what is just and lawful in music; raging like bacchanals and possessed with inordinate delights—mingling lamentations with hymns, and paeans with dithyrambs; imitating the sounds of the flute on the lyre, and making one general confusion; ignorantly affirming that music has no truth, and, whether good or bad, can only be judged of rightly by the pleasure of the hearer. And by composing such licentious works, and adding to them words as licentious, they have inspired the multitude with lawlessness and boldness, and made them fancy that they can judge for themselves about melody and song. And in this way the theaters from being silent have become vocal, as though they had understanding of good and bad in music and poetry; and instead of an aristocracy, an evil sort of theatrocracy has grown up. For if there had been a democracy in music alone, consisting of free men, no fatal harm would have been done; but in music there first arose the universal conceit of omniscience and general lawlessness;—freedom came following afterwards, and men, fancying that they knew what they did not know, had no longer any fear, and the absence of fear begets shamelessness. For what is this shamelessness, which is so evil a thing, but the insolent refusal to regard the opinion of the better by reason of an over-daring sort of liberty?[28]

[28] *Laws*, 700ff.

Plato concluded that the artist makes a Faustian compromise when he decides to create or perform according to the dictates of the masses. How, he wondered, can the artist 'allow himself to be dazzled by the foolish applause of the world, and heap up riches to his own infinite harm?'[29]

[29] *Republic*, IX, 591d.

> And in what way does he who thinks that wisdom is the discernment of the tempers and tastes of the motley multitude, whether in painting or music, or, finally, in politics, differ from him whom I have been describing? For when a man consorts with the many, and exhibits to them his poem or other work of art or the service which he has done the State, making them his judges when he is not obliged, the so-called necessity of Diomede will oblige him to produce whatever they praise. And yet the reasons are utterly ludicrous which they give in confirmation of their own notions about the honorable and good.[30]

[30] ibid., VI, 493d.

Bruno Walter had similar concerns for the long-range impact of entertainment on the culture.[31]

[31] Bruno Walter, op. cit., 202ff.

> The cataracts of music pouring forth from radio stations and other sources day in and day out; the assimilation of musical and literary works to what is supposed to be the taste of the age; the inundation of the masses with entertainments, amusements, diversion, distractions—all this endangers the serious inner life today and spiritual aspirations of those who are exposed to it.

He believed he could see the direct effects all around him.

> Thus the climate of our world becomes colder; with the increasing perfection of the external conditions of life goes the impoverishment of its intrinsic conditions; cordiality becomes politeness, the desire for education a craving for sensationalism; conversation gives way to television; books to newspapers or illustrated journals; music-making to radio-listening.

For other philosophers, the concern was not so much the influence on society as simply one of the waste of time and talent. Euripides (484–406 BC), in a discussion of 'idle music,' wonders why, when musicians have the potential for doing so much good ('to heal men's wounds by music's spell'), do they waste their talents on entertaining at a banquet, when the banquet itself is sufficient entertainment?[32]

[32] *Medea*, 179.

Shakespeare made a similar comment regarding popular music. In *As You Like It* a rather light love song is performed ('With a hey, and a ho …'). Upon being criticized by Touchstone, the singer says 'You are deceived, sir. We kept time; we lost not our time.' Touchstone answers,

> By my troth, yes. I count it but time lost to hear such a foolish song.[33]

[33] *As You Like It*, act 5, scene 3, line 34ff.

One finds some very similar expressions during the nineteenth century, as for example by Robert Schumann:

> When you grow older, avoid playing what is merely fashionable. Time is precious. It would require a hundred lives merely to get acquainted with all the good music that exists.[34]

[34] 'Maxims for Young Musicians.'

And Felix Weingartner:

> A good performance of a poor work is of no artistic consequence, and regrettable both because it furthers bad taste and because it means time and labor unprofitably squandered.[35]

[35] Felix Weingartner, *On Conducting* (New York: Kalmus), 19.

Are there other ethical considerations in programming?

The long history of testimonials to the ethical powers of music has been thoroughly documented, beginning with ancient Greece. One of the most passionate of these testimonials is found in a famous letter from Cassiodorus (480–573 AD) to Boethius (475–524 BC), both important medieval philosophers who wrote on the subject of music.

> For what is more glorious than music, which modulates the heavenly system with its sonorous sweetness, and binds together with its virtue the concord of nature which is scattered everywhere? For any variation there may be in the whole does not depart from the pattern of harmony. Through this we think with efficiency, we speak with elegance, we move with grace. Whenever, by the natural law of its discipline, it reaches our ears, it commands song.
>
> The artist changes men's hearts as they listen; and, when this artful pleasure issues from the secret place of nature as the queen of the senses, in all the glory of its tones, our remaining thoughts take to flight, and it expels all else, that it may delight itself simply in being heard. Harmful melancholy he turns to pleasure; he weakens swelling rage; he

makes bloodthirsty cruelty kindly, arouses sleepy sloth from its torpor, restores to the sleepless their wholesome rest, recalls lust-corrupted chastity to its moral resolve, and heals boredom of spirit which is always the enemy of good thoughts. Dangerous hatreds he turns to helpful goodwill, and, in a blessed kind of healing, drives out the passions of the heart by means of sweetest pleasures.[36]

In terms of our own society, perhaps the most important ethical question for the conductor is whether he has an obligation to program for the purposes of raising the level of culture of his audience. This is an important question due to the potential power which music contains in its universality. Lenin, for instance, was quoted as observing, 'Music is a means of unifying broad masses of people.'[37] One can see this same concern for the powerful influence of music in a passage by St. Ambrose (fourth century) in which he seems to be pleading for musicians to be responsible for their choice of repertoire.

> Therefore play what is honorable, that your compassion may be honorable. For one who sees is much affected by what he sees, and one who hears by what he hears.[38]

Beginning with the nineteenth century, one begins to find much interest in using music to raise the general culture. Henry Cleveland wrote in 1840,

> Music must be made popular, not by debasing the art; but by elevating the people.[39]

Wagner wrote to Von Bülow contending that their purpose was to,

> persuade our audiences, by means of the correct illusion, to acquire, without noticing it, a greater refinement of taste.[40]

Weingartner wonders,

> will the courts, states and towns never understand that the [opera] theater must be a place not of luxury and thoughtless amusement, but of *popular education* like the school, only in a more spiritualized sense, and at any rate of a higher ethical significance than the church?[41]

[36] Letter to Boethius, in *Variae*, trans., Thomas Hodgkin (London: Frowde, 1886), II, xl.

[37] Quoted by Dimitri Shostakovich, in Nat Shapiro, op. cit., 236.

[38] Saint Ambrose, 'Death as a Good,' in *Seven Exegetical Works*, trans., Michael P. McHugh (Washington, DC: The Catholic University of America Press), 89.

[39] *National Music* (1840), quoted in Nat Shapiro, op. cit., 233.

[40] Letter of December 27, 1868.

[41] Felix Weingartner, op. cit., 49.

We are especially fond of a passage by Bruno Walter:

> There are people for whom life begins anew every morning. It is they who are ever more deeply touched by every renewed encounter with Schubert's *Unfinished*, it is they whom the perusal of a familiar Goethe poem moves with the force of a first impression; people over whom habit has no power; people who, in spite of their increasing years and experience, have remained fresh, interested, and open to life. And there are others who, when they watch a most glorious sunset or listen to the Benedictus in Beethoven's *Missa Solemnis*, feel scarcely more than 'I know this already'; and who are upset by everything new and unusual—in other words, people whose element is habit and comfort. It is for the former that our poets have written, our artists created, and our musicians composed; and it is for them, above all, that we perform our dramas, our operas, oratorios, and symphonies. As regards the latter, we artists must try, time and time again, to burst open the elderly crust they have acquired, or with which many of them may have been born; our youthful vigor must call upon theirs or revive whatever is left of it.[42]

[42] Bruno Walter, quoted in Carl Bamberger, *The Conductor's Art* (New York: McGraw-Hill, 1965), 176ff.

Bruno Walter reminds us of something very important here: we are not merely giving concerts, we are also crusaders who have the obligation to pass on the great gift of understanding which we have been given to those whom, for what ever reason, have not had the opportunity we have had to be exposed to great music.

It is in this context that another important question arises: Does the conductor have an obligation to program new music? Erich Leinsdorf believed programming was done for one of three basic purposes: serving oneself, educating the public, and encompassing the great repertoire.[43] Of the second of these, he observed that the idea 'sounds admirable, yet I am somewhat skeptical of the whole principle. Is this a performer's task?'

[43] Erich Leinsdorf, *The Composer's Advocate* (New Haven: Yale University Press, 1981), 206.

> The phrase 'educating the public' is too often mouthed to explain a repertoire that most listeners will dislike.

Many composers feel that just because they have written an orchestral composition, society owes them a performance. But no clarinet player feels the world owes him a performance with an orchestra just because he has learned a new concerto. The fact is only music worth playing deserves to be played. It does not matter whether it is new or old. In most cases, for better or worse, the conductor makes this decision.

Again, the question must be asked, Is the general audience capable of understanding new music? In answer to this question, the critic, Ernest Newman (1868–1959), has written,

> There is not a single case in musical history of a composer being a century ahead of his time: the greatest composers have all been perfectly comprehensible to the average instructed music lover of their day.[44]

[44] Sir Ernest Newman, *A Musical Critic's Holiday* (1925).

If there is any validity to the ancient aesthetic premise that art is a mirror of life, then he is probably correct. The twentieth century stands alone in history as a time when many composers had no interest in communicating with listeners and some have believed their music will be understood in some century in the future.

On programming for music education

One would hope that everyone would agree that only the best music should be used in music education, that our children be given the best we have. In fact, not every educator or conductor believes this, nor have they ever. Wagner once addressed this very issue.

> Why make such a fuss about the falsification of artistic judgment or musical taste? Is it not a mere bagatelle, compared with all the other things we falsify: commercial goods, sciences, food, public opinions, State culture-tendencies, religious dogmas, clover seeds, and what not? Are we to grow virtuous all of a sudden in Music? …
>
> The acceptance of the empty for the sound is stunting everything we possess in the way of schools, academies, and so on, by ruining the most natural feelings and misguiding the faculties of the rising generation … But that we should pay for all this, and have nothing left when we come to our senses … this, to be frank, is abominable![45]

[45] *Prose Works of Wagner*, op. cit., VI, 146ff.

Plato, in a discussion of his concern that in sampling entertainment one tends to become like the gourmand who, 'snatches a taste of every dish which is successively brought to the table, without having allowed himself time to enjoy the one before,'[46] also mentioned his concern over the potential for harm in the concept of music as amusement within the educational environment.

[46] *Republic*, I, 354b.

> Then, I said, our guardians must lay the foundations of their fortress in music?
> Yes, he said; the lawlessness of which you speak too easily steals in.
> Yes, I replied, in the form of amusement, and as though it were harmless.
> Why, yes, he said, and harmless it would be; were it not that little by little this spirit of license, finding a home, imperceptibly penetrates into manners and customs; whence issuing with greater force it invades contracts between man and man, and from contracts goes on to laws and constitutions, in utter recklessness, ending at last, Socrates, by an overthrow of all rights, private as well as public.
> Is that true? I said.
> That is my belief, he replied.
> Then, as I was saying, our boys should be trained from the first in a stricter system, for if childish amusement becomes lawless, it will produce lawless children, who can never grow up into well-conducted and virtuous citizens.[47]

[47] ibid., IV, 424d.

Another author, Donald Roach, had a similar concern, in particular for the substitution of 'interesting' for quality.

> Educational practice during the past half century has been greatly influenced by pragmatic philosophy. This 'cash value' theory puts great emphasis on practicality in learning experiences. John Dewey emphasized growth that leads to more growth, and his value system was humanistically oriented toward consensus. The Tanglewood Declaration called for all types of music to be included in the public school curriculum. The Contemporary Music Project has called for a nonfragmented 'common elements' approach that includes music of all types and times, with instruction centered around experiences with performance, listening (analyzing), and creative composition. Educational psychologists would have music teachers capitalize on the in-life learning experiences of students because of the interest that is generated and the increased learning that transpires.
> The crucial point is whether we can afford to sacrifice content for interest. Any innovative approach will be successful only if it does the job at least as well as some other instructional mode. In making the music curriculum relevant to contemporary society, we should not be too hasty to substitute expedience for quality.[48]

[48] Donald Roach, 'Contemporary Music Education: A Comprehensive Outlook,' *Music Educators Journal*, September, 1973.

In conclusion, the educational conductor must have the integrity to select the best music available to him and to reject everything else. Archibald T. Davison, the famous conductor of the Harvard University Glee Club, was making this argument already in 1945—which suggests we, as a profession, have made little progress in a half-century in providing a sense of aesthetics in our teacher training programs.

> The most serious demand is for teachers whose knowledge and experience of music is wide enough to guarantee a sound musical taste. Only when there is intelligent revolt against much educational material that now passes for music will there be hope for a productive music education in this country.[49]

[49] Quoted in Willi Apel, *Harvard Dictionary of Music* (Cambridge: Harvard University Press, 1947), 472.

Having the good taste to understand the difference between good music and inferior music is probably more common than having the honesty and integrity to engage in what Davison calls, 'intelligent revolt.' Schumann was another who called upon musicians to fight this fight.

> You ought not help to spread bad compositions, but, on the contrary, help to suppress them with all your force.
>
> ...
>
> Never play bad compositions and never listen to them when not absolutely obliged to do so.
>
> ...
>
> Never play anything of which in our own heart you feel ashamed.[50]

[50] 'Maxims for Young Musicians.'

Is programming a personal affair?

Erich Leinsdorf, as we have mentioned, believed programming was done for one of three basic purposes: serving oneself, educating the public, and encompassing the great repertoire.[51] The first, he says is rarely admitted, but the most frequently employed. We are happy to admit it and, in fact, think it an important principle. If a conductor, in planning repertoire, makes a list of the works he is desperately wanting to play next, any choice from this list guarantees that he will walk into the rehearsal hall filled with enthusiasm. Further, what-

[51] Erich Leinsdorf, op. cit., 206. Leinsdorf mentions [ibid., 205] some conductors try to program works all in the same key, a practice with he strongly disagrees with. We once had dinner in Vienna with a young European conductor who firmly believed, from his own experience, that if he began a concert with a composition in the key of D Major the success of the concert was assured.

ever there is in the music which creates his enthusiasm will also have, to some degree, the same effect on the players. This, alone, is a very big step towards an effective rehearsal process.

In any case, it is the conductor's perfect right to select his repertoire from his own perspective, whatever it may be. This is the long acknowledged right of any musician, as we see already in an anonymous poem from the period of Homer. Hermes, in giving the gift of music to Apollo, also gives him advice on the use of music. The choice he holds out to Apollo is the same choice offered to musicians today.

> You may choose to learn whatever you desire.[52]

However, all 'rights' come with strings attached and in this case there is a very important qualification. While the conductor has the right to choose his repertoire, he must understand that his choices *will* reflect on his own character. One sees this documented already in Aristophanes (448–380 BC), where a character in *The Thesmophoriazusae*, tells us,

> Answer me. But you keep silent. Oh! just as you choose; your songs display your character quite sufficiently.[53]

In an autobiographical poem by the Baroque poet, Antonio Abbatini, we have a first-hand description of one of the academies, which in this case, met in his home. His description is similar to other reports of these gatherings of upper class and noble gentlemen for an evening with music and discussion of intellectual topics of the day, but he adds that all the gentlemen took turns performing *for the purpose* of demonstrating their character.

> Then to the harpsichord the company transfers,
> and each man takes upon himself to show, with song
> and sound, his virtue, which binds the heart and soul.[54]

Among more recent testimonials is one by Pablo Casals (1876–1973):

> The artist is responsible for the music he performs.[55]

---

[52] 'To Hermes,' trans., Apostolos N. Athanassakis, *The Homeric Hymns* (Baltimore: Johns Hopkins University Press, 1976), 474–489. The translator observes, 'The artistic sensitivity and the truly genteel nature of the advice that Hermes gives Apollo are remarkable. It is small wonder that the best practitioners of the art of singing and playing the lyre were called *theioi* (divine).'

[53] Line 143.

[54] Quoted in Lorenzo Bianconi, *Music in the Seventeenth Century*, trans., David Bryant (Cambridge: Cambridge University Press, 1989), 290ff.

[55] *Conversations with Casals* (1956).

The most outspoken musician on this subject was Richard Wagner, who repeatedly, in his prose writings, condemns the artist who does not take responsibility for the moral implications of his work.

> The man who strays into the realm of triviality must pay for his transgression at the cost of his own more noble nature. But he who seeks it deliberately, that man is fortunate, for he has *nothing* worth losing.[56]
>
> ...
>
> To take a last look back upon the picture afforded us by the public astir in Time and Space, we might compare it with a river, as to which we must decide whether we will swim against or with its stream. Who swims with it, may imagine he belongs to constant progress; it is so easy to be borne along, and he never notes that he is being swallowed in the ocean of vulgarity. To swim against the stream must seem ridiculous to those not driven by an irresistible force to the immense exertions that it costs.[57]

[56] Letter to Eduard Hanslick, January 1, 1847.

[57] *Wagner's Prose Works*, op. cit., VI, 94.

In his last word on this subject, Wagner offers a parody of a familiar church Credo, which he concludes with a forecast of the punishment sure to await those who willingly propagate poor music.

> I believe in God, Mozart and Beethoven, and likewise their disciples and apostles;
> I believe in the Holy Spirit and the truth of one, indivisible Art;
> I believe that this Art proceeds from God, and lives within the hearts of illumined men;
> I believe that he who once has bathed in the sublime delights of this high Art, is consecrated to Her forever, and never can deny Her; I believe that through this Art all men are saved; ...
> I believe in a last judgment, which will condemn to fearful pains all those who in this world have dared to play the huckster with chaste Art, have violated and dishonored Her through evilness of heart and ribald lust of senses; I believe that these will be condemned through all eternity to hear their own vile music.[58]

[58] ibid., VII, 66ff.

Memorial to Richard Wagner, Berlin, ca. 1904

Frederick Fennell and David Whitwell, 1972

Afterword

IN 1998 I FINISHED THE FIRST EDITION of this book on conducting, an unusual book in that it contains none of the usual diagrams for the baton to follow, pictures of poses for the conductor, nomenclature and transpositions of the various instruments, etc., et. al. Rather, as the title suggests, it is a conducting book which deals with the mental and genetic aspects of conducting, that is to say, emotions and motion. Perhaps it is fair to say that after decades of watching the great conductors, as well as the less successful, I generally concluded that what makes a musical conductor is not how he looks, but how he thinks.

Writing the book allowed me the opportunity to pull together a variety of material which I have been using with students and in conducting clinics for many years. I sent a copy in advance to Frederick Fennell, who was most enthusiastic.

Frederick Fennell to David Whitwell
Sarasota, Florida, 22 April 1998

> Before you are launched into the printing you have to know that 'your book' will be major among your writings. You know this, of course. What jumps up as it is read rather staggers, for among those who should read it are certain to be among that endless legion of the un-read, the intellectually un-washed who stand in high places—not perhaps as shoulder to shoulder as some years ago, but the absence of places (and people) for today's 'Dialogues' remains a sad fact to us. And you must write as you do. I have some idea of how long this book has been cooking in the oven of that brain of yours. And you have not lost faith in it, ever as—all about you is seen a 'Berlin-type' wall of ignorance—even false leadership. I have read and reread … Thank you again for the best I have yet read. Write on! Ethics!!

The following month Fred wrote again having been quite taken by a passage from Plato which I quoted in Chapter 17, 'On Programming' [in this second edition it is in Chapter 15, p. 268]. Fred found in this passage the philosophical and aesthetical argument against Rock and Roll and its impact on society. He writes,

Frederick Fennell to David Whitwell
Sarasota, Florida, 19 May 1998

> Leafing thru Chapter 17, on programming, it exposed exactly in Plato's words pp. 210–211 the scene with Rock—more than exposed—it explodes! Allowing the society of them—Lord knows who today would speak it with the power to have it received? I'm so glad it is in your book.

Frederick Fennell wrote once more about the book, the following week.

Frederick Fennell to David Whitwell
Sarasota, Florida, 25 May 1998

> Again I found myself reading your great book. It is, of course, unique and extraordinary in the way that this expression was generated to be. Among those, stating this as purpose, there is none like this one known to me.

I was very pleased with the response the conducting book had, considering how different it is from the usual conducting texts. I received many kind notes and will conclude with one more, from my dear friend, Frank Battisti, who wrote,

Frank Battisti to David Whitwell
Boston, Massachusetts, 16 June 1998

> I am now reading your *The Art of Musical Conducting* and the latest issue of the WASBE Journal which you edited. Both are EXCELLENT and VERY STIMULATING. BRAVO! and congratulations on both!

About the Author

Dr. David Whitwell is a graduate ('with distinction') of the University of Michigan and the Catholic University of America, Washington DC (PhD, Musicology, Distinguished Alumni Award, 2000) and has studied conducting with Eugene Ormandy and at the Akademie fur Musik, Vienna. Prior to coming to Northridge, Dr. Whitwell participated in concerts throughout the United States and Asia as Associate First Horn in the USAF Band and Orchestra in Washington DC, and in recitals throughout South America in cooperation with the United States State Department.

At the California State University, Northridge, which is in Los Angeles, Dr. Whitwell developed the CSUN Wind Ensemble into an ensemble of international reputation, with international tours to Europe in 1981 and 1989 and to Japan in 1984. The CSUN Wind Ensemble has made professional studio recordings for BBC (London), the Koln Westdeutscher Rundfunk (Germany), NOS National Radio (The Netherlands), Zurich Radio (Switzerland), the Television Broadcasting System (Japan) as well as for the United States State Department for broadcast on its 'Voice of America' program. The CSUN Wind Ensemble's recording with the Mirecourt Trio in 1982 was named the 'Record of the Year' by The Village Voice. Composers who have guest conducted Whitwell's ensembles include Aaron Copland, Ernest Krenek, Alan Hovhaness, Morton Gould, Karel Husa, Frank Erickson and Vaclav Nelhybel.

Dr. Whitwell has been a guest professor in 100 different universities and conservatories throughout the United States and in 23 foreign countries (most recently in China, in an elite school housed in the Forbidden City). Guest conducting experiences have included the Philadelphia Orchestra, Seattle Symphony Orchestra, the Czech Radio Orchestras of Brno and Bratislava, The National Youth Orchestra of Israel, as well as resident wind ensembles in Russia, Israel, Austria, Switzerland, Germany, England, Wales, The Netherlands, Portugal, Peru, Korea, Japan, Taiwan, Canada and the United States.

He is a past president of the College Band Directors National Association, a member of the Prasidium of the International Society for the Promotion of Band Music, and was a member of the founding board of directors of the World Association for Symphonic Bands and Ensembles (WASBE). In 1964 he was made an honorary life member of Kappa Kappa Psi, a national professional music fraternity. In September, 2001, he was a delegate to the UNESCO Conference on Global Music in Tokyo. He has been knighted by sovereign organizations in France, Portugal and Scotland and has been awarded the gold medal of Kerkrade, The Netherlands, and the silver medal of Wangen, Germany, the highest honor given wind conductors in the United States, the medal of the Academy of Wind and Percussion Arts (National Band Association) and the highest honor given wind conductors in Austria, the gold medal of the Austrian Band Association. He is a member of the Hall of Fame of the California Music Educators Association.

Dr. Whitwell's publications include more than 127 articles on wind literature including publications in Music and Letters (London), the London Musical Times, the Mozart-Jahrbuch (Salzburg), and 39 books, among which is his 13-volume *History and Literature of the Wind Band and Wind Ensemble* and an 8-volume series on *Aesthetics in Music*. In addition to numerous modern editions of early wind band music his original compositions include 5 symphonies.

David Whitwell was named as one of six men who have determined the course of American bands during the second half of the 20th century, in the definitive history, *The Twentieth Century American Wind Band* (Meredith Music).

A doctoral dissertation by German Gonzales (2007, Arizona State University) is dedicated to the life and conducting career of David Whitwell through the year 1977. David Whitwell is one of nine men described by Paula A. Crider in *The Conductor's Legacy* (Chicago: GIA, 2010) as 'the legendary conductors' of the 20th century.

'I can't imagine the 2nd half of the 20th century—without David Whitwell and what he has given to all of the rest of us.' Frederick Fennell (1993)

www.ingramcontent.com/pod-product-compliance
Lightning Source LLC
Chambersburg PA
CBHW081417230426
43668CB00016B/2265